IMAGES
of America

CORAL SPRINGS

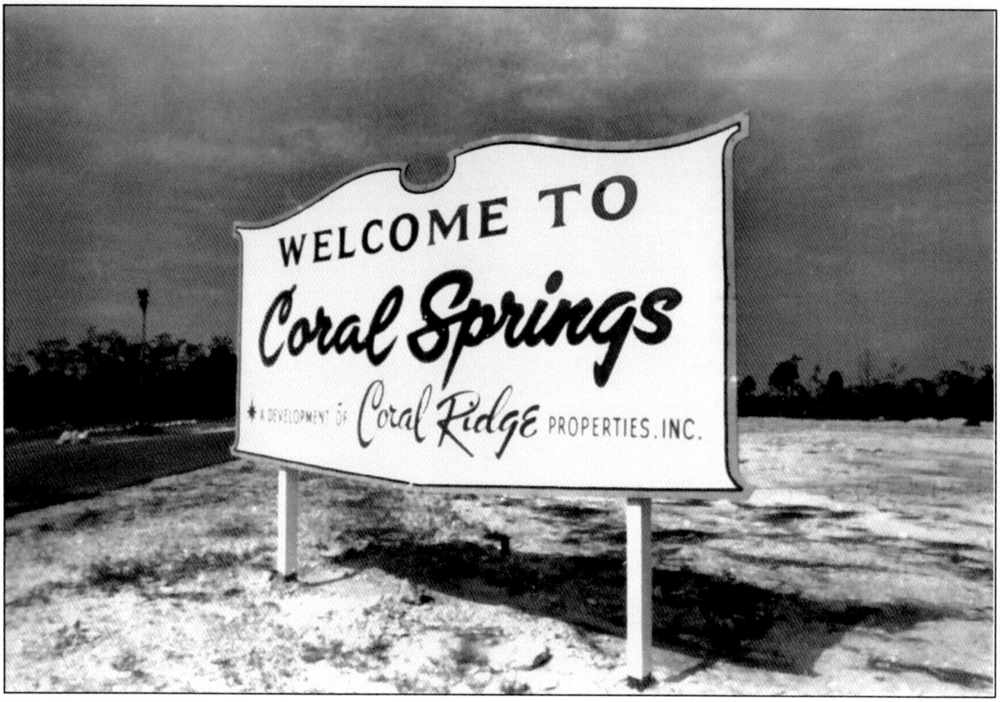
WELCOME TO
Coral Springs
A DEVELOPMENT OF Coral Ridge PROPERTIES, INC.

IMAGES
of America

CORAL SPRINGS

Wendy Wangberg and Kevin Knutson

ARCADIA
PUBLISHING

ISBN 978-0-7385-1505-2

Published by Arcadia Publishing
Charleston, South Carolina

Printed in the United States of America

Library of Congress Catalog Card Number: 2002117161

For all general information contact Arcadia Publishing at:
Telephone 843-853-2070
Fax 843-853-0044
E-mail sales@arcadiapublishing.com
For customer service and orders:
Toll-Free 1-888-313-2665

Visit us on the Internet at www.arcadiapublishing.com

To my husband Paul, who is always ready for the next adventure. —WW

To my daughter Zoë—so you can know where you come from.

And to my wife Kim, who continues to inspire me. —KK

Proceeds from the sale of this book will benefit the Coral Springs Historical Advisory Committee and the Museum of Coral Springs History.

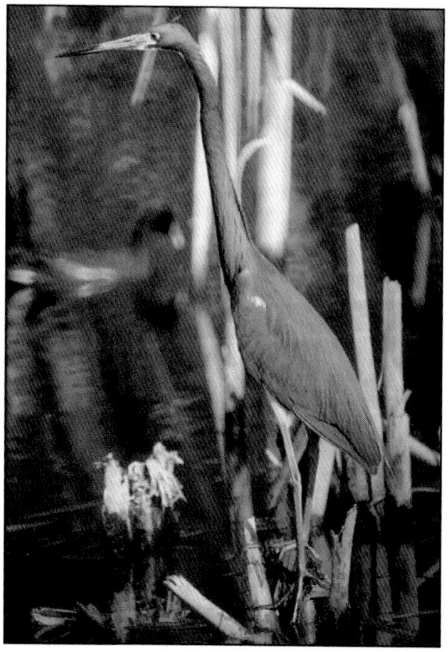

Located along the Everglades, Coral Springs is visited daily by our western neighbors, including this Great Blue Heron. (Courtesy of the City of Coral Springs.)

Contents

ACKNOWLEDGMENTS

A project of this scope could not be completed without the knowledge, skills, and passion of many people. Thank you to the following individuals who provided assistance to us:

City History—Former Mayor Edward Heafy and Emily Heafy, former president of Coral Ridge Properties Robert Hofmann, Mayor John Sommerer, Janis Humpage, Bruce Harner, Sandy Cugno, Frank Szymanski, Roy Gold, Linda Weiner, Steve Scali, Stuart McIver (author of *Coral Springs: The First Twenty-Five Years*), Susan Hess, Rick Engle, William Wolf, Gail Dixon, Korey Meckes, and Joyce Campos.

Project Support—Mike Levinson, Susan Grant, Gina Salinsky, and Sheri Chadwick.

Technical Support—Matt Hoffman, Christine Parkinson, and Rita Lanning-Radziwon.

Photo Sources—City of Coral Springs, George Miller, Christine Parkinson, Sheri Chadwick, Coral Ridge Properties, the Heafy Collection, the Coral Springs Historical Advisory Committee, Broward County Historical Commission, Lyons-Inez Fisher Collection, Smith Aerials & Associates, Broward County Archeological Society, Richard C. Reilly, *Miami Herald*, the Coral Springs *Forum*, Dillon Aerial Photography, and the Broward County Library.

Dedicated to the memory of former Mayor Edward Heafy, who spent a lifetime fostering the city as a sports enthusiast, commissioner, and mayor.

INTRODUCTION

How did 13,400 acres of bean fields and grazing land become a city of 122,000 people in just 40 years? When Coral Ridge Properties ran out of land to develop in Ft. Lauderdale in the early 1960s, it looked for enough land to develop an entire city from scratch. It located a vast tract in northwest Broward County and drew up a complete development plan before a shovel hit the soil. Just as with a first child, Coral Springs' growth was photographed every step of the way from the ground and from the air starting in 1963. The city inherited these photographs and took up where the founders left off, amassing a total of 20,000 photographs, 60,000 slides, and a myriad of maps, plats, and publications.

This totally planned city features a covered bridge as its centerpiece, as the developer wanted to project a vision of the Old South on the empty landscape. The earliest office buildings were Williamsburg-style with brick facades and white columns, but these belied the modern nature of the city. Land for schools and parks was set aside before a street was paved. Restrictions governed the size and quality of every building. When Westinghouse acquired Coral Ridge Properties in 1966, Coral Springs became its urban laboratory. The company built a series of state-of-the-art "Electra Lab" houses with such revolutionary conveniences as dimmer switches, motion detectors, and intercoms, as well as a prototype electric car.

Coral Springs also attracted the attention of equestrians, with its open stretches of land for stabling, showing, and racing horses. Golfers flocked to the city's four courses and the whole country could watch the annual Honda Classic Golf Tournament on television. Tennis and aquatics facilities held annual meets and the Florida Panthers Hockey Team practices at "Incredible Ice."

Although the master plan evolved over time to reflect the most current techniques in urban development, prohibition of large signs and overt advertising has been a constant. This resulted in headlines and a question in the board game *Trivial Pursuit*: "What did Coral Springs, Florida, officials not allow a new McDonald's to build in 1965?" Answer: "Golden Arches." The city also gained attention, and a spot on the *Good Morning, America*, on its 25th anniversary in 1988 when it grilled the world's largest hamburger, according to the *Guinness Book of World Records*.

Masterminding the astounding growth of this manicured city is a municipal government with the following mission: "We want to be the premier city in Florida in which to live, work and raise a family." To that end they are totally responsive to annual satisfaction surveys administered by an independent marketing firm hired by the City. The results have spawned everything from additional schools and a senior center to more flowers along the boulevards.

Proactively, the city has developed localized town meetings, called "Slice of the Springs," a "City Hall in the Mall" annex, as well as a free community bus service. In 1997, Coral Springs won the Florida Governor's Sterling Award for Excellence, the first state-sanctioned Baldrige Quality Award–based honor won by a municipality. The founders' dream of a city full of well-maintained houses, parks, and schools—with every mile landscaped—has been realized. But rather than a fanciful version of the Old South, it is now a picture of everything modern. We hope you enjoy this scrapbook of how Coral Springs grew from a bean patch to one of the most progressive cities in the country.

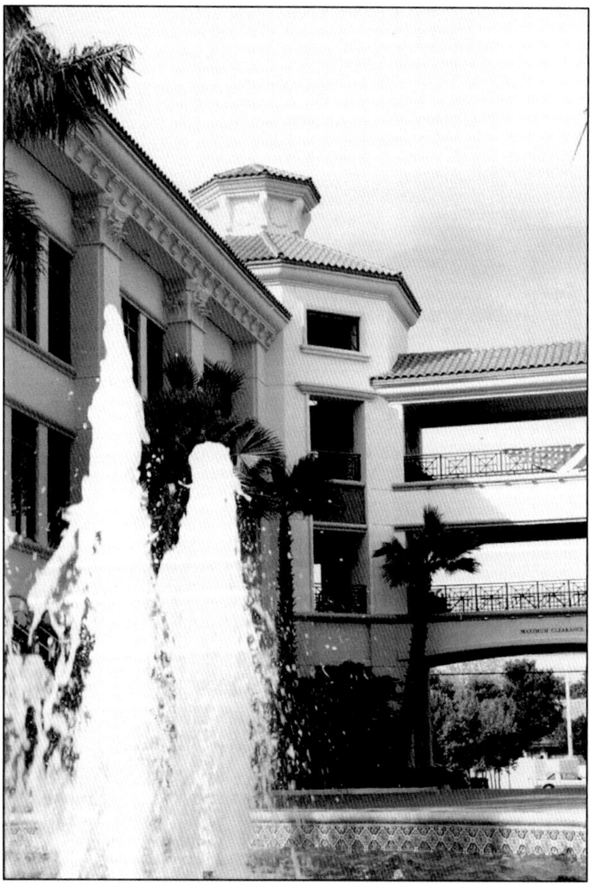

Now that Coral Springs has reached "build-out"—meaning that most of the available land has been developed—the focus of planning has turned to renovation and redevelopment. This building is part of "The Walk" on University Drive, the first phase of a decade-long revitalization of the downtown area currently taking place. (Courtesy of the City of Coral Springs.)

One

Enough Land

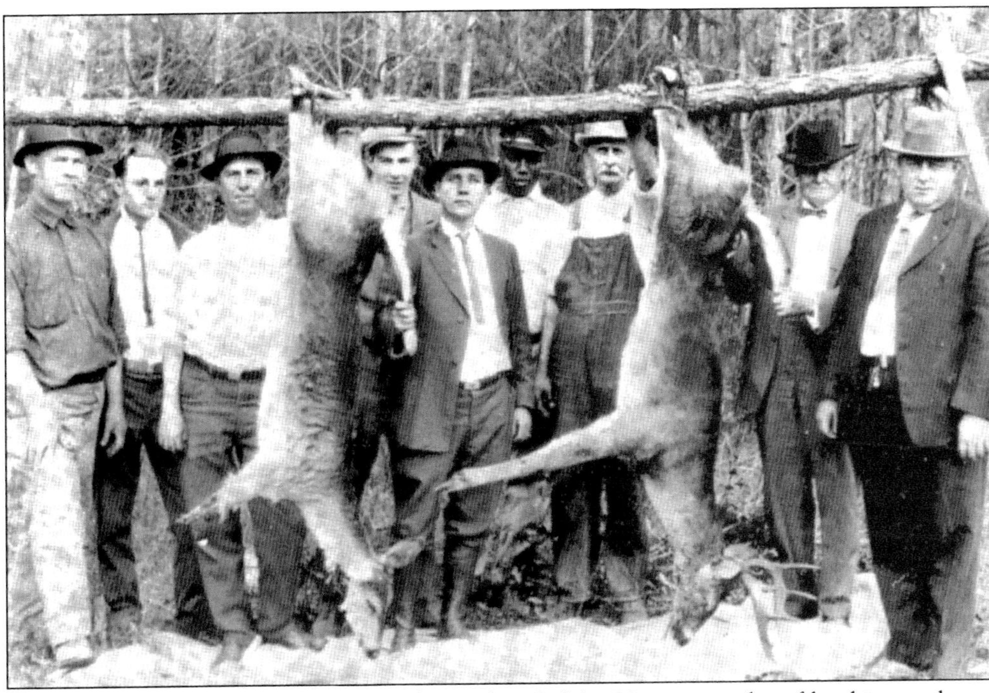

Henry L. (Bud) Lyons bargained, bought, and traded for 20 square miles of land in northwest Broward County between 1911 and 1939, sometimes for $20 per 20-acre lot. He used the wilderness for hunting, farming, and cattle grazing, digging ditches and dikes for irrigation by hand alongside his Bahaman laborers. He can be seen at the far right in the picture, standing next to his father. Much of western Broward County looked like this all the way to the Everglades. (Courtesy Broward County Historical Commission, Lyons-Inez Fisher Collection.)

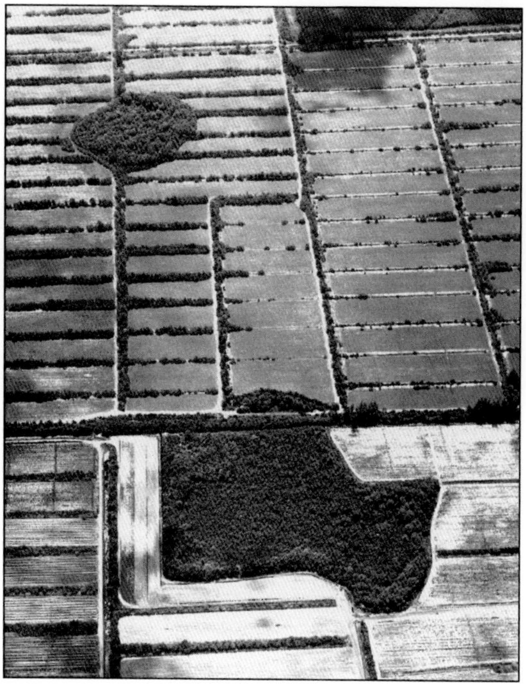

This aerial shot shows the land as Lyons left it for planting beans and cucumbers with hedgerows of guava trees. He was referred to as "The Titan of the Bean Patch" and his packing plant in Pompano Beach kept hundreds of people employed during the Great Depression by sorting, crating, and shipping produce. Hurricanes in 1945 prompted the formation of the Central and South Flood Control District (now the South Florida Water Management District) that further enhanced drainage with canals, levies, and pump houses. (Courtesy of Smith Aerials & Associates.)

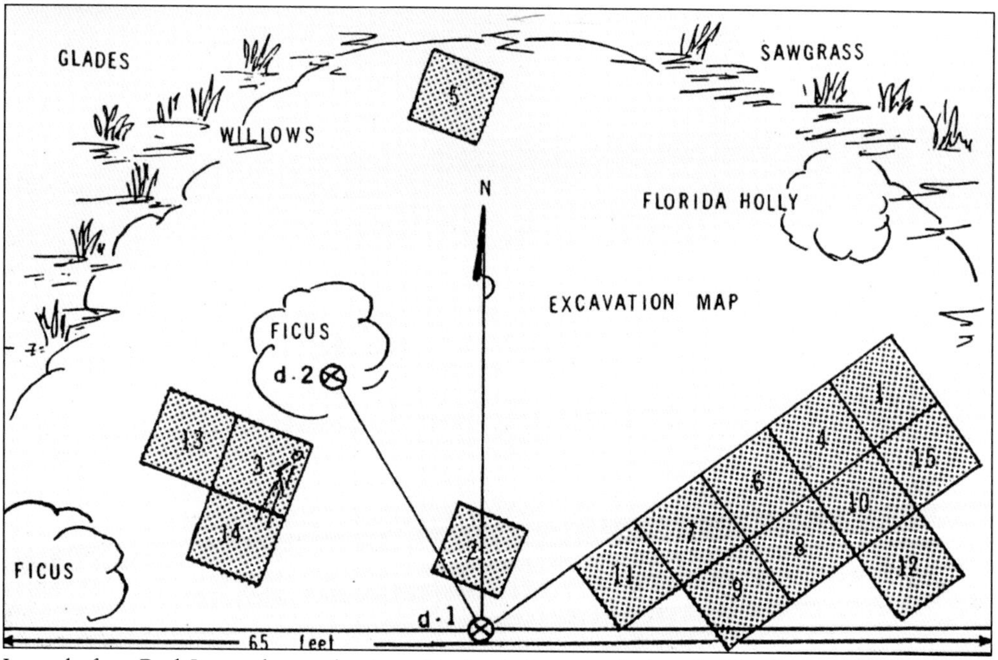

Long before Bud Lyons began buying this land, it was inhabited. "Cagles Hammock . . . is situated on the wild southwest corner of the City of Coral Springs . . . a rather small mound on the north end of the wooded hammock. The unusual ficus tree clump indicates the slight elevation that made habitation possible in the wet Glades, before modern drainage." So reads the result of one of the Broward County Archaeological Society's Coral Springs digs of 1967, revealing the lay of the land primarily during the Glades II Period, c. 1500 B.C. (Courtesy of Coral Ridge Properties.)

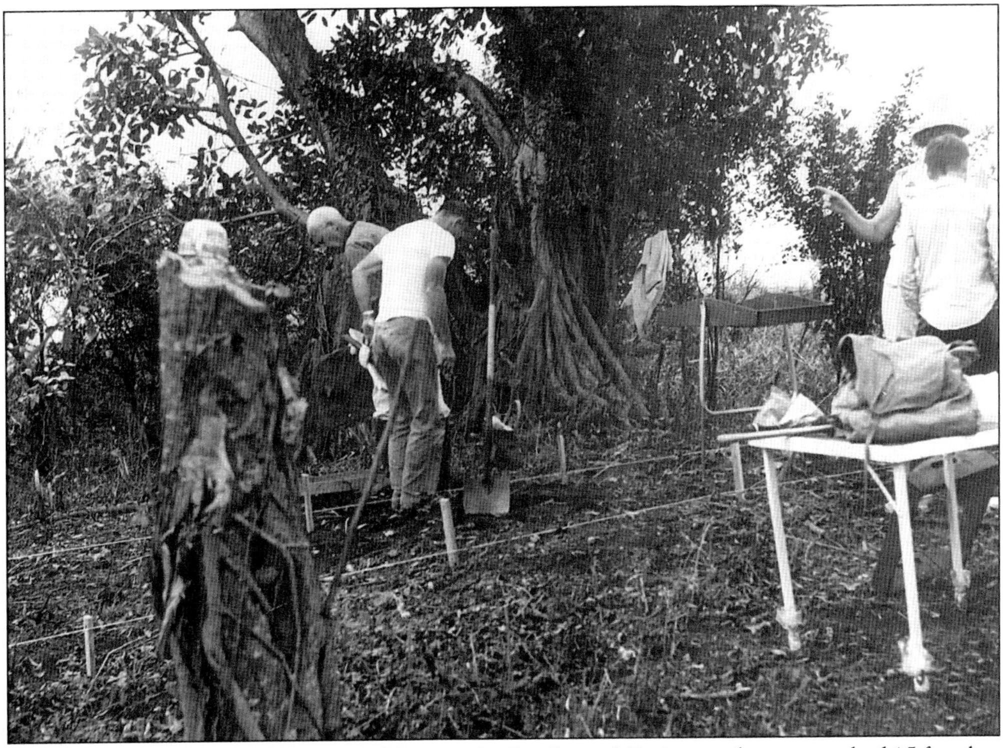

Under the supervision of the Broward County Archeological Society, volunteers staked 15 five-by-five-foot squares, dug to six-inch levels, and sifted all material, which was then washed, classified, and catalogued. "The large number of shark teeth and vertebrae indicates full participation in a coastal economy," the report continues. (Courtesy of Coral Ridge Properties.)

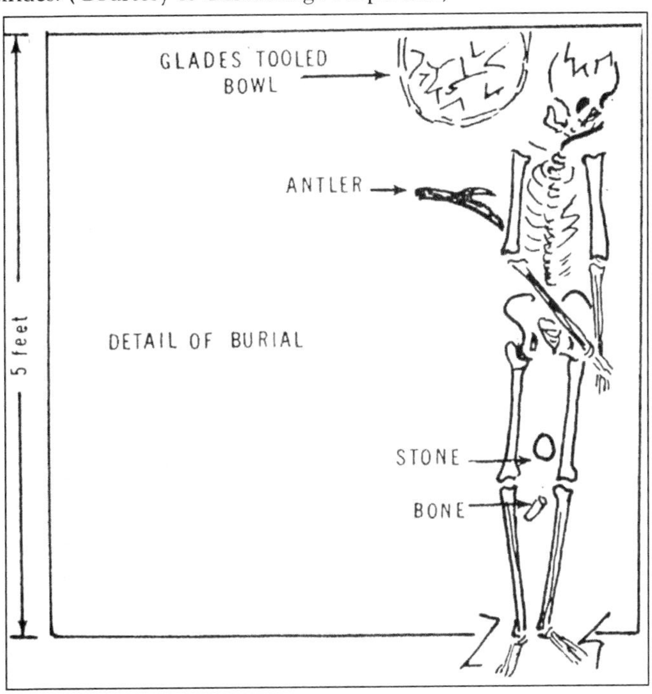

"Midden burials are the exception in Glades hammock sites. The skeleton was extended NNE-SSW direction, skull to the north, lying on its back, skull turned to the left. This was probably a ceremonial burial, with the body laid in a shallow grave dug into the midden material, and accompanied by a killed bowl of food, a symbolic antler and some of the deceased's worldly goods." (Courtesy of Broward County Archeological Society.)

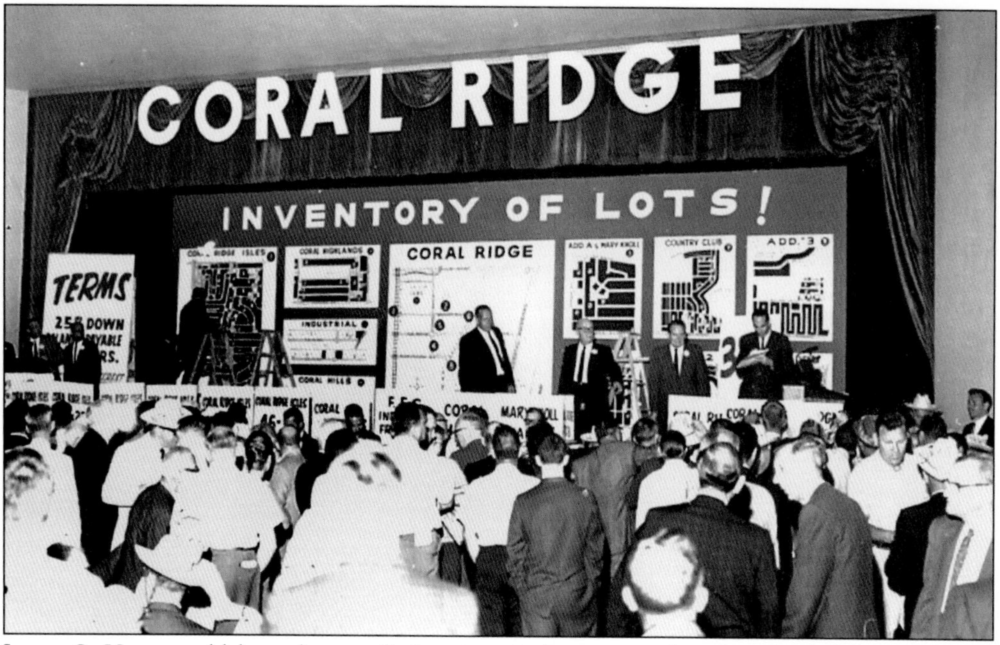

James S. Hunt could have been called a titan in his own right when he left Detroit—and the biggest Chevrolet dealership in the country—looking for investment opportunities in Ft. Lauderdale in 1946. It did not take him long to hone in on the real estate market. By 1947, Coral Ridge Properties was founded. After developing the Galt Ocean Mile and the subdivision of Coral Ridge, representing one-third of Ft. Lauderdale's tax roll, Hunt looked for "enough land" to build an entire city. Here the ever-dapper Mr. Hunt stands in front of the easel with a flower in his lapel. (Courtesy of Coral Ridge Properties.)

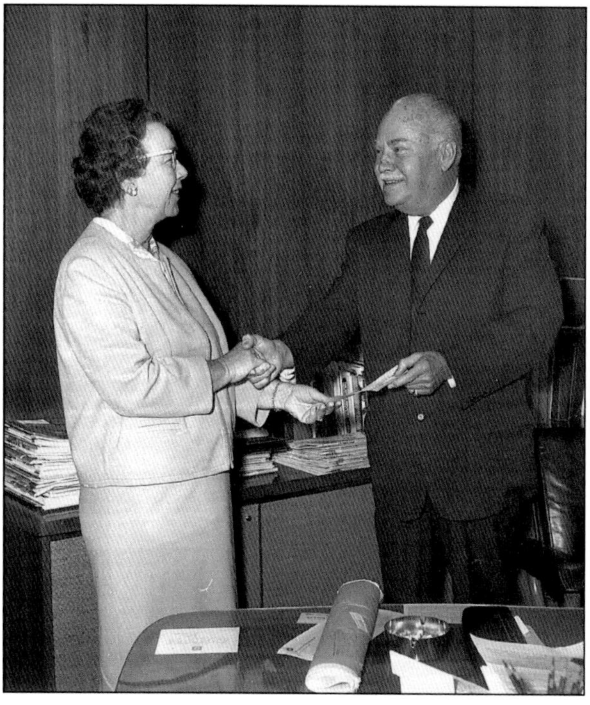

The result of Hunt's search for land was recorded on December 14, 1961. A check for $1 million, handed to Lena Lyons, marked the transfer of 3,869 acres—the first part of what eventually became a 10,000-acre purchase. Four hundred additional acres bought from Rodman Rockefeller allowed Coral Springs to reach Royal Palm Boulevard. The final 3,000 acres were purchased in 1971 from Remsburg Ranch. (Courtesy of Coral Ridge Properties.)

The first printed master plan was for a large retirement community named Curran Village. When moderately priced housing for younger families took off, the retirement village idea was dropped. The name of "Quartermore" was considered for the City as an enticement (buy three acres and get a fourth free), as was the name of Pompano Springs, to link the new city to neighboring Pompano Beach. But Hunt did not want his dream to be named after a "damn fish," so he named his new creation after his development company, with a twist—Coral Springs. (Courtesy of Richard C. Reilly.)

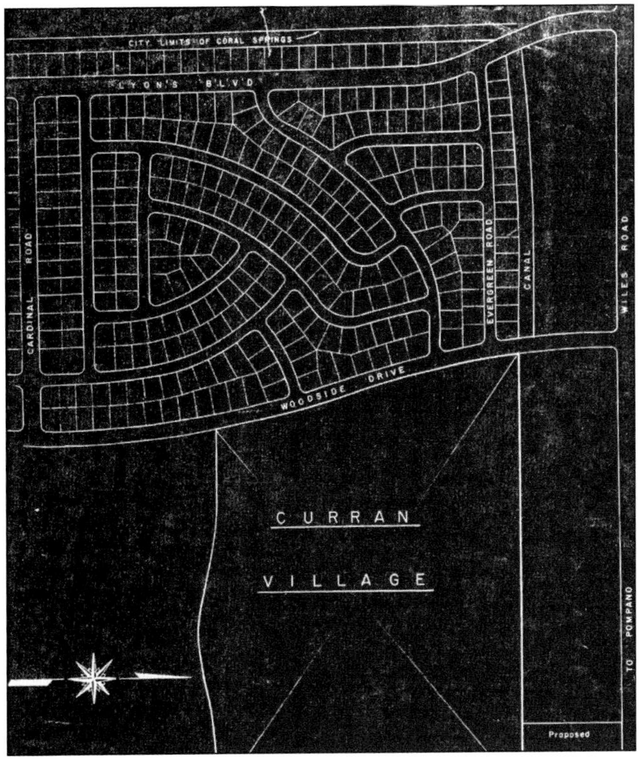

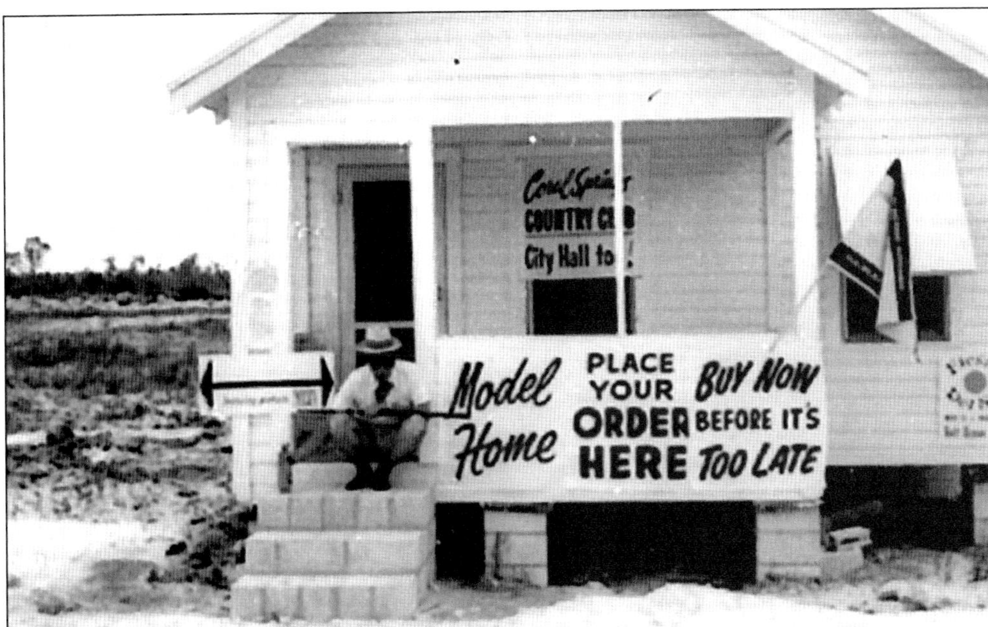

Creating a city required more than acreage—it had to be populated by at least five citizens. Since there were no houses in 1963, three cabins were towed to the area of Riverside Drive for Coral Ridge employees to take up residence, and the requirement was thus fulfilled. Gordon Ickes not only moved in but also appeared to take over. His rifle was not a prop, as there were poisonous snakes, wildcats, and stray cattle to discourage. (Courtesy of Coral Ridge Properties.)

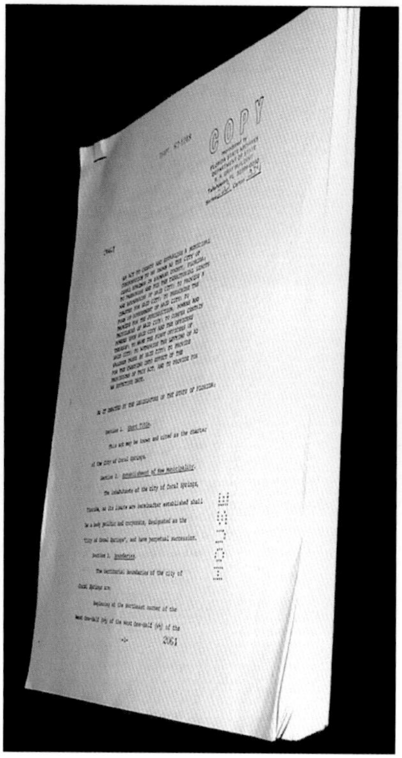

After assembling the acreage and populace, a city charter was needed. The ever-practical (and impatient) Hunt took the 105-page Ft. Lauderdale charter and changed the city name and boundaries. That is why Section 5, "Powers of the City," provides for "the regulating of condition of all dairies, butcher pens, and slaughter houses" in this bedroom community, as well as the right to borrow money for "the erection of seawalls." It was passed by Special Act of the Florida Legislature on May 25, 1963 and filed on July 10, 1963, the city's anniversary date. (Courtesy of the City of Coral Springs.)

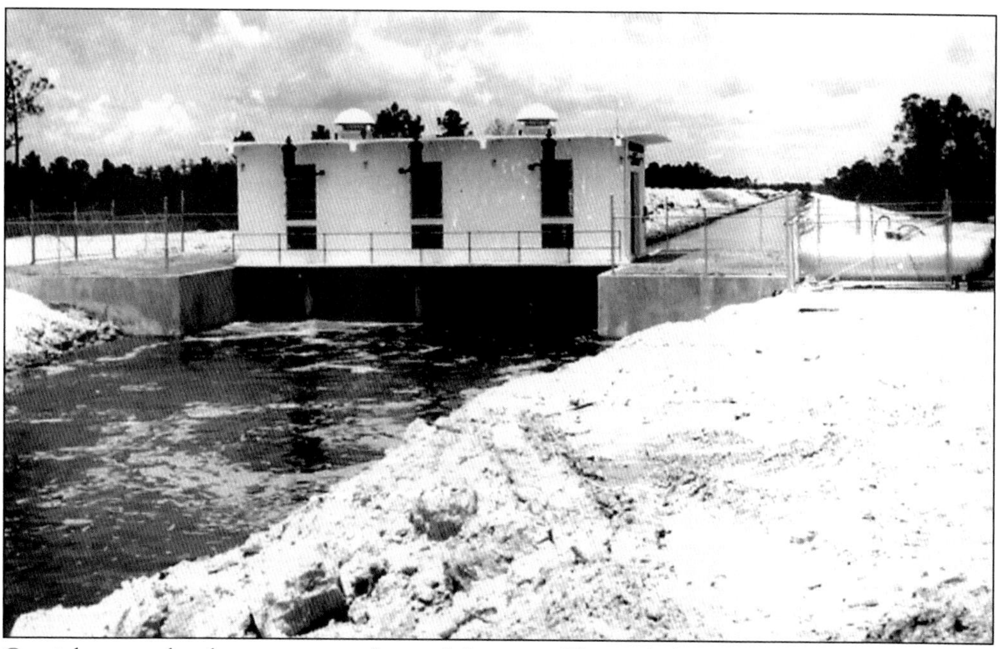

Crucial to any development was enhanced drainage. The underlying cap rock (exposed coral) held water like a plate. Bud Lyons's dikes and the Central and South Flood Control pump stations did not provide adequate drainage for a city. The C-14 canal dredged at the south end of the city was part of the county's Sunshine Drainage District reclamation plan. (Courtesy of Coral Ridge Properties.)

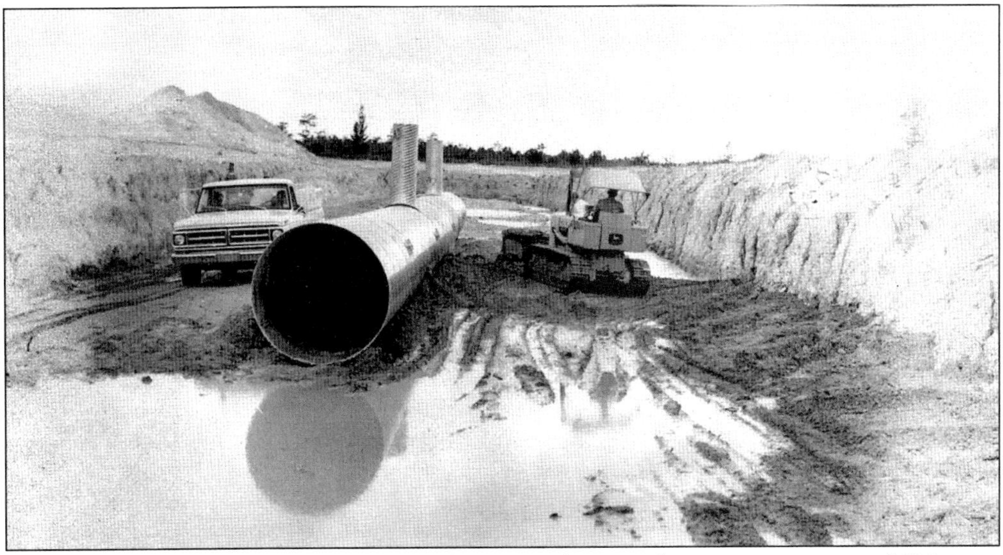

Coral Ridge Properties built canals along the section lines, each section consisting of 650 acres. The residue was used to build roads. The 40 miles of canals, streams, and lakes allowed for a significant percentage of water-view properties in the city and serve as a habitat for native wildlife, including an occasional errant alligator. (Courtesy of Coral Ridge Properties.)

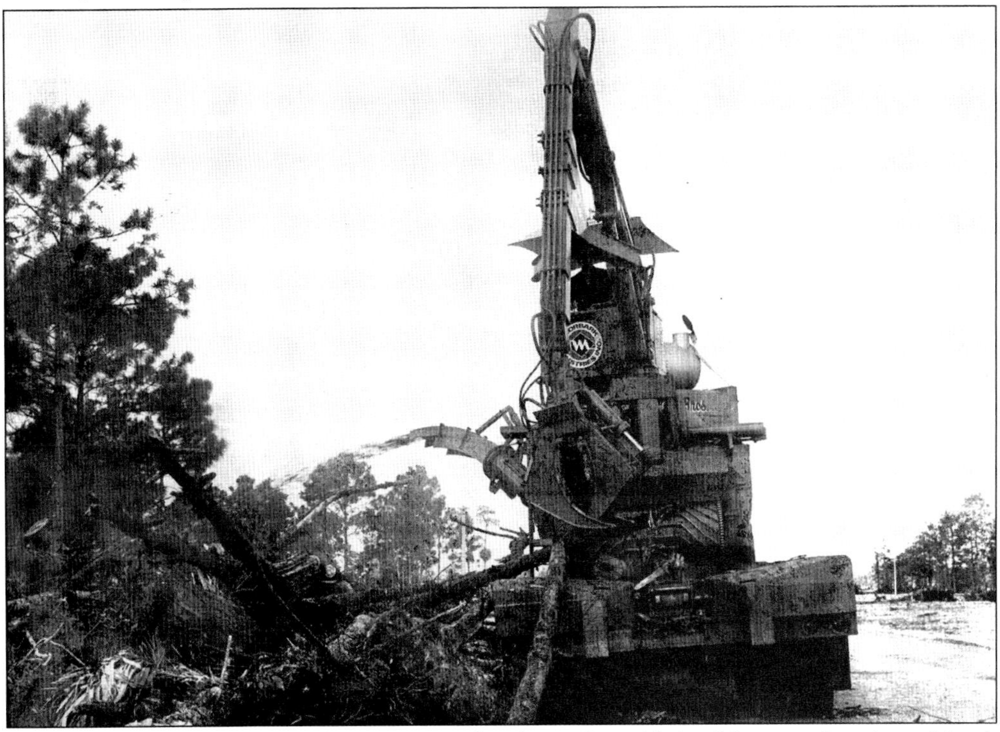

This large chipper was "part of the expense in developing" useable land from scrub and marshland. It can be deduced that the area pictured is scrub because of the pine trees. Cypress trees would indicate marshland and the underlying muck would have to be removed before any building could commence. The residue was used for landscaping "mountains" and berms. (Courtesy of Coral Ridge Properties.)

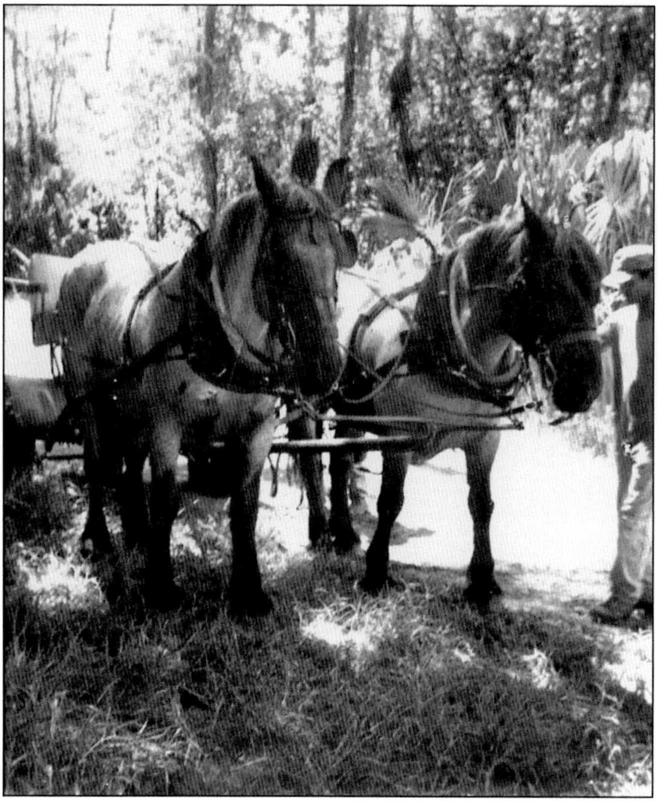

A number of jobs required a gentler touch. Horses were employed from time to time to clear selected trees from a site, leaving others intact. Entire stands of trees were left in place in some areas to retain the natural environment. (Courtesy of the Heafy Collection.)

University Drive, now the main artery running north and south, had to be cleared and graded. In anticipation of its importance, it was planned as a four-lane thoroughfare with room for expansion. Hunt had been to Hawaii and was struck by the boulevards full of flowering plants, and that was part of his plan for Coral Springs. (Courtesy of Coral Ridge Properties.)

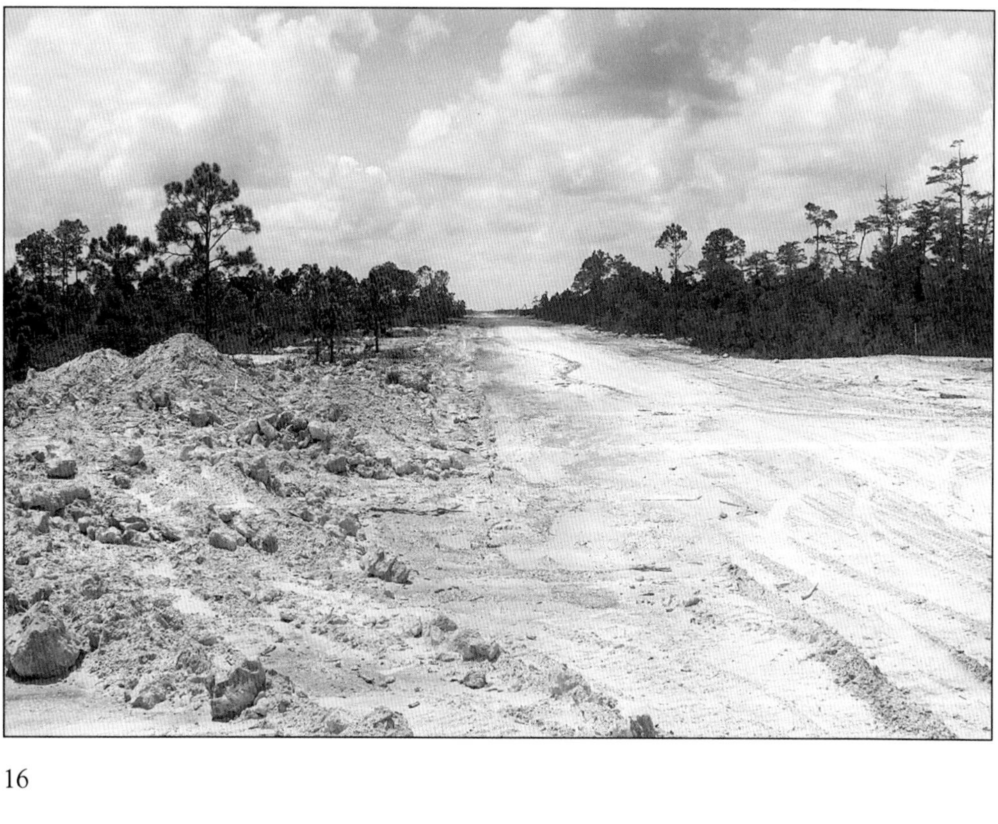

Two

"One of the Last Pieces of Gold on the Gold Coast"

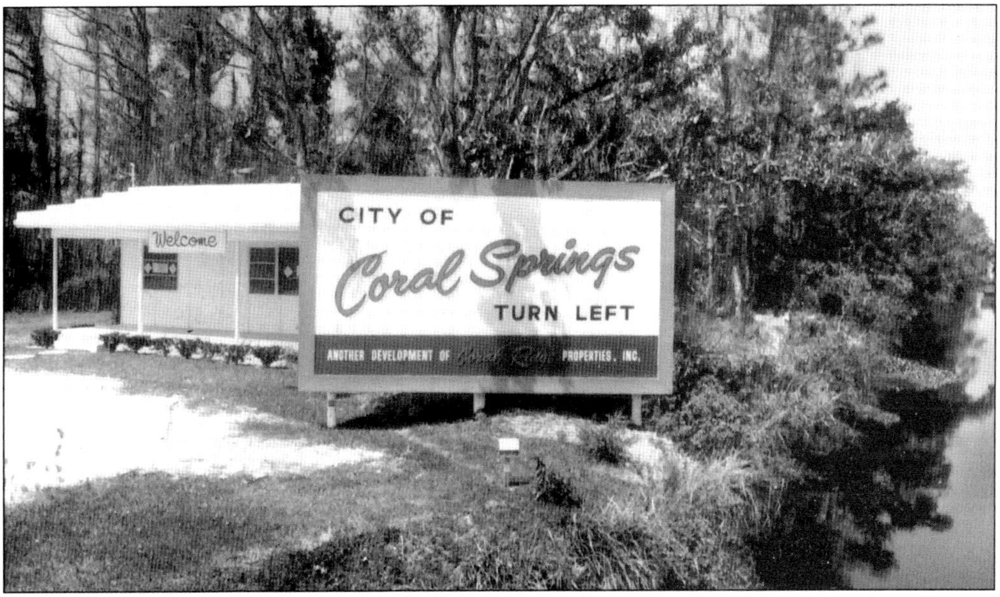

Coral Ridge Properties built the city's first real estate office in 1964 at the intersection of Route 441 and Wiles Road, just outside the city limits. It was a 30-by-20-foot single-room wooden structure, furnished with a desk, several chairs, a floor fan, filing cabinet, and a manual typewriter to complete purchase contracts. The walls were covered with subdivision plats so prospective buyers could choose a site. Wiles Road was the only road (albeit gravel) into the city. This one-room building was moved several times as it became the first police station, a club house, fire department training site, the Mini Museum, and finally the Museum of Coral Springs History. Notice the original Bahaman-style roof. (Courtesy of Coral Ridge Properties.)

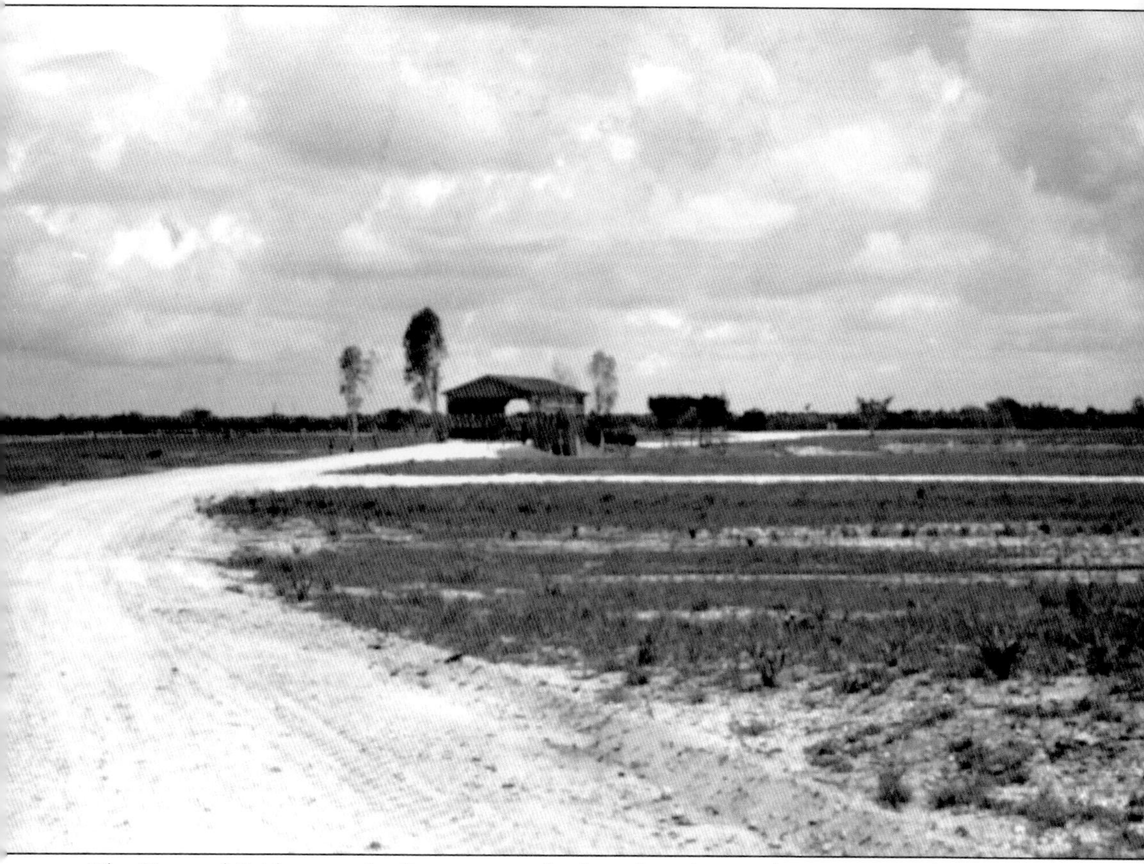

The Covered Bridge was the first structure built within the city by contractor George Porter, who was hired by Lewie Mullins, vice president of the building division of Coral Ridge Properties, in early 1964. It withstood the eye of Hurricane Cleo, which passed over in August 1964 without any damage. The 40-foot bridge has a single steel span. Its roof is composed of 25 truss rafters, cross braces, and stringers and is covered with shingles. It is the only covered bridge in Florida along the public right-of-way. James S. Hunt wanted to project a sense of the South on the otherwise barren landscape. Originally painted barn red, snuff advertisements were painted on either side to make it appear appropriately seasoned. (Courtesy of Coral Ridge Properties.)

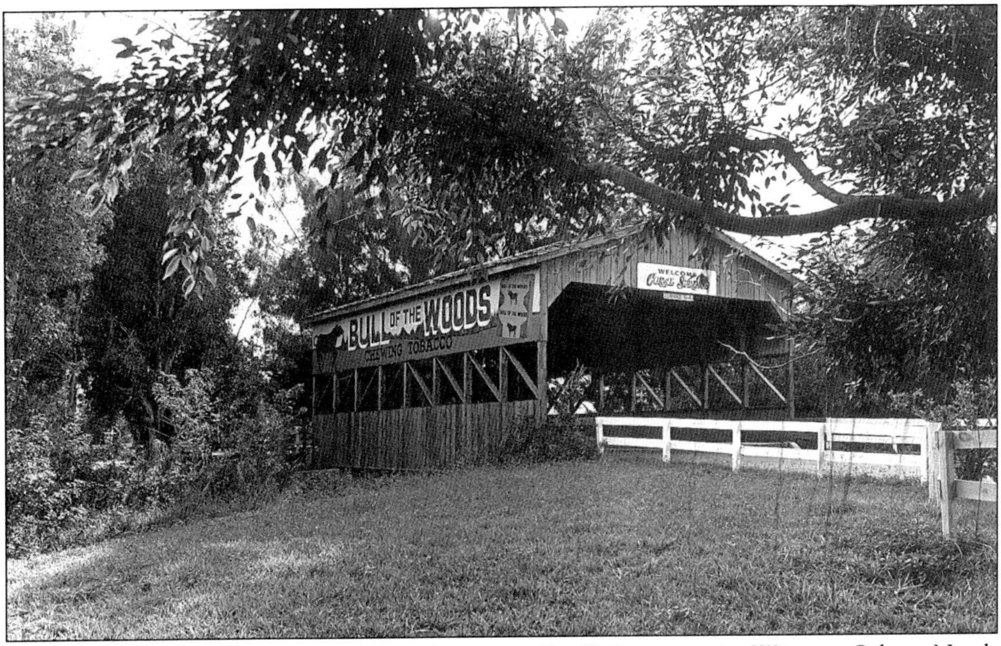

Coral Ridge Properties contacted the American Snuff Company in Winston-Salem, North Carolina, for chewing tobacco designs to use on the Covered Bridge. They supplied two designs plus an artist to paint the murals. The Bull of the Woods logo was first used in 1876. (Courtesy of the Heafy Collection.)

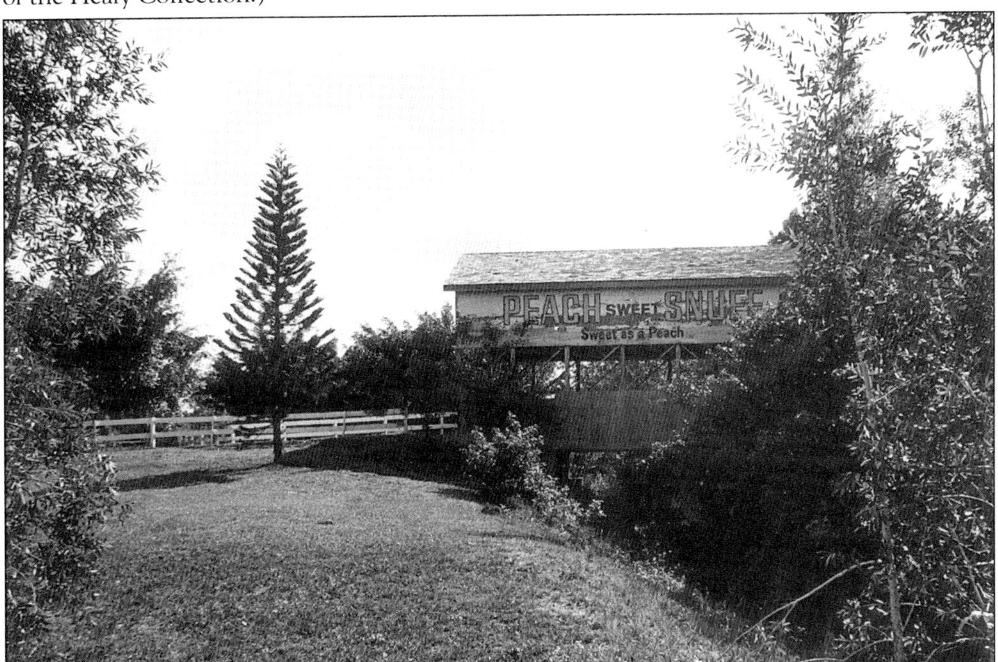

The Peach Sweet Snuff logo, made to appeal to ladies when introduced in 1950, was painted on the west side of the bridge. Over the years, the murals have been restored but are difficult to see as trees have grown along the sides of the canal. This leads many people to suspect that the "Bridge Clearance" signs along Wiles Road are misplaced. (Courtesy of Coral Ridge Properties.)

This is it! *This is it!*

Brokers and Investors

SPECTACULAR FIRST PRE-DEVELOPMENT SALE OF

City of Coral Springs Lots !

GALT OCEAN MILE HOTEL — WEDNESDAY — JULY 22nd — 8:30 A. M. !!

NOW! ***Read the following reprints carefully:***

The Miami Herald BROWARD COUNTY EDITION

Saturday, July 11, 1964 No. 223 *Florida's Most Complete Newspaper* 54th Year 62 Pages 10 Cents

A Latin American Edition is Published Daily

New City to Get $3.2 Million Sendoff

By DON BEDWELL
Assistant Broward Bureau Chief

FORT LAUDERDALE — Coral Ridge Properties Inc. plans to channel 3.2 million dollars "immediately" into land development of a northwest Broward city ultimately capable of absorbing a population of 70,000.

Spokesmen for the giant firm said Friday they will outline their blueprint for the already incorporated city of Coral Springs before county brokers and investors July 22.

Five hundred sixty-three modestly priced lots are to be placed on the market at that time, according to J. P. Taravella, executive vice president of the corporation.

Taravella said triple-faceted construction plans will convert 5,000 acres of virgin land north and west of Margate into:

CORAL SPRINGS proper, a residential community of the 563 lots being marketed next week.

CORAL SPRINGS HILLS, a more affluent cluster of 1½ and two-acre tracts with prices ranging from $19,600 up to around $50,000.

CORAL SPRINGS VILLAGE, a retirement complex incorporating 3,700 apartment units blended into a golf course.

Corporation officials said the 3.2 million dollars will be poured into land development of the massive 5,000-acre package, providing lakes, artificial hills and canals.

Work already has started at the site — west of State Road 7 between Wiles Road and Sample Road abutting Margate — according to Taravella.

Coral Ridge Properties, a firm with an estimated 155 million dollars' worth of investments in Broward County, bought the 5,000 acres three years ago in what Taravella said was a cash transaction.

"We're lighting three fires at once," he said. "We hope to hit three markets with this one, including the only slightly touched retirement market."

He expressed hope the retirement community, Coral Springs Village, can be underway by December.

That complex of single story apartments grouped around a lake and waterways will be interlaced with a nine-hole golf course, according to plans.

It will feature medical facilities and personnel, including ambulance service, Taravella said. The rental price — presently envisioned at under $100 monthly — is to cover hospitalization insurance as well.

Coral Springs itself, the only portion of the development incorporated by the State Legislature, should come into its own around 1966 or 1968, Taravella believes.

That's when he expects Florida to be besieged with young married couples, by-products of the World War II baby boom, seeking moderately priced housing.

Coral Springs Hills is foreseen as an area of widely spaced luxury homes amid rolling hills, reached through a covered bridge in the primitive tradition.

Officials said the new development will be protected by strict building restrictions patterened after those in the firm's existing Coral Ridge section.

FORT LAUDERDALE NEWS AND SUN-SENTINEL, Saturday, July 11, 1964 1C

-LOCAL- -STATE- -NATIONAL- -WORLDWIDE-

REAL ESTATE AND BUILDING HIGHLIGHTS

'Spectacular' Scheduled For July 22

Coral Springs Land Sale Coming Up

A discount land sale to celebrate the birth of the City of Coral Springs will be held by Coral Ridge Properties, Inc., in the Galt Ocean Mile Hotel at 8:30 a.m. July 22.

There will be free breakfast, entertainment, dancing girls, jazz, and investment opportunities in building lots.

It will be the sixth in a series of discount land sales "spectaculars" held by the Ft. Lauderdale development firm over the past 16 years. The first was held to inaugurate the Coral Ridge section which has become approximately one-third of the city of Ft. Lauderdale. More than $15,000,000 have passed hands in the sales which Life and other national magazines have described as wild and spectacular jamborees.

The sales, unlike anything held anywhere else, are the brainchild of James S. Hunt Sr., founder, president and board chairman of Coral Ridge Properties. Hunt believes in doing things in a dramatic, big-scale manner and his methods have made the firm one of the most profitable land developers in the country.

NO CHANGE

Hunt sees no reason for changing a successful formula, and so the upcoming sale will follow the pattern set by its forerunners, except that it will be held in the ballroom of one of the three hotels owned by the Hunt organization instead of at the War Memorial Auditorium as in the past. In former years, as many as 6,000 persons have attended the sales, but fewer than 2,000 are expected this year.

Whatever the number, they can expect to be greeted by a troupe of Scottish bagpipers out front. Though many find the wail of a bagpipe a bit hard to take shortly before dawn, Hunt thinks their music enchanting, and they will be there.

At the entrance, girls will preside over long tables of juice, coffee, danish rolls and doughnuts and visitors will be invited to have all they wish. From the inside will come the rollicking blare of the Dixieland jazz — the Preacher Rollo Quintet doing its best to wake 'em up and shake 'em up.

DANCING GALS

The entertainment will consist mainly of a motion picture showing growth of Ft. Lauderdale and the Gold Coast, with consequent rapid increases in realty values. Girls will dance, the band will play and suddenly a bell will ring.

James S. Hunt will then step forward and announce the terms of the sale, including the discount from established plat prices, amount of down payment and length of amortization period. Another bell will sound, and for the next ten minutes or so, pandemonium will break loose as the crowd surges forward to the sellers to get "hold" certificates for the lots they wish.

The lots to be sold on July 22 comprise Subdivision 1 of the City of Coral Springs, to soon be opened about 2½ miles west of Pompano on Sample Rd. Extension. Only 536 lots are offered, and among them are apartment and single-family residence lots.

Plans for the City include 3,700 apartments, a golf course, stores and all community facilities, including 30 miles of roads and 20 miles of canals winding among the hills and lakes that are now being built at a cost of more than $7,000,000.

BROKERS AND SALESMEN! Pick up your "Advance Copy" Plats and invitations at the Coral Ridge Sales Office immediately! Start lining up your customers who like "GOOD BUYS"!

NOTICE TO OUT-OF-TOWN INVESTORS!! Contact one of our local brokers about this investment of a lifetime!! Attend this big meeting with him! It will be one you'll remember!!

Coral Ridge PROPERTIES, INC.

2787 East Oakland Park Blvd. Fort Lauderdale, Florida 564-5222

The first land sale for brokers occurred on July 22, 1964 at the Galt Ocean Mile Hotel in Ft. Lauderdale. There were Scottish bagpipers playing out front, a free breakfast, "dancing gals," a Dixieland jazz band, and investment opportunities. Fifteen-hundred brokers bought 536 lots for $1.6 million in 14 minutes. (Courtesy of *The Miami Herald*.)

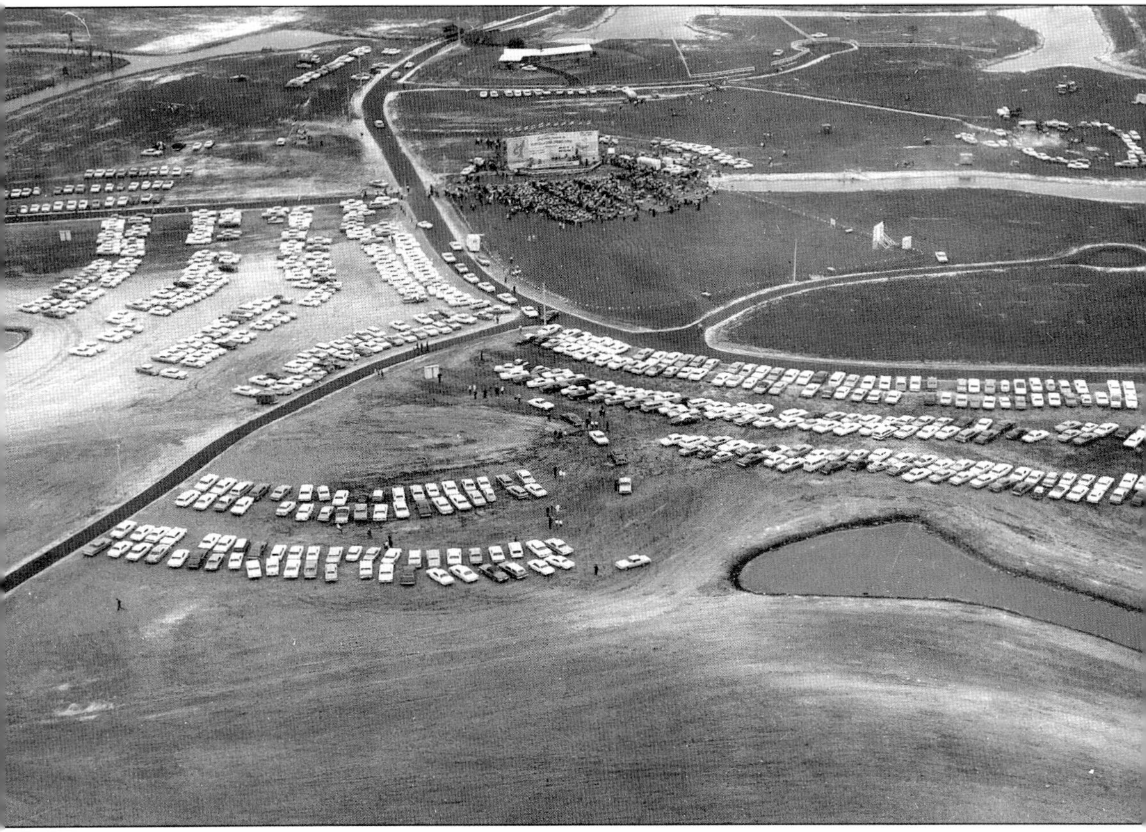

The second land sale, for brokers and the general public, took place on March 25, 1965 in Coral Springs. Five-and-a-half miles of roads had to be laid just to gain access to sites. Eight model houses were also built for the event. Hunt again proved his powers of persuasion. Ten thousand people drove through the Covered Bridge that day, pictured at the top of the photograph. (Courtesy of Coral Ridge Properties.)

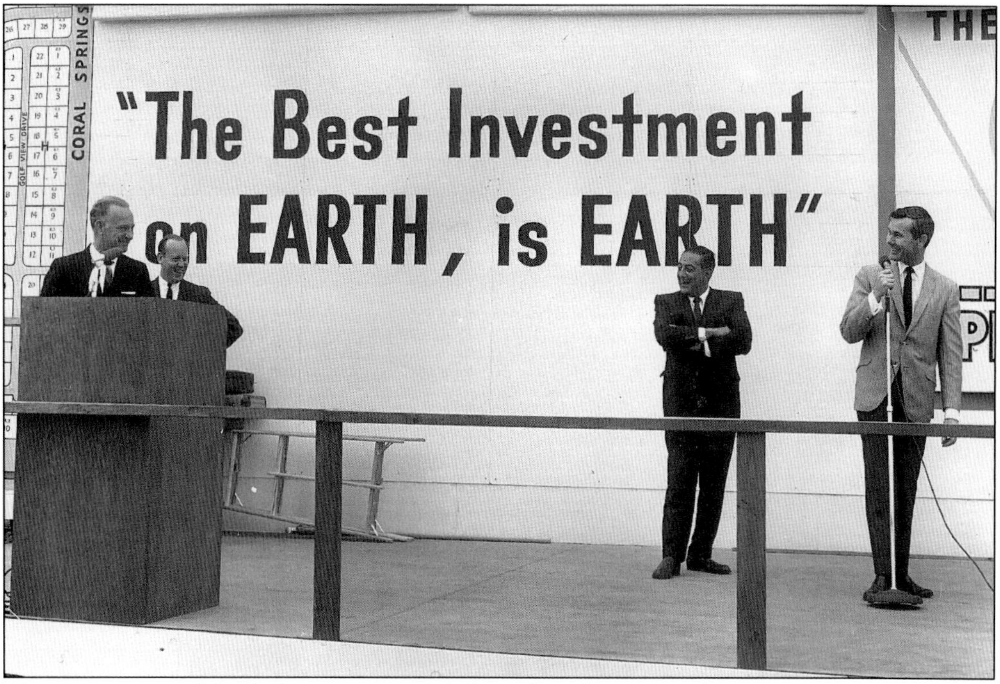

The "Largest Land-Rush Discount Land Sale and Barbecue" in then-desolate Coral Springs brought in $5 million for the sale of 1,100 lots and served up three tons of barbecue. Even host Johnny Carson bought 54.6 acres along Royal Palm Boulevard, selling them five years later for five times the purchase price. Guy Lombardo, appearing at the Galt Ocean Mile Hotel, came along for the ride. (Courtesy of Coral Ridge Properties.)

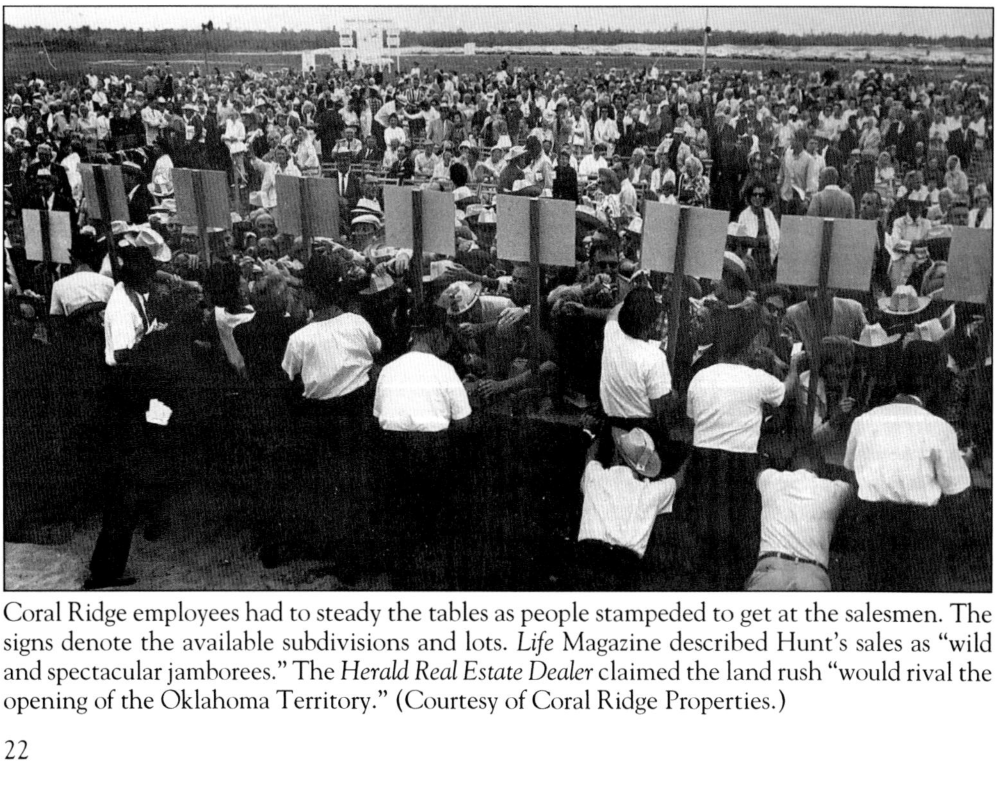

Coral Ridge employees had to steady the tables as people stampeded to get at the salesmen. The signs denote the available subdivisions and lots. *Life* Magazine described Hunt's sales as "wild and spectacular jamborees." The *Herald Real Estate Dealer* claimed the land rush "would rival the opening of the Oklahoma Territory." (Courtesy of Coral Ridge Properties.)

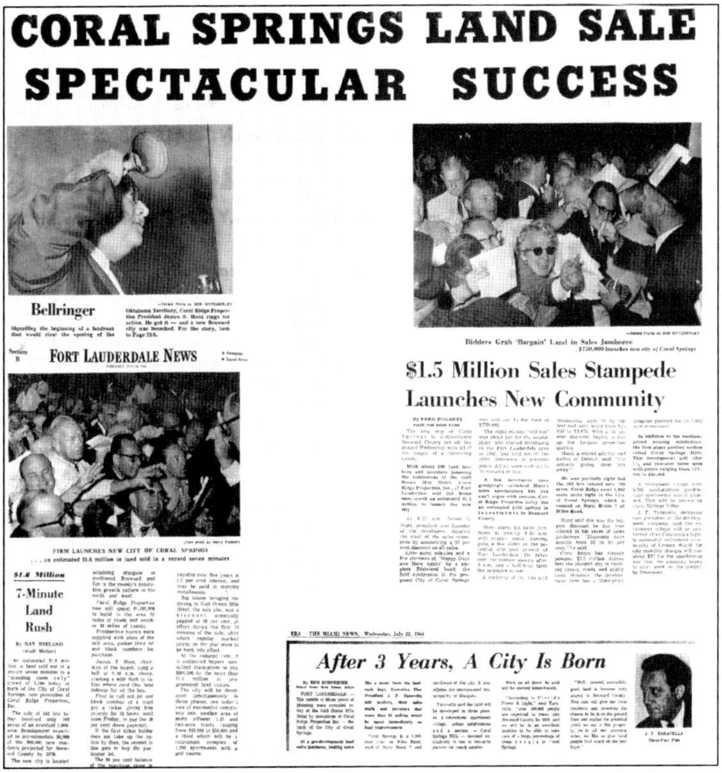

CORAL SPRINGS LAND SALE SPECTACULAR SUCCESS

Bellringer

Signalling the beginning of a landrush that would rival the opening of the Oklahoma Territory, Coral Ridge Properties President James S. Hunt rings for action. He got it — and a new Broward city was launched. For the story, turn to Page 23A.

FORT LAUDERDALE NEWS

Section B

FIRM LAUNCHES NEW CITY OF CORAL SPRINGS

. . . an estimated $1.6 million in land sold in a record seven minutes

$1.6 Million

7-Minute Land Rush

By RAY WIELAND (Staff Writer)

Bidders Grab 'Bargain' Land in Sales Jamboree

$750,000 launches new city of Coral Springs

$1.5 Million Sales Stampede Launches New Community

By FRED FOGARTY

THE MIAMI NEWS, Wednesday, July 22, 1964

After 3 Years, A City Is Born

J. P. TARAVELLA

This collage of newspaper articles illustrates the carnival atmosphere at the land sale, including James Hunt ringing the opening bell. Coral Ridge Properties had everything riding on the success of this event. As usual, Hunt picked the right horse. (Courtesy of Coral Ridge Properties.)

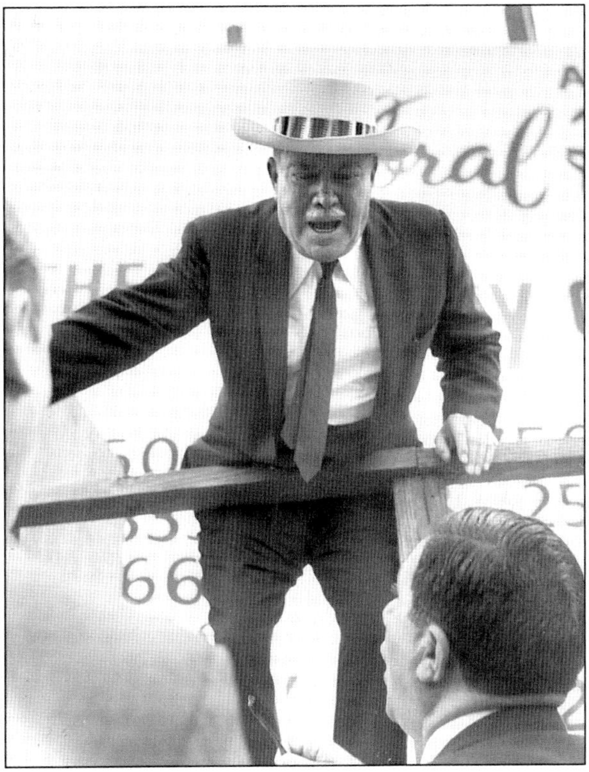

James Hunt and his executive vice president Joseph Taravella had many animated conversations about the development of their planned city, in public as well as in private, and sometimes at 3 a.m. Hunt had the ideas and Taravella the know-how to carry them out. (Courtesy of Coral Ridge Properties.)

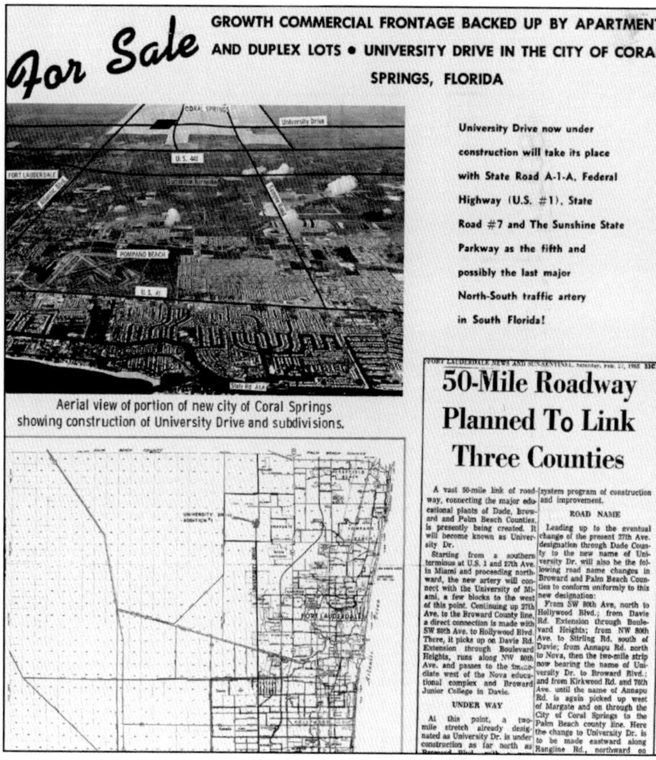

50-Mile Roadway Planned To Link Three Counties

A vast 50-mile link of roadway, connecting the major educational plants of Dade, Broward and Palm Beach Counties, is presently being created. It will become known as University Dr.

Starting from a southern terminus at U.S. 1 and 27th Ave. in Miami and proceeding northward, the new artery will connect with the University of Miami, a few blocks to the west of this point. Continuing up 27th Ave. to the Broward County line, a direct connection is made with SW 80th Ave. to Hollywood Blvd. There, it picks up on Davie Rd. Extension through Boulevard Heights, runs along NW 80th Ave. and passes to the immediate west of the Nova educational complex and Broward Junior College in Davie.

UNDER WAY

At this point, a two-mile stretch already designated as University Dr. is under construction as far north as

system program of construction and improvement.

ROAD NAME

Leading up to the eventual change of the present 27th Ave. designation through Dade County to the new name of University Dr. will also be the following road name changes in Broward and Palm Beach Counties to conform uniformly to this new designation:

From SW 80th Ave. north to Hollywood Blvd.; from Davie Rd. Extension through Boulevard Heights; from NW 80th Ave. to Stirling Rd. south of Davie; from Annapu Rd. north to Nova, then the two-mile strip now bearing the name of University Dr. to Broward Blvd.; and from Kirkwood Rd. and 78th Ave. until the name of Annapu Rd. is again picked up west of Margate and on through the City of Coral Springs to the Palm Beach county line. Here the change to University Dr. is to be made eastward along Rangline Rd., northward on

Coral Springs was so remote in the early 1960s that all sales literature included a map with directions. People in Ft. Lauderdale called the new city "T.F.O."—Too Far Out. Annapu Road was to become part of a 50-mile link of roadways connecting schools of Dade, Broward, and Palm Beach Counties, including a proposed college in Coral Springs. It was later renamed University Drive. (Courtesy of Coral Ridge Properties.)

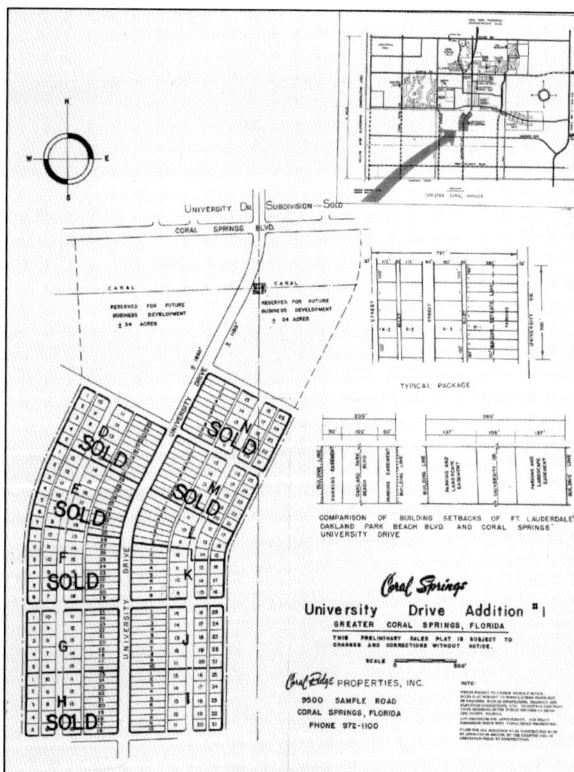

Coral Ridge Properties filed this University Drive Addition plat on April 15, 1966. Construction along that thoroughfare was to be commercial. Notice that Royal Palm Boulevard had been originally named Coral Springs Boulevard. Many street names were changed to make them unique to the City, but some were changed to match what the roads were called in neighboring cities, such as Royal Palm Boulevard. The original University Drive subdivision had already sold out. (Courtesy of Coral Ridge Properties.)

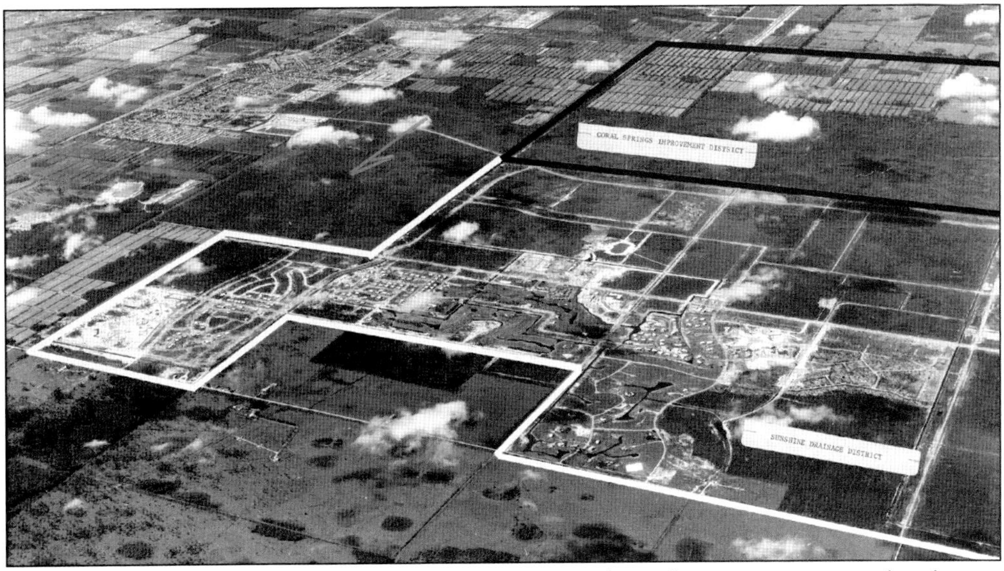

In 1969 the Coral Springs Improvement District was formed to manage water distribution to the area adjacent to the original Sunshine Drainage District. When the north side of town was developed, the North Springs Improvement District was formed. (Courtesy of Coral Ridge Properties.)

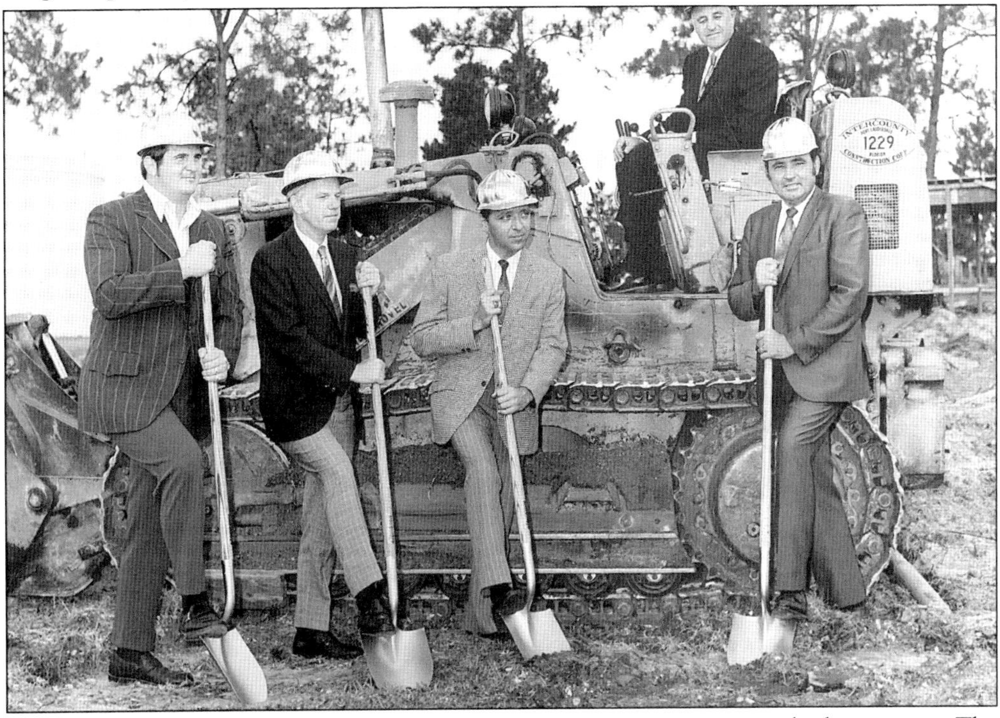

An expansion of the sewage and water plants was underway in 1971 to triple the capacity. The Coral Springs Water District has always owned its facilities, making them cost effective to its customers. The following gentlemen started the construction: Commissioners Richard Hunt, Edward Heafy, unknown, Dr. Paul Hughes (Broward County Health Director), and Mayor George MacGregor. (Courtesy of Coral Ridge Properties.)

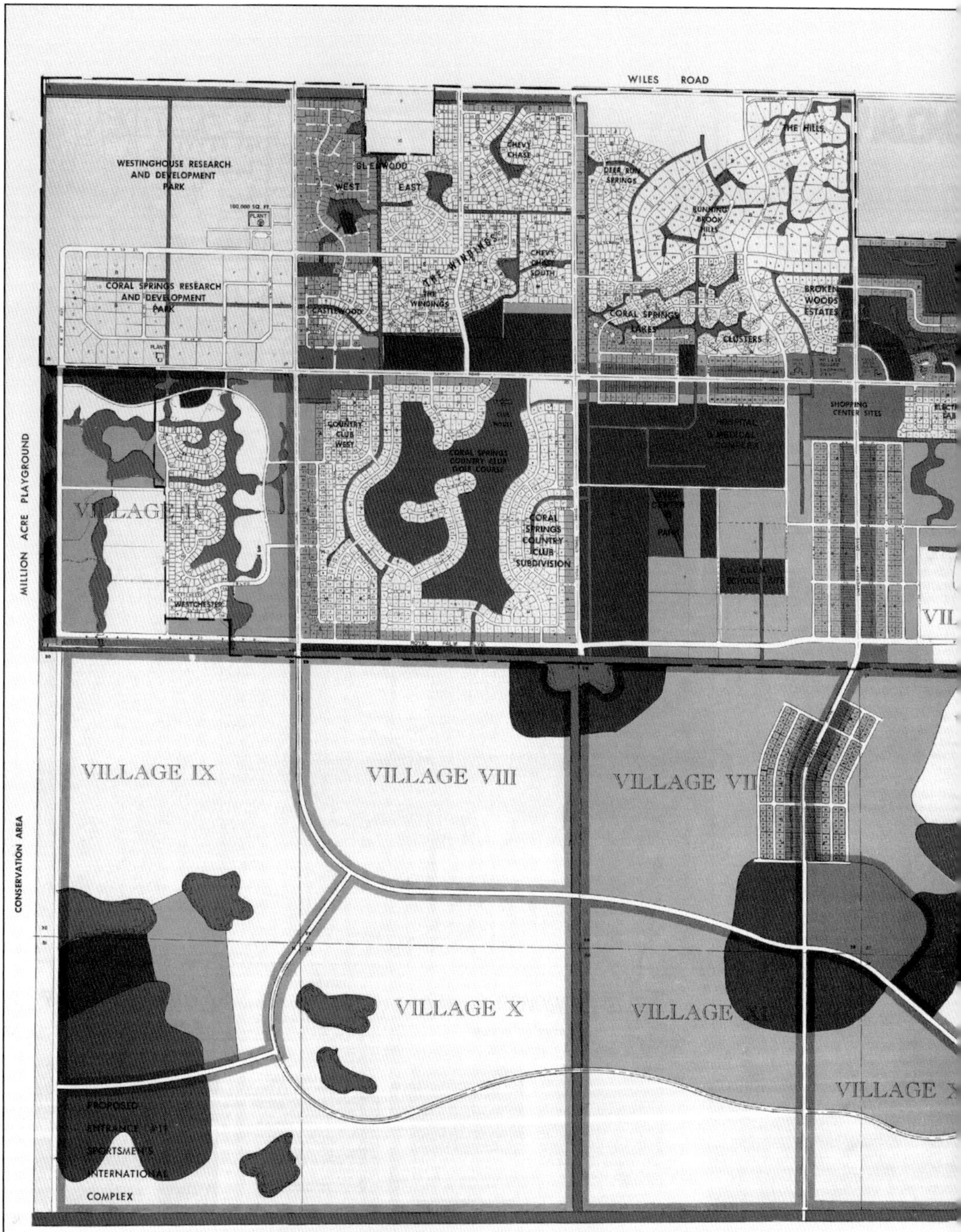

FORT LAUDERDALE'S NEW "NEIGHBOR CITY" O

In 1971, with a population of 7,800, the master plan evolved into the controlled development of twelve distinct villages, each with its own shops, schools, and parks. Nothing was yet planned for anything north of Wiles Road. By 1979 the population hit 37,000 and the plan was expanded

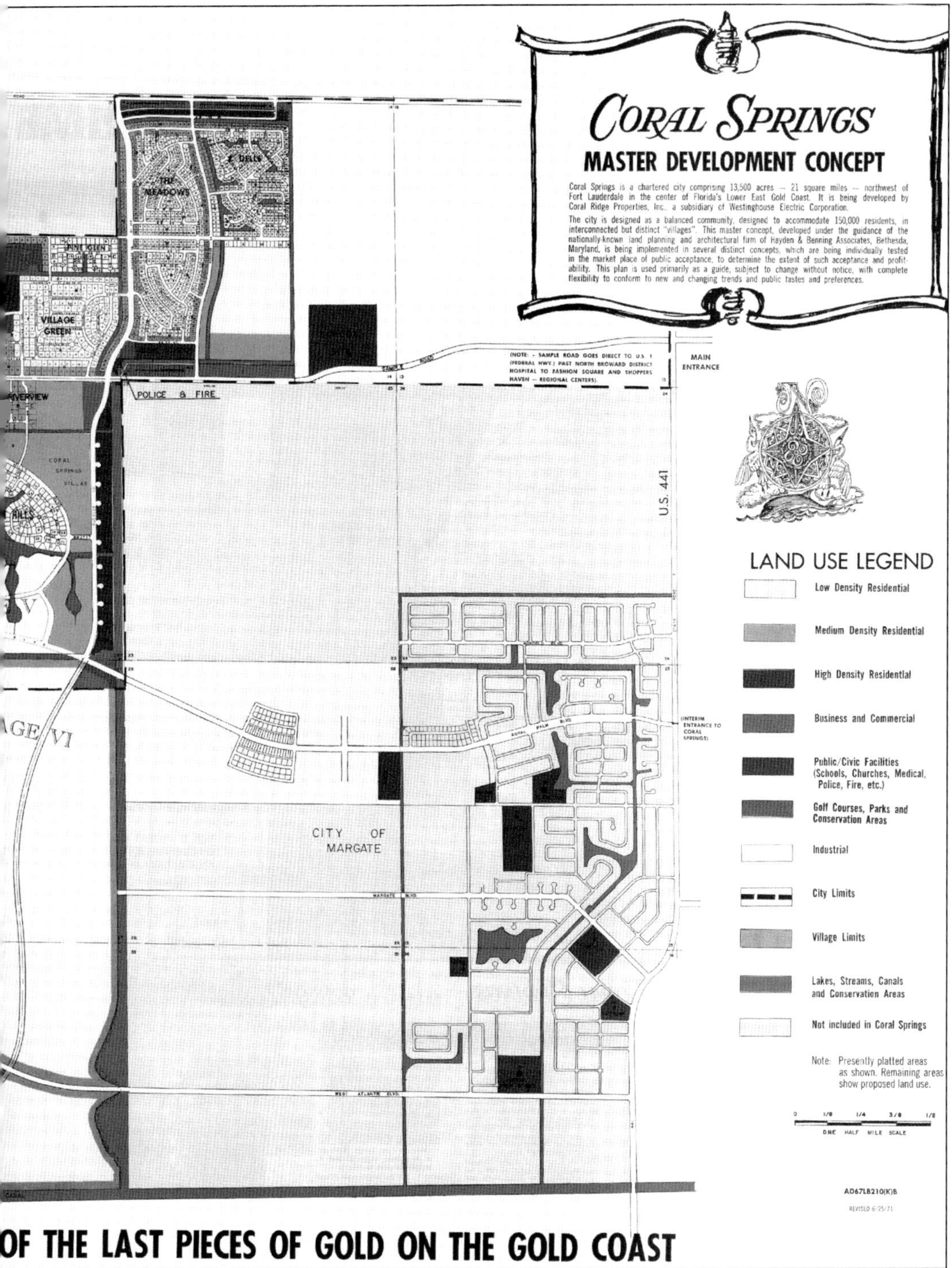

to include sixteen villages. It wasn't until 1982 that plats with subdivisions north of Wiles Road were filed. (Courtesy of Coral Ridge Properties.)

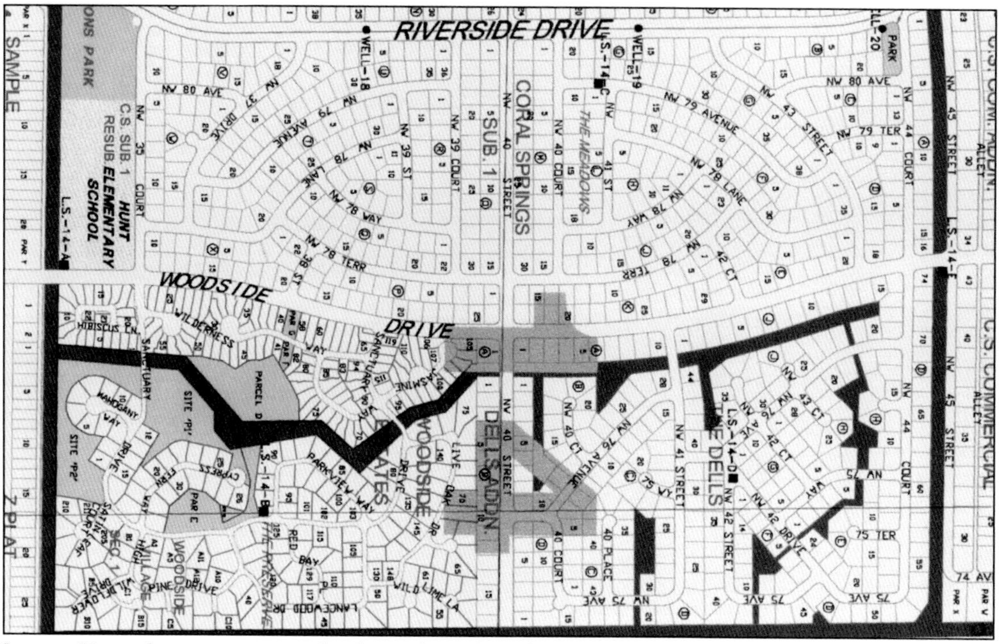

James Hunt became irritated when the plan for the very first subdivision was causing writer's block among his executives. He took a plat of the Coral Ridge Isles subdivision in Ft. Lauderdale, cut it to size, rotated it 180 degrees and announced, "There's your plat!" It became the Meadows along Riverside Drive, south of Wiles Road. (Courtesy of the City of Coral Springs.)

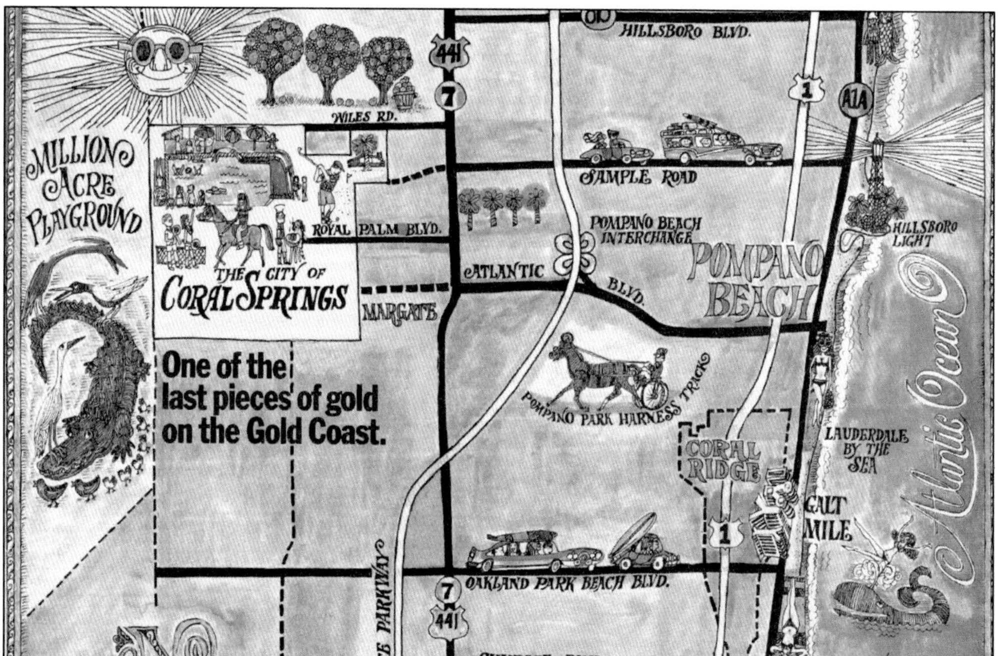

This charming map of Broward County was created by Harvey Olsen, city commissioner from 1963 to 1965. It uses Coral Ridge Property's favored moniker for Coral Springs at the time: "One of the last pieces of gold on the Gold Coast." (Courtesy of the City of Coral Springs.)

Three

"The City in the Country"

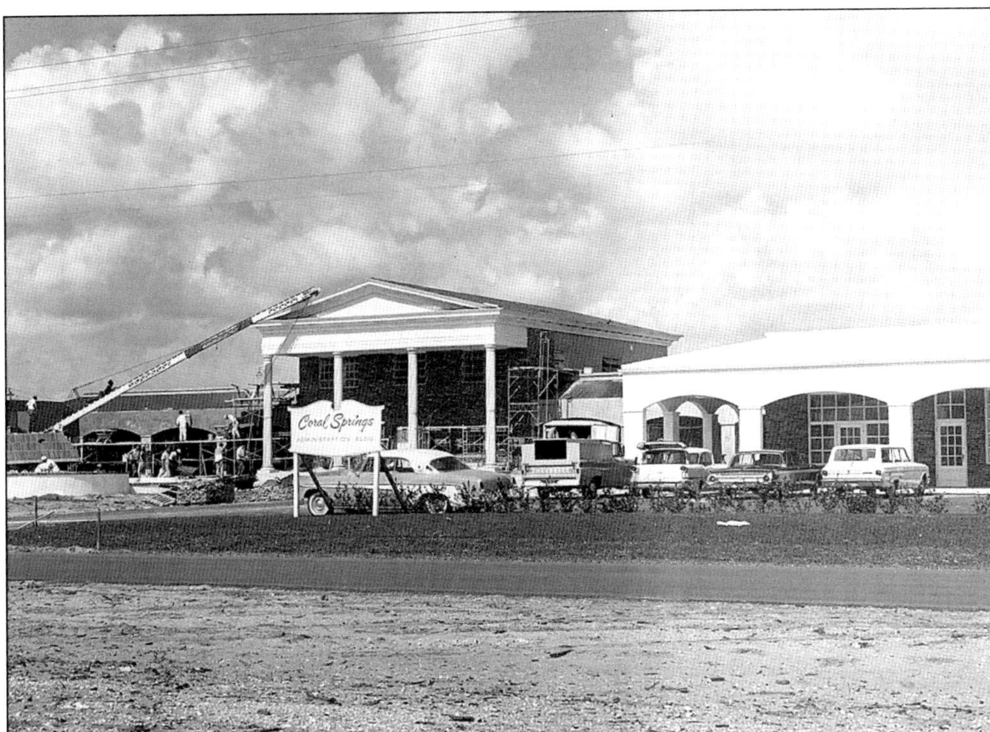

The construction of Coral Ridge Properties Administration Building on Sample Road in 1966 was a far cry from the one-room office at the foot of Wiles Road erected just two years earlier. The two-story central building housed the office staff. The west and east wings served various uses, from employee lunchroom to city library to offices for independent realtors. This was to be the hub of what James Hunt imagined as his graceful "City in the Country." (Courtesy of Coral Ridge Properties.)

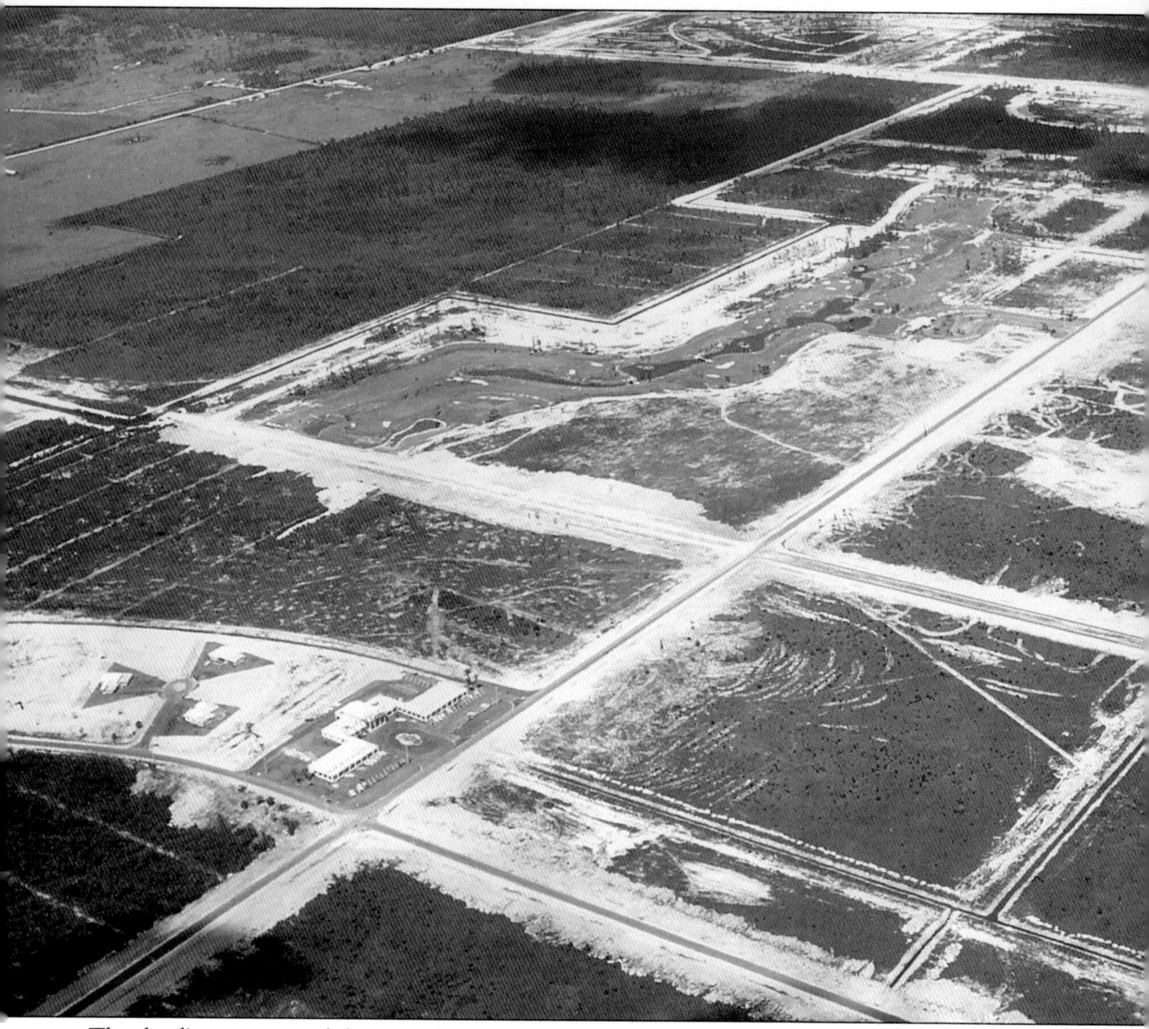

This bird's-eye view of the completed Coral Ridge Properties Administration Building shows more country than city. Red bricks and white columns were used in the design to represent colonial ambiance. To the east is Broken Woods Country Club; to the north are three houses in the Clusters, and to the south, nothing. One had to drive to the neighboring city of Margate for gas or groceries. (Courtesy of Coral Ridge Properties.)

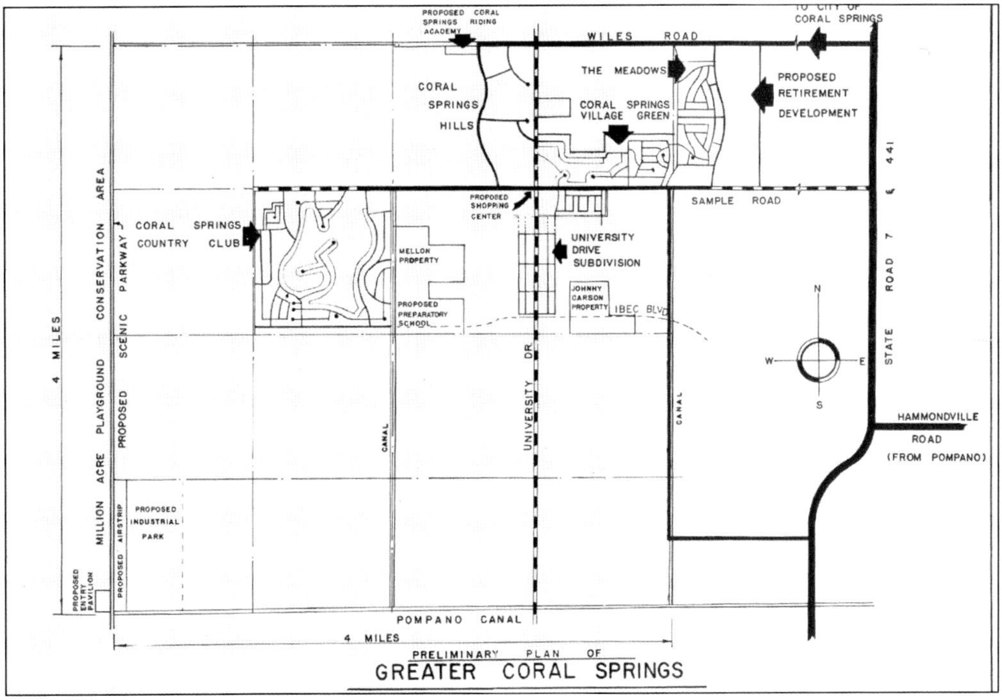

This is the extent of Coral Springs after the land rush. Sample Road is not completed nor is University Drive started, and a million-acre playground and conservation area is planned out west, as well as an airstrip and the Coral Springs Country Club. Johnny Carson owns property along Ibec Boulevard, which would become Royal Palm Boulevard. (Courtesy of Coral Ridge Properties.)

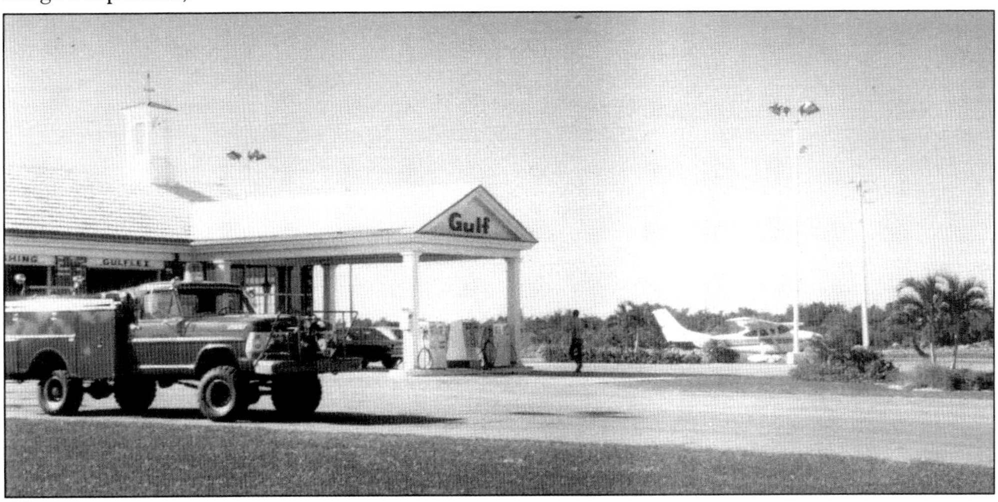

Shortly afterwards, a brick Gulf Station with a colonial-style cupola was built directly across the street—without the large oval sign that is suspended over all other Gulf stations. Note the city's only fire truck and a private plane parked in what was then the "center of town." James Hunt enforced signage covenants from the start, which was a result of what he admired about Honolulu—no advertising in the front of businesses. He also mandated large setbacks from the road, restricted paint colors for building exteriors, and outlawed clotheslines in residential areas. (Courtesy of Coral Ridge Properties.)

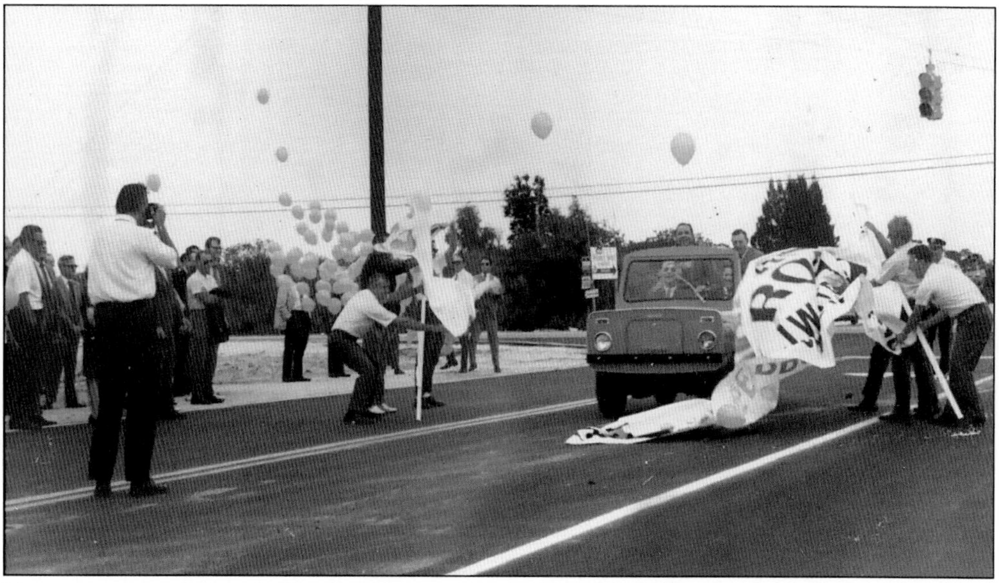

The extension of Sample Road to Route 441 on May 27, 1970 was a significant milestone. Before this, Sample Road had ended before Rock Island Road, necessitating a trip over to Wiles Road or through Margate to access or leave the city. The grand ceremony included a parade with City and Coral Ridge Properties officials. Joseph Taravella, now president of Coral Ridge Properties, is driving Mayor George MacGregor and others in the red Westinghouse Marketeer electric car, which could accelerate to 30 mph. (Courtesy of Coral Ridge Properties.)

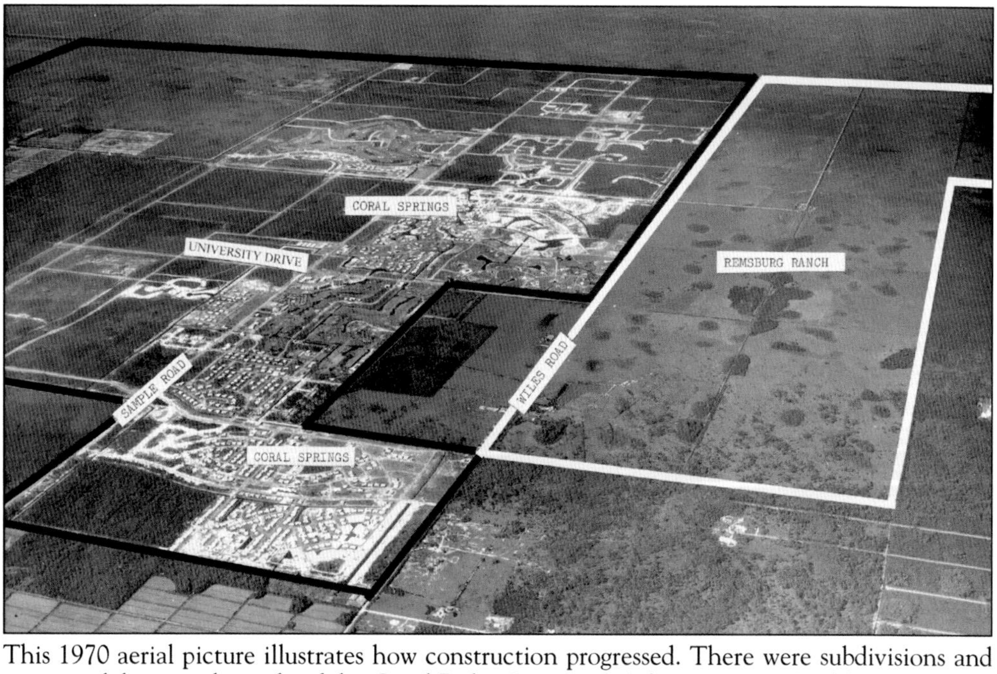

This 1970 aerial picture illustrates how construction progressed. There were subdivisions and country clubs on either side of the Coral Ridge Properties Administration Building. For three years, Robert Hofmann, executive vice president of Coral Ridge Properties, tried to purchase 3,000 acres of ranch land from Luther Remsburg. One year after this aerial photograph was taken, the deal was done. (Courtesy of Dillon Aerial Photography.)

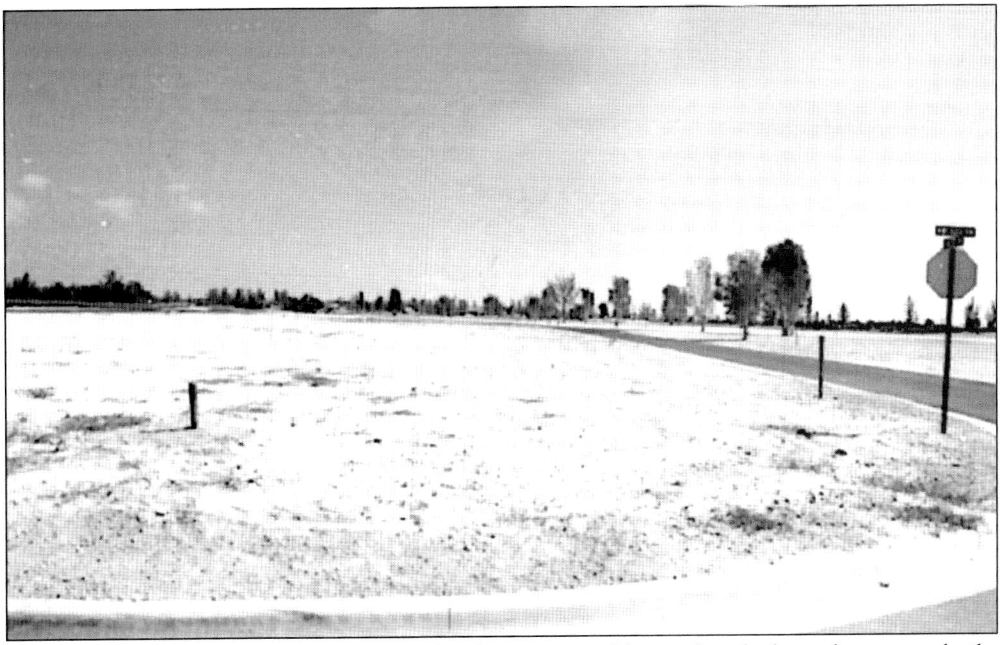

Streets and street signs, water, sewer, and utilities were tidily in place before a house was built. One departure from the colonial design favored by Hunt was curving roads instead of a grid pattern. Broward County had some concerns about the unorthodox layout, but his goal was to slow down traffic. (Courtesy of Coral Ridge Properties.)

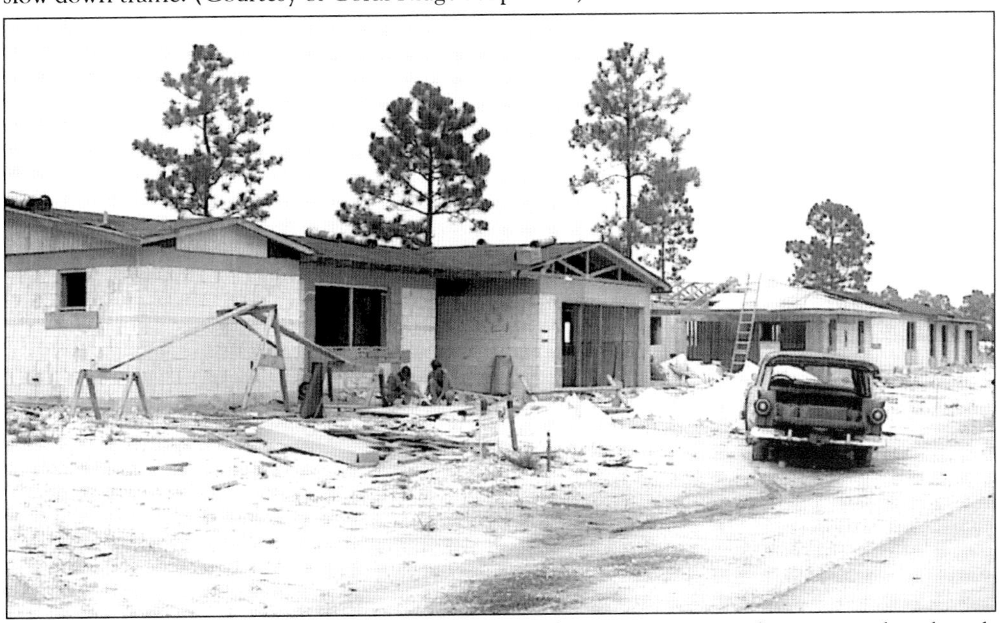

Although the subdivisions were opened in a planned sequence, it must have seemed as though the entire city was under construction at the same time. Bulldozers, cement trucks, framers, cranes, and trucks laden with rolls of sod and palm trees monopolized the roads. Flat tires from roofing nails and the pungent smell of tar were constant assaults. Finally, the approach of moving trucks signaled an end to the mayhem, for one subdivision at least. This shows Broken Woods under construction. (Courtesy of Coral Ridge Properties.)

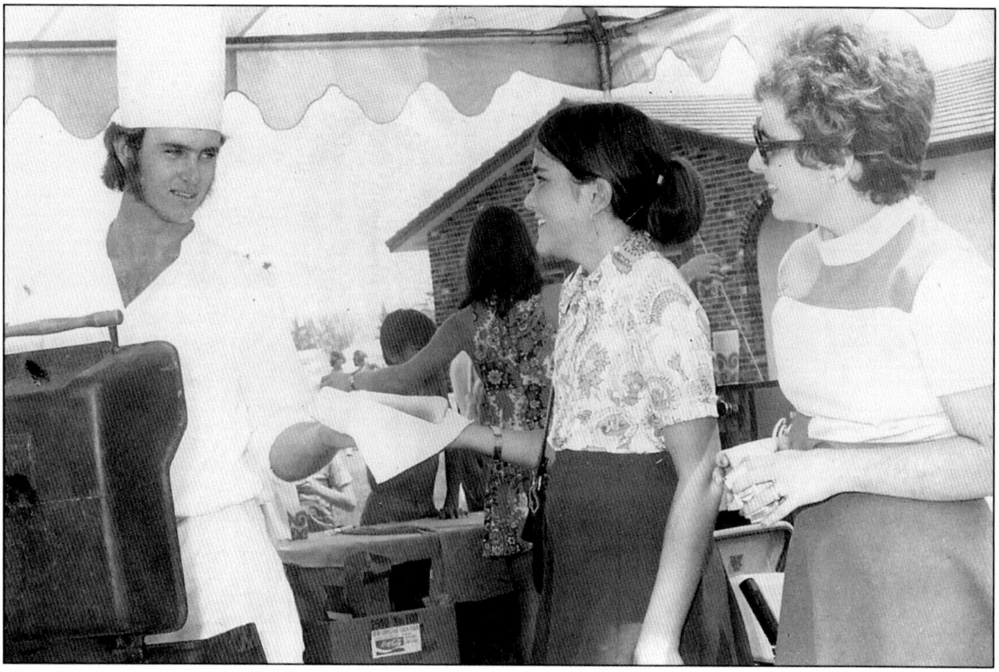

The Forum reported, "Refreshments were part of the fun this weekend when builders opened models in the Ramblewood Subdivision of Coral Springs. Ten homes in the $35,000 to $59,500 price range [exclusive of lots] are featured. Pictured at the home tour [and enjoying a hot dog] are Lisa and Mrs. Joe Ruggiero." (Courtesy of *The Forum*, c. 1974. Photograph by Larry Mailloux.)

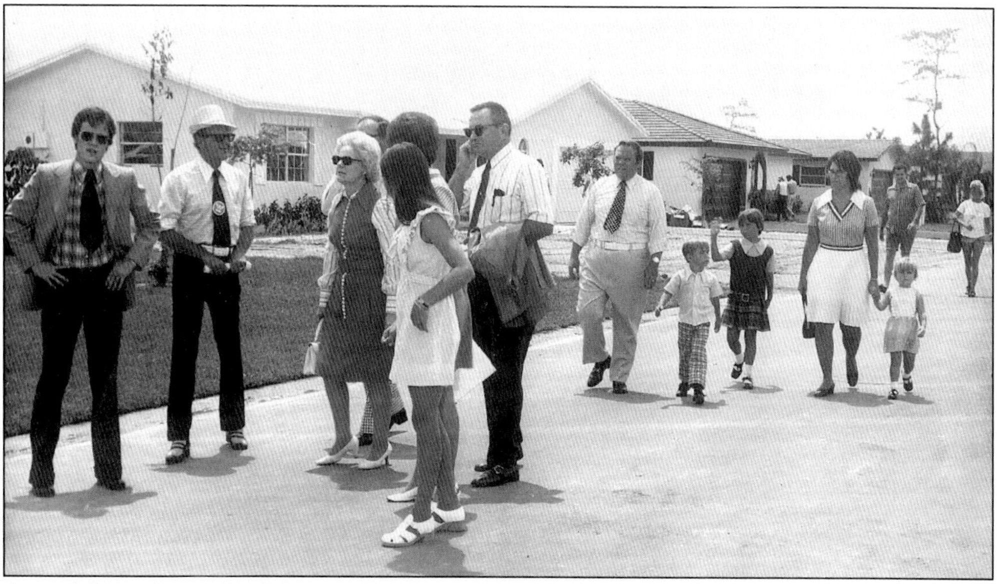

A model row for each subdivision displayed a variety of houses from several contractors, who were not allowed to buy land for speculation. Westinghouse salesmen, representing the 150 independent builders contracted to do business in Coral Springs, were on hand to answer any questions. There were dozens of model rows and grand openings across the city as it grew. (Courtesy of Coral Ridge Properties.)

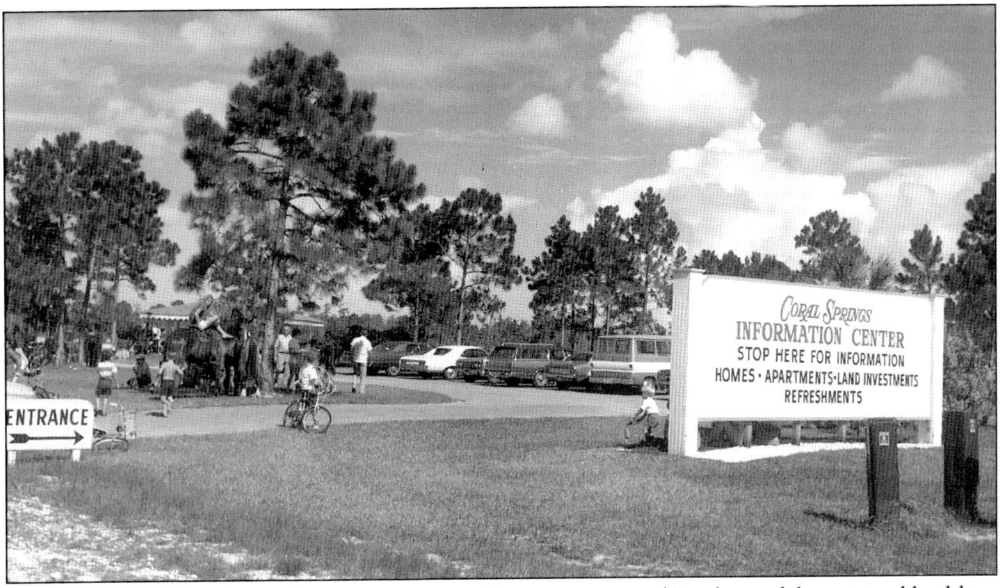

A new Information Center for prospective residents was erected in place of the original building at Route 441 and Wiles, at the southwest corner of Riverside Drive and Sample Road (now occupied by a Shell Station). This is where realtors met most of their prospects. It was also a free watering hole for locals, gathered here with their horses and bicycles. (Courtesy of Coral Ridge Properties.)

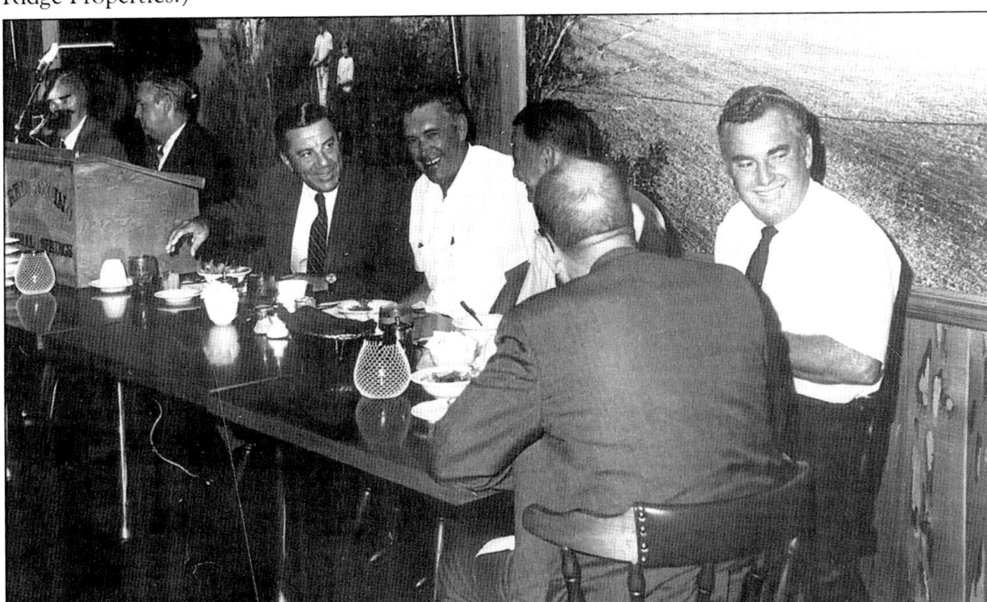

At first held daily, Coral Ridge Properties held a Friday brokers' breakfast at the Red Fox Inn, the city's first restaurant. There are photographic murals of the city sites on the walls—including the Covered Bridge and Broken Woods golf course. They had even more breakfasts in Ft. Lauderdale, as getting to Coral Springs was a trek before the Sawgrass Expressway was built. Joseph Taravella, president of Coral Ridge Properties, is to the right of the microphone and James Hunt Jr., vice president of Coral Ridge Properties, is at the far right. (Courtesy of Coral Ridge Properties.)

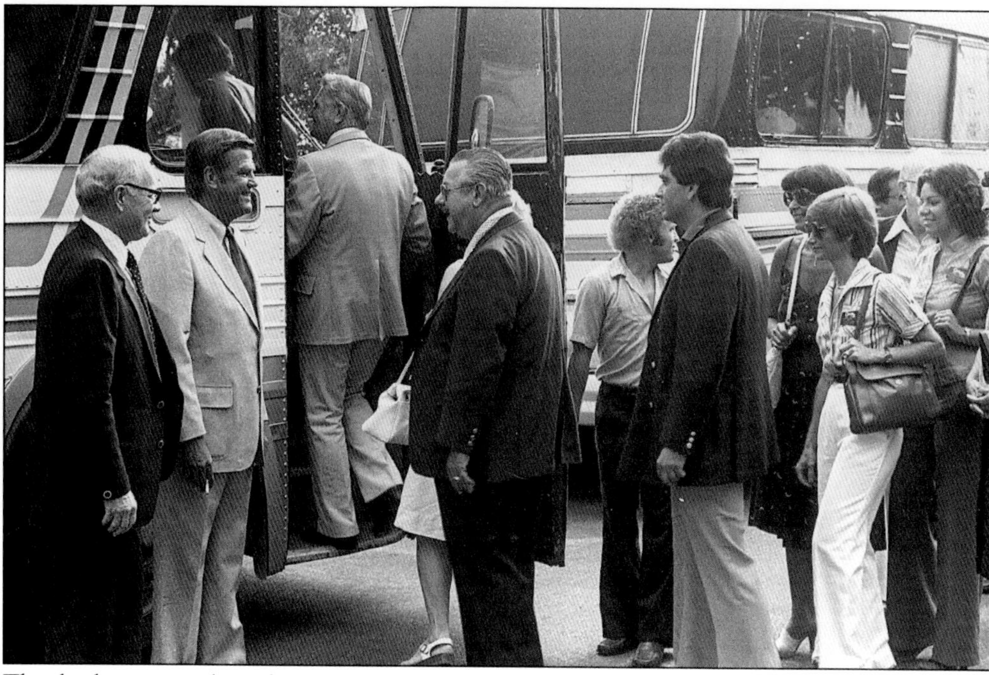

The brokers were brought to see the newest subdivisions in comfort via a fleet of air-conditioned buses. Coral Ridge Properties also provided transportation from Ft. Lauderdale. The brokers would bring back their prospects and hand them over to the Coral Ridge sales force who would show the models, answer questions, make the sale, and pay brokers their commission. (Courtesy of Coral Ridge Properties.)

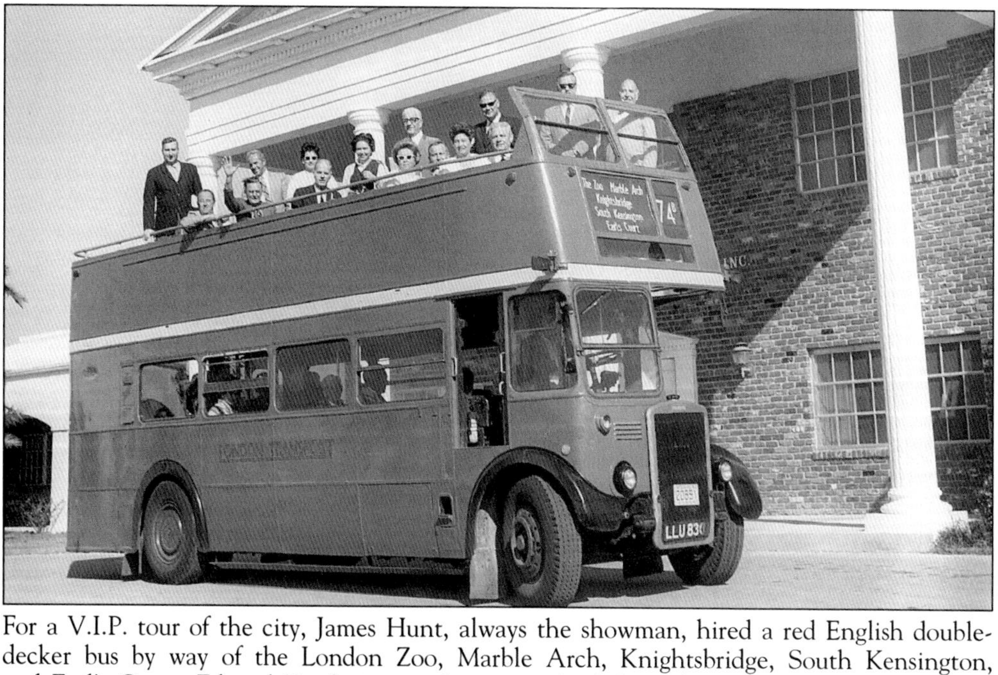

For a V.I.P. tour of the city, James Hunt, always the showman, hired a red English double-decker bus by way of the London Zoo, Marble Arch, Knightsbridge, South Kensington, and Earl's Court. Edward Heafy is seated on top, third from the right. (Courtesy of Coral Ridge Properties.)

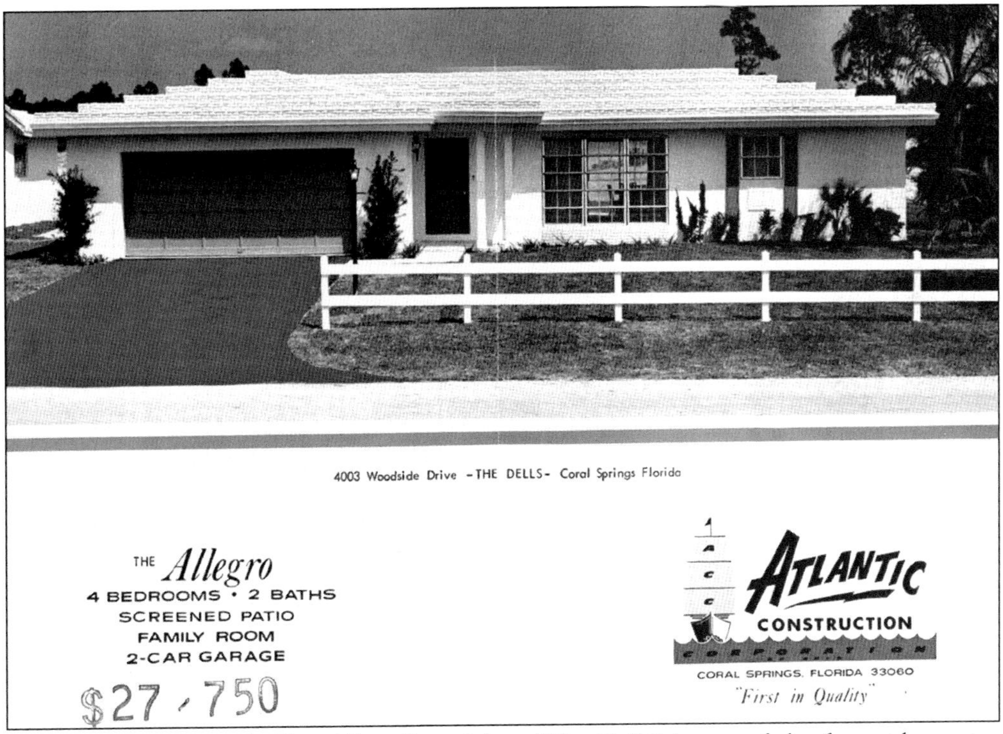

This 1968 brochure of "The Allegro" model in "The Dells" is one of the few with a price stamped on it. Salesmen carried price sheets for the houses in all the model rows that ranged from $17,900 to $70,000. This four-bedroom, two-bath home featured a screened patio, family room, and two-car garage—with pool optional—and cost $27,750. (Courtesy of the City of Coral Springs.)

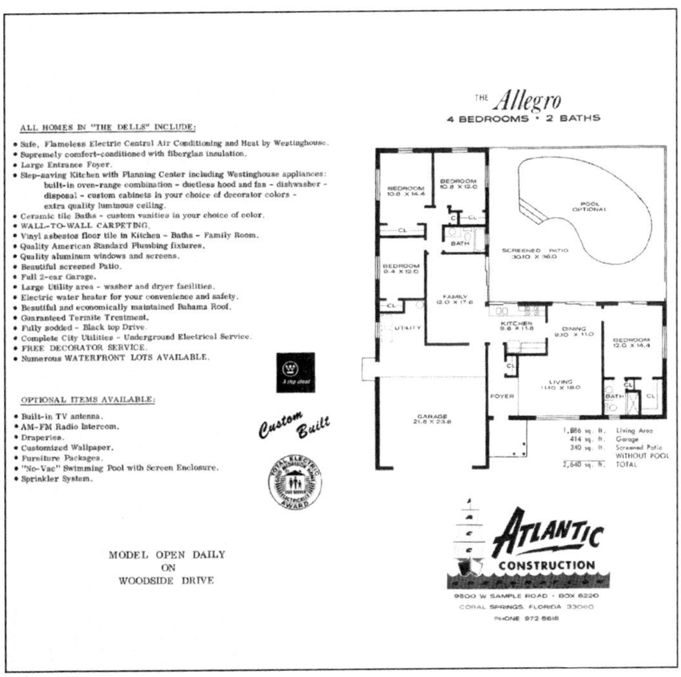

All houses in "The Dells" had Westinghouse appliances, including a "step-saving kitchen," built-in oven-range combination, dishwasher, disposal, "safe, flameless electric central air conditioning and heat," and "an extra quality luminous ceiling." As options, a built-in TV antenna, AM-FM radio intercom, draperies, wallpaper, sprinkler system, and furniture packages were available as well. Atlantic Construction was the builder. (Courtesy of the City of Coral Springs.)

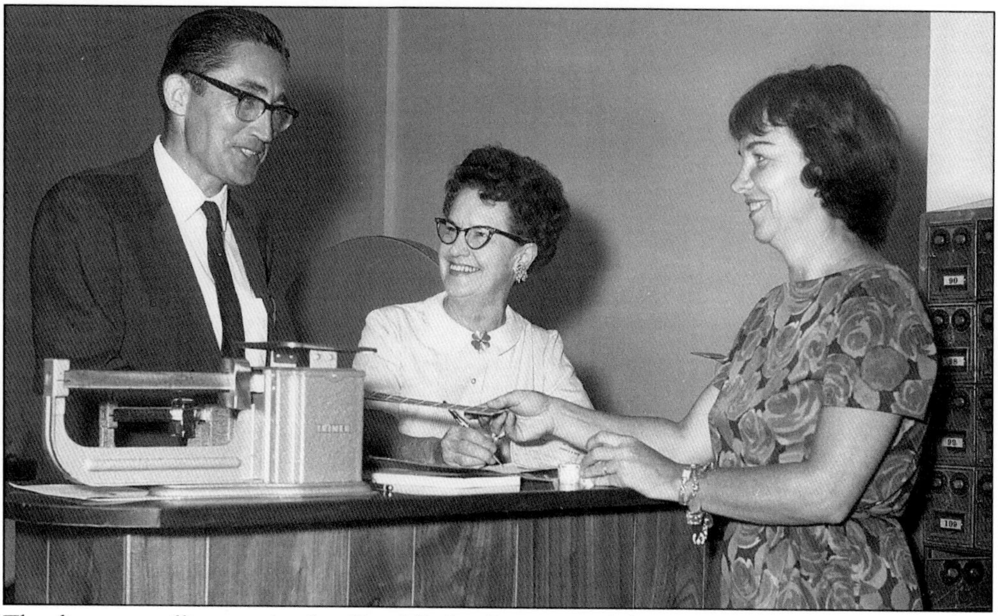

The first post office was in the Coral Ridge Properties Administration Building. The boxes are still used by City Hall for municipal mail. Streets used to have descriptive names but as the city mushroomed, the main post office requested that they be changed to numbers for the sake of efficiency. Locals had to remember that CBSs (Courts, Boulevards, and Streets) ran east and west, while TWAs (Terraces, Ways, and Avenues) ran north and south. Here Werner Buntemeyer of Coral Ridge Properties buys stamps from a postal employee (unknown) as postmistress Dorothy Connors looks on. (Courtesy of Coral Ridge Properties.)

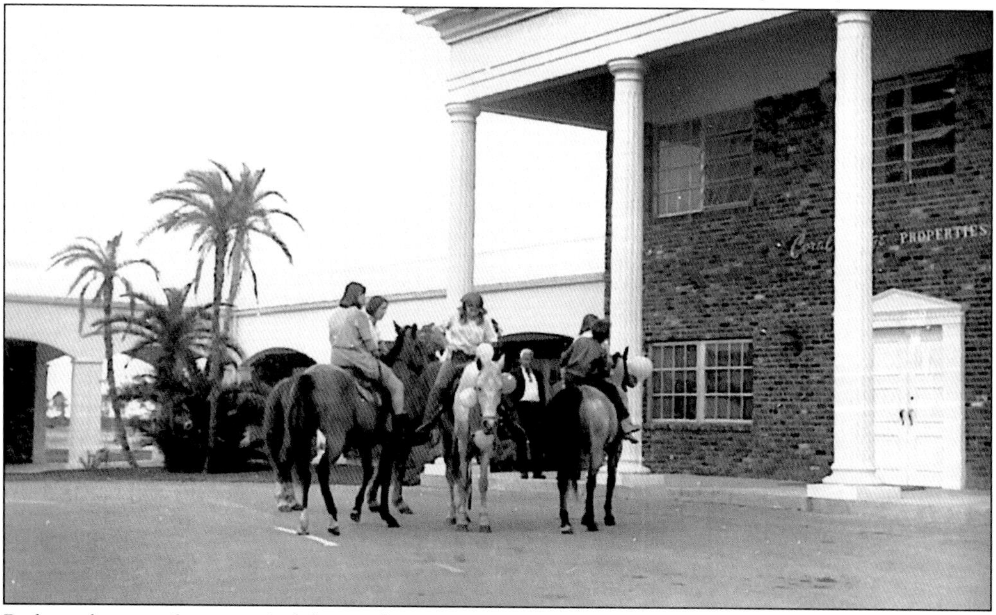

Before door-to-door mail delivery began in 1970, one distribution option was the "pony express." Residents with horses could leave their mounts by the flag poles in front of the Coral Ridge Administration Building, pick up their letters, and have a chat. (Courtesy of Coral Ridge Properties.)

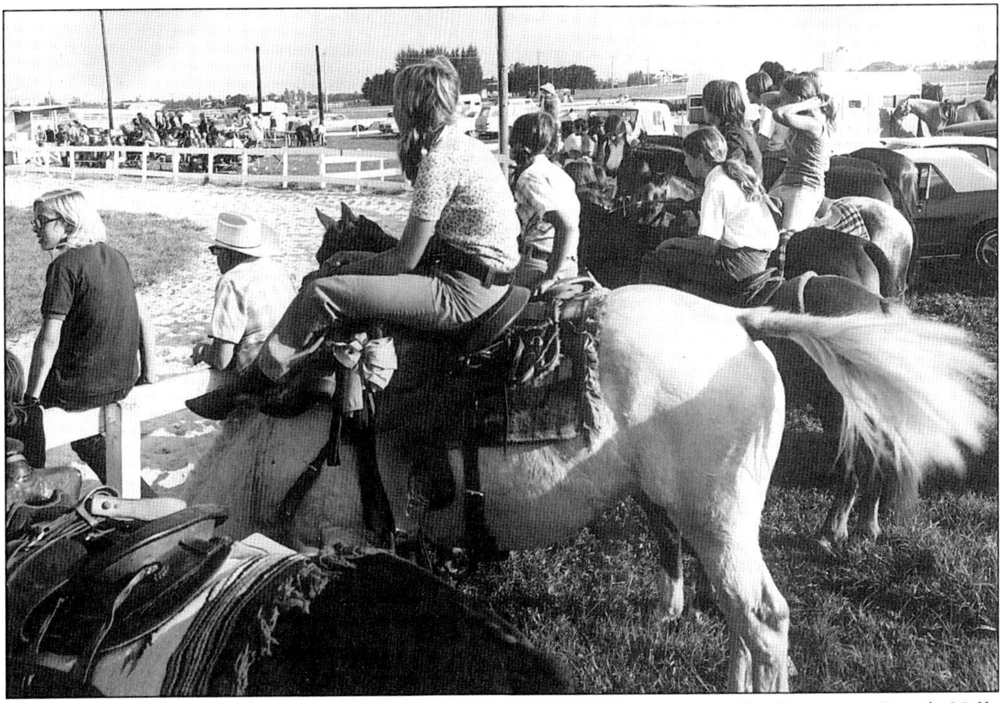

There was a riding ring on Wiles Road and Coral Hills Drive, now the Running Brook Hills subdivision. Lessons were given and the Saddle Club held monthly horse shows that included the surrounding communities. Many people bought houses in Coral Springs in order to have enough property to keep horses. (Courtesy of Coral Ridge Properties.)

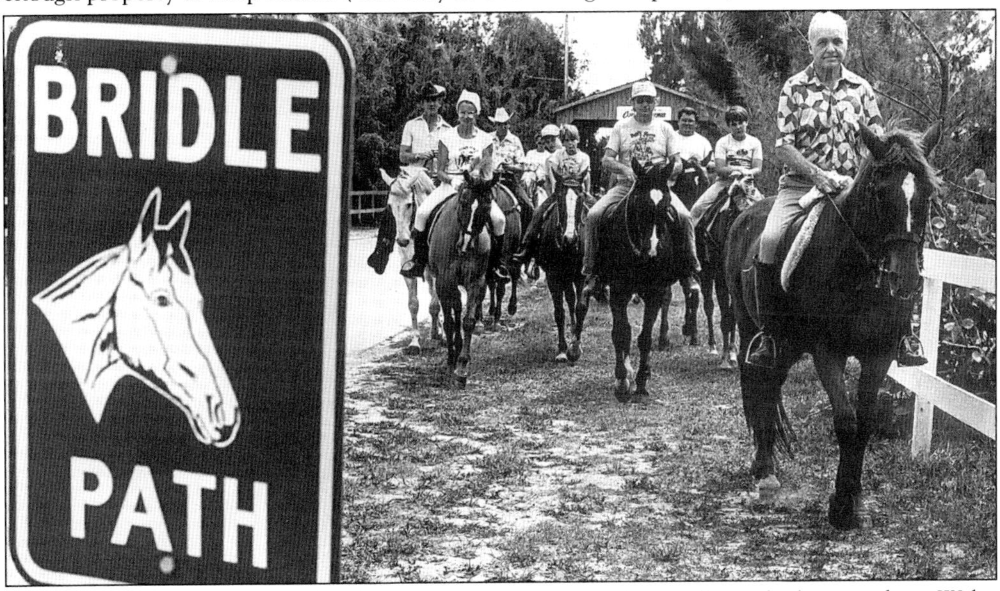

Another excursion with the family could be taken along the Bridle Path that ran from Wiles Road to the Village Green and back. The route went from the riding ring to NW 95th Avenue, through the Covered Bridge, to a small bridge at University Drive. The trail continued across University Drive to the Village Green. Here Mayor James Edwards leads the charge. (Courtesy of Coral Ridge Properties.)

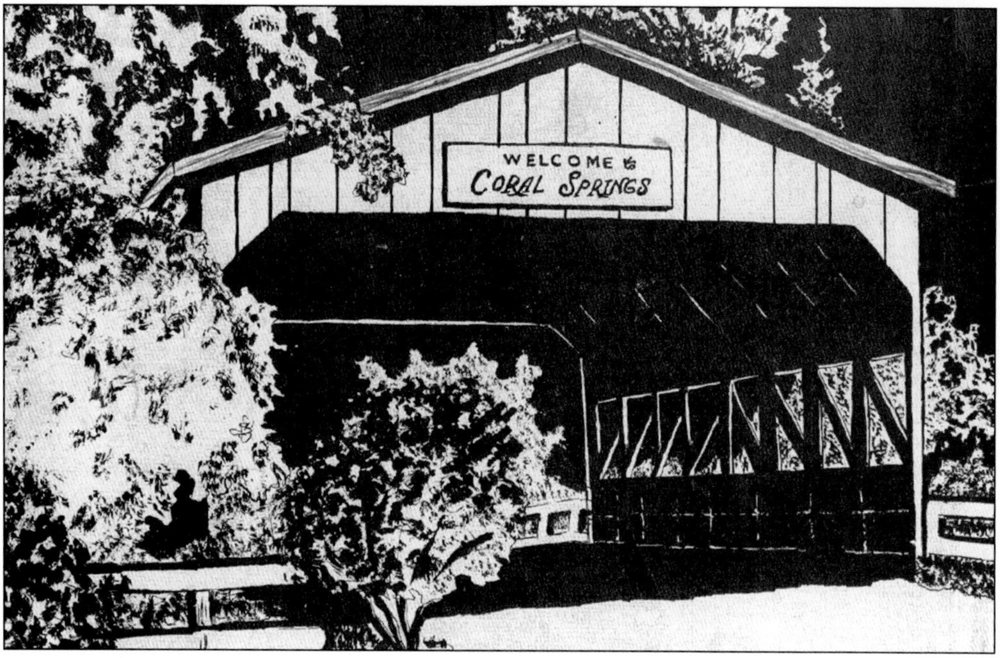

In 1971, the Civic Association printed a phone directory listing not only 1,000 names, addresses, and phone numbers, but also each person's occupation, the names and ages of the family's children, and (at the end of the "white pages") people who did odd jobs or baby sat, all by subdivision. There were 35 yellow pages. The back cover featured a Publix advertisement, "where shopping is a pleasure." (Courtesy of the City of Coral Springs.)

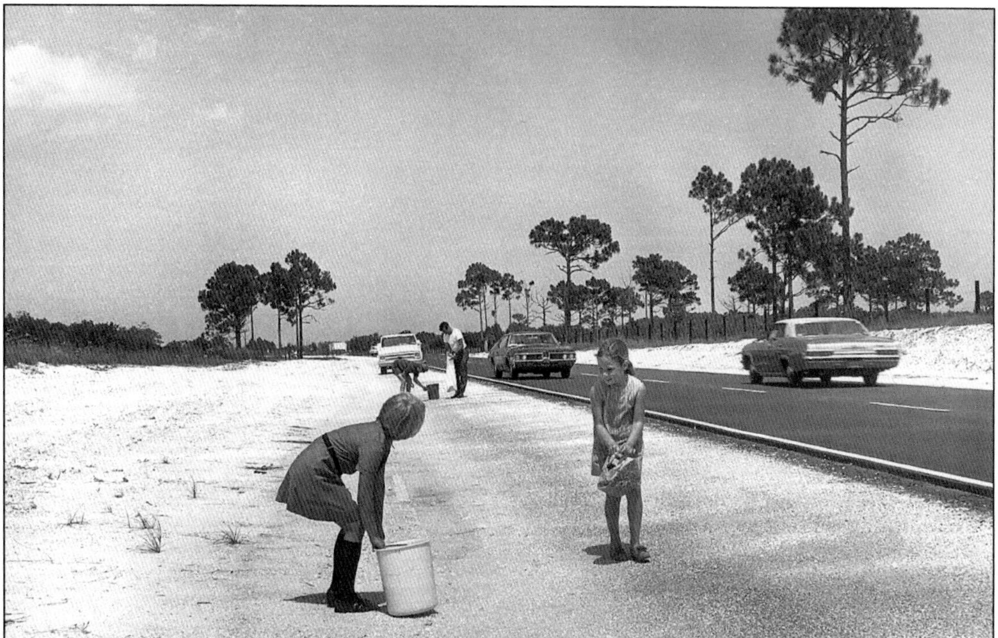
The Coral Springs Brownie Troop clean-up detail along Sample Road looks more like a day at the beach. The Coral Springs Water and Sewer Department was there to assist. (Courtesy of Coral Ridge Properties.)

Four

The City of The Future

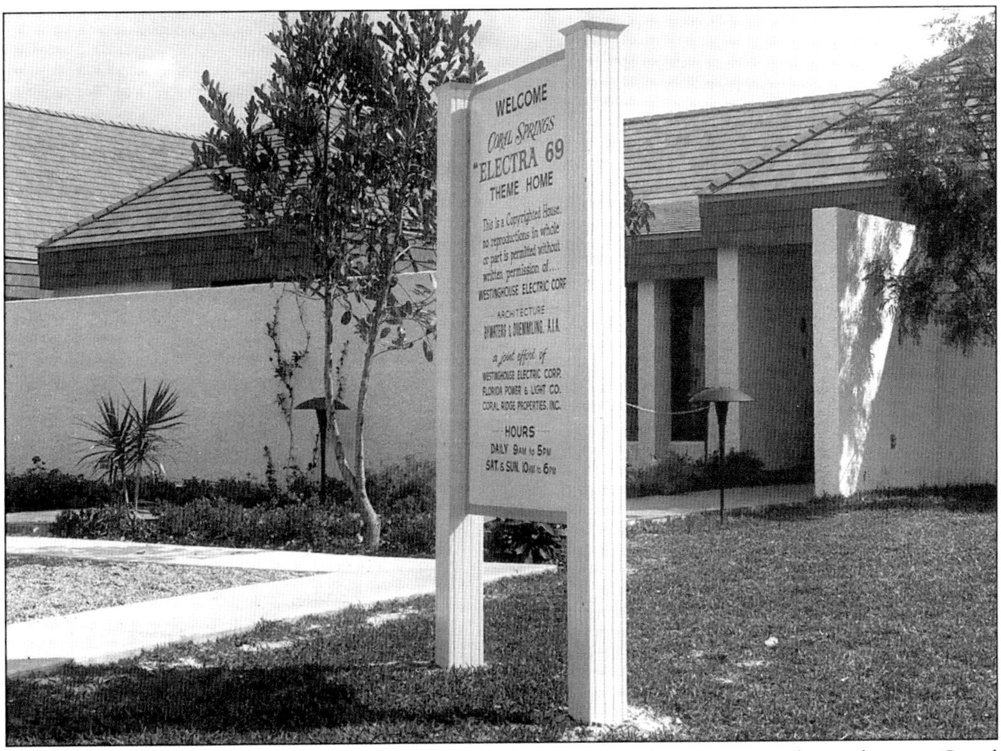

When Westinghouse purchased Coral Ridge Properties on July 1, 1966, it planned to use Coral Springs as its urban laboratory. It touted its "Electra Lab" subdivision as "the only community of its kind in the world! A unique joint effort of the Florida Power and Light Co., Westinghouse Electric Corporation and Coral Ridge Properties, Inc. . . . the Electralab introduces a totally new way of living electrically—the first in a series of small clustered communities in Coral Springs, to market-test new concepts as they evolve for ever-increasing better environments." (Courtesy of Coral Ridge Properties.)

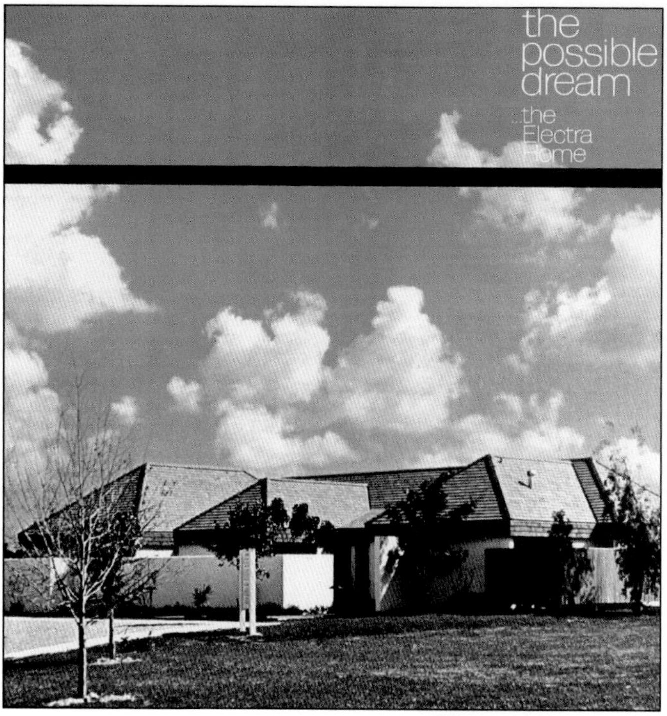

The "Electra 69" theme home was advertised as "not just a place to live but a WAY to live," and as "A dream-you-couldn't-dream-house." This totally electric house in the Electra Lab subdivision featured futuristic landscaping, exterior moonglow lighting, window and door sensors, exterior grill with a refrigerator, and sauna in the pool area. It attracted 75,000 visitors, including Arnold Palmer—who stayed there when he competed in the 1970 Coral Springs Open—and Astronaut Gordon Cooper. (Courtesy of Coral Ridge Properties.)

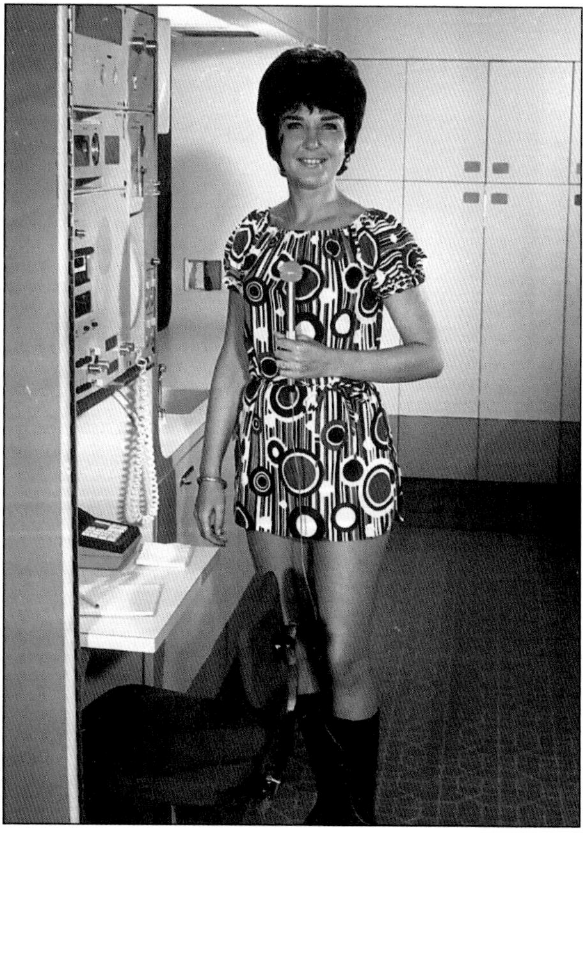

Mission control for the house of the future was the kitchen "Communication Center" with telephone, television, security alarm, AM/FM inter-room radio control, file drawers, and an adding machine. The master bath boasted a marble pool and shower, a whirlpool with temperature and pressure controls, marble vanity, and "electric beauty bar." (Courtesy of Coral Ridge Properties.)

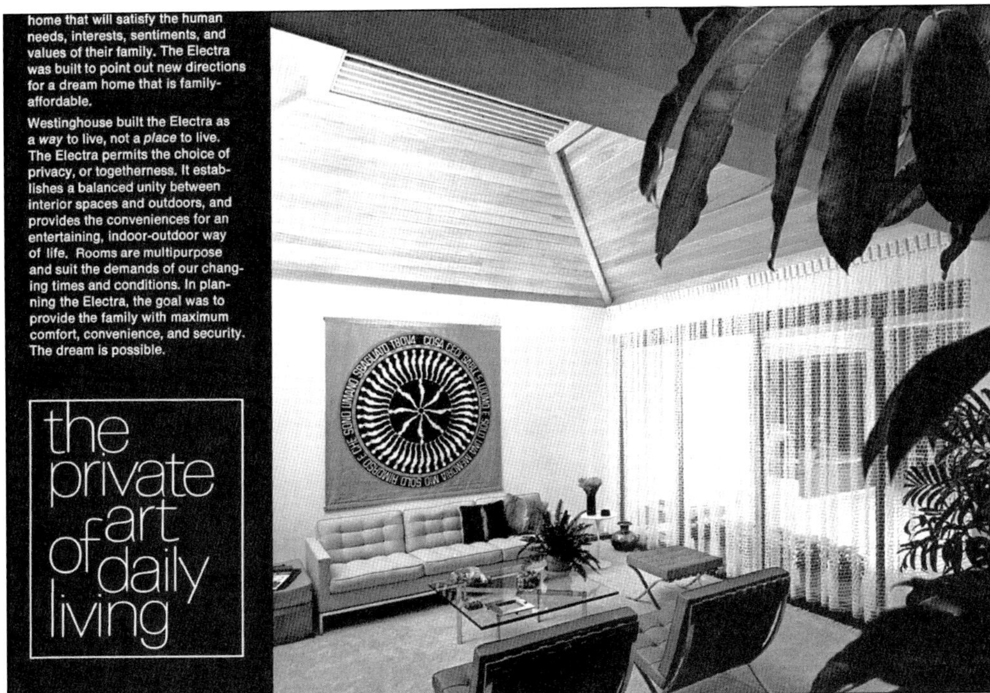

The sales brochure points out how "the living room and atrium combine to give privacy and a feeling of spaciousness to its residents. Together, the rooms overlooking the screened-in pool and patio achieve a sensitive unity between inside and outdoors. As each day advances from daybreak into evening, the changing rhythms of light and shadow create an infinite variety of optical surprises." (Courtesy of Coral Ridge Properties.)

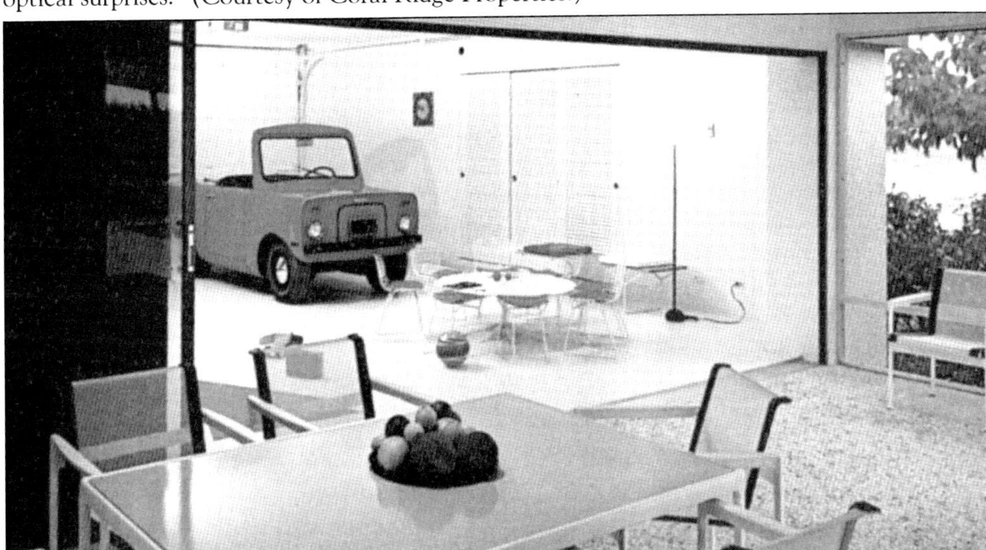

"One of the most exciting innovations in the Electra is the convertible garage/game room. Shown here is the Marketeer electric vehicle. With the garage empty . . . you have an attractive, easy-to-care-for game room. An experimental Micarta floor with built-in shuffleboard is decorative and grease resistant. A sliding glass wall opens one entire end of the room to expand the patio/outdoor living area." (Courtesy of Coral Ridge Properties.)

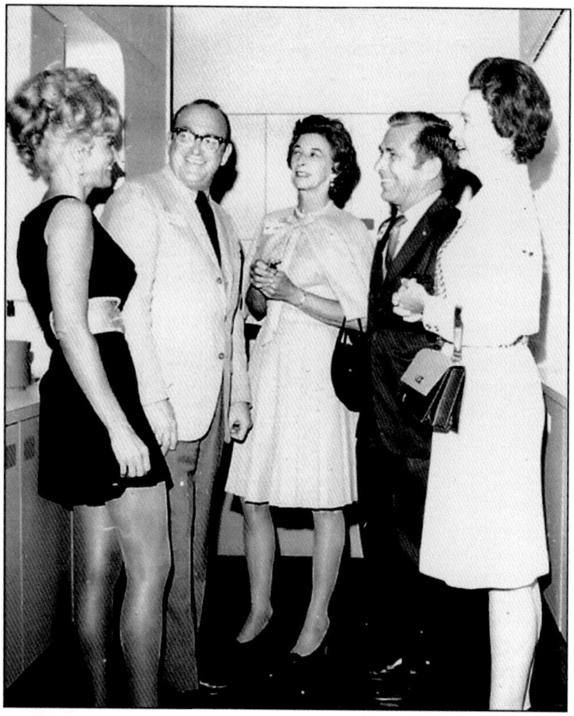

The galley provided food service for the den and screened patio area. It had copious storage, a small sink, refrigerator, and a flat cooktop stove—a novelty. The Electra I stove featured coil burners. (Courtesy of Coral Ridge Properties.)

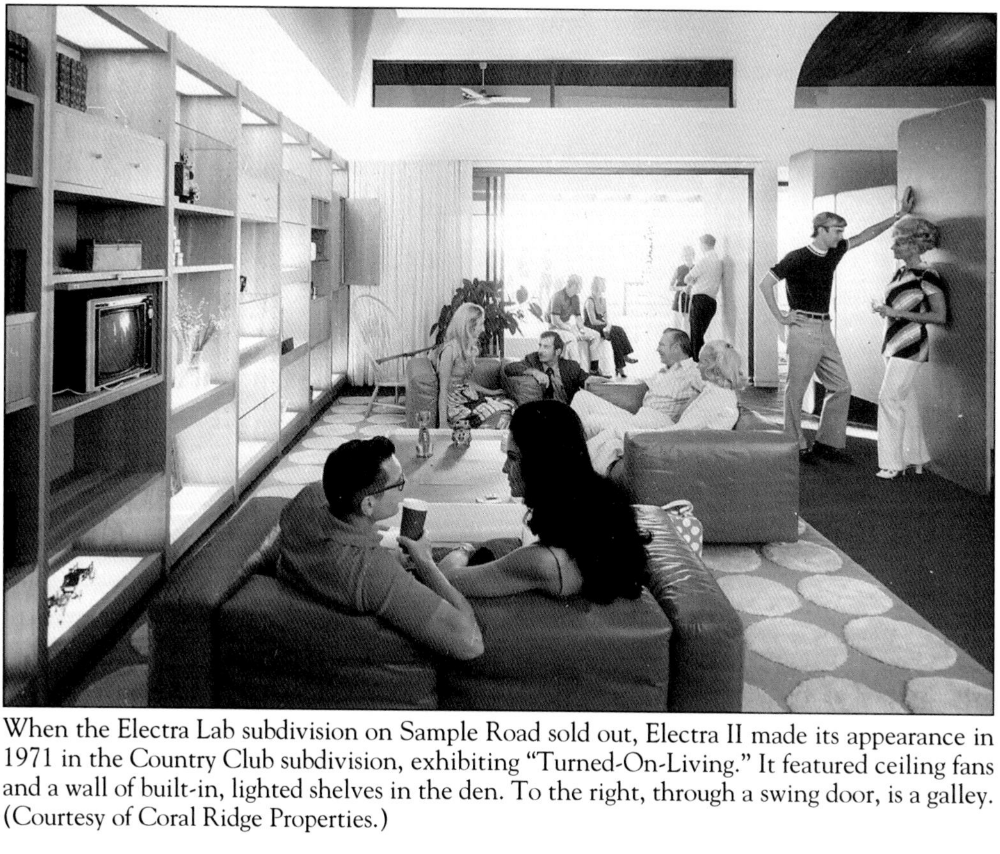

When the Electra Lab subdivision on Sample Road sold out, Electra II made its appearance in 1971 in the Country Club subdivision, exhibiting "Turned-On-Living." It featured ceiling fans and a wall of built-in, lighted shelves in the den. To the right, through a swing door, is a galley. (Courtesy of Coral Ridge Properties.)

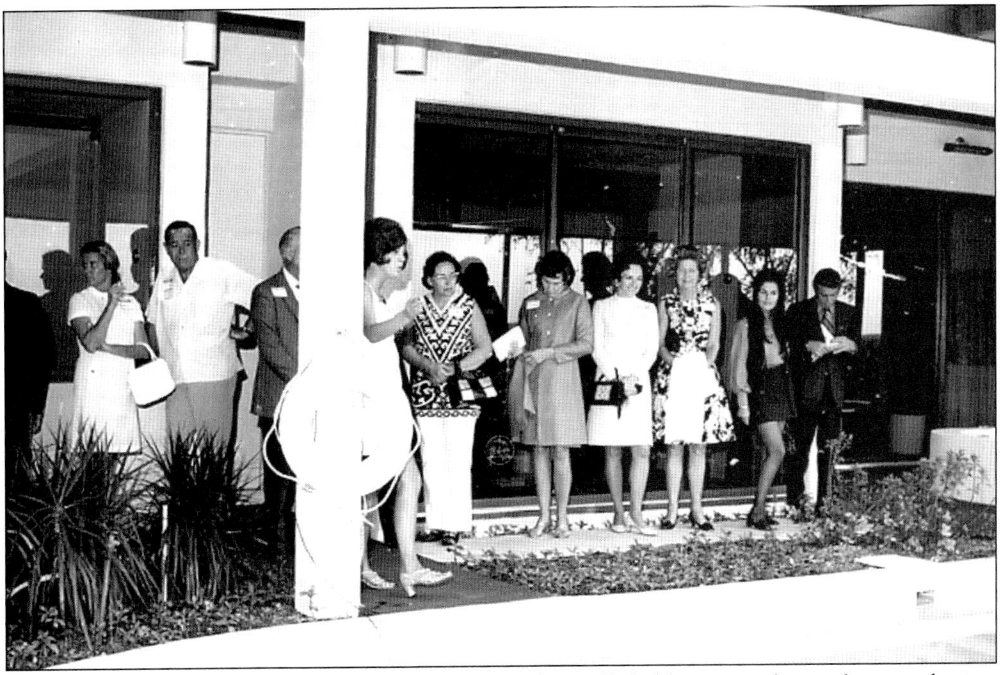

Another innovation, of great interest to parents with small children, was the pool sensor device. When armed, an alarm would sound if anything fell in the water. The water itself was warmed by solar panels. (Courtesy of Coral Ridge Properties.)

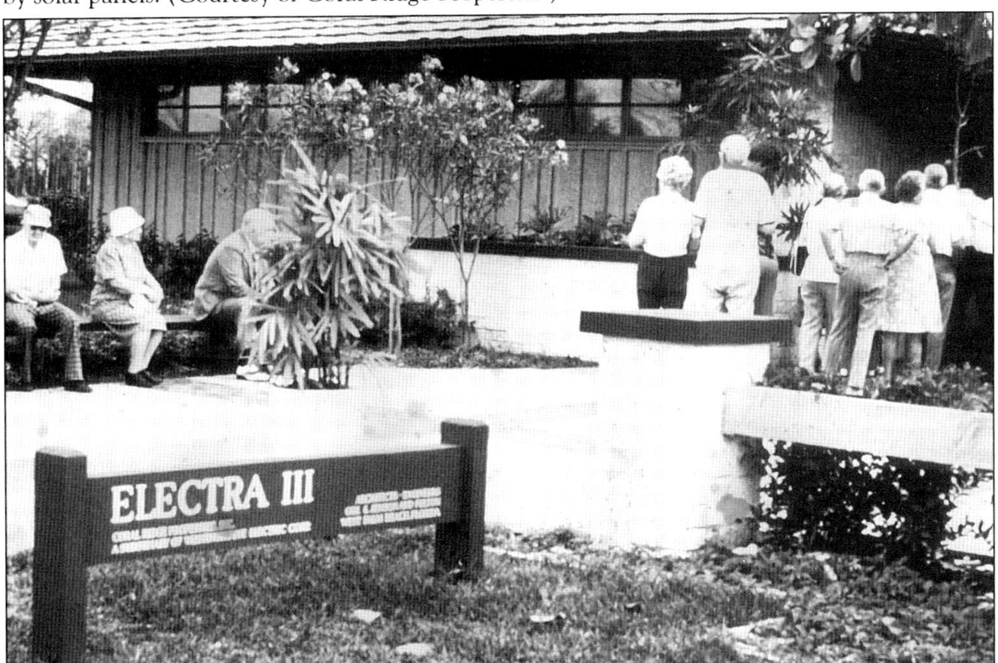

When the Electra III was built in the mid-1970s in the Ramblewood II subdivision, it still drew crowds willing to stand, or sit, in line. The cedar shake roof shingles were relatively uncommon in the area. Residents considered a tour of the new model as a "must see." (Courtesy of Coral Ridge Properties.)

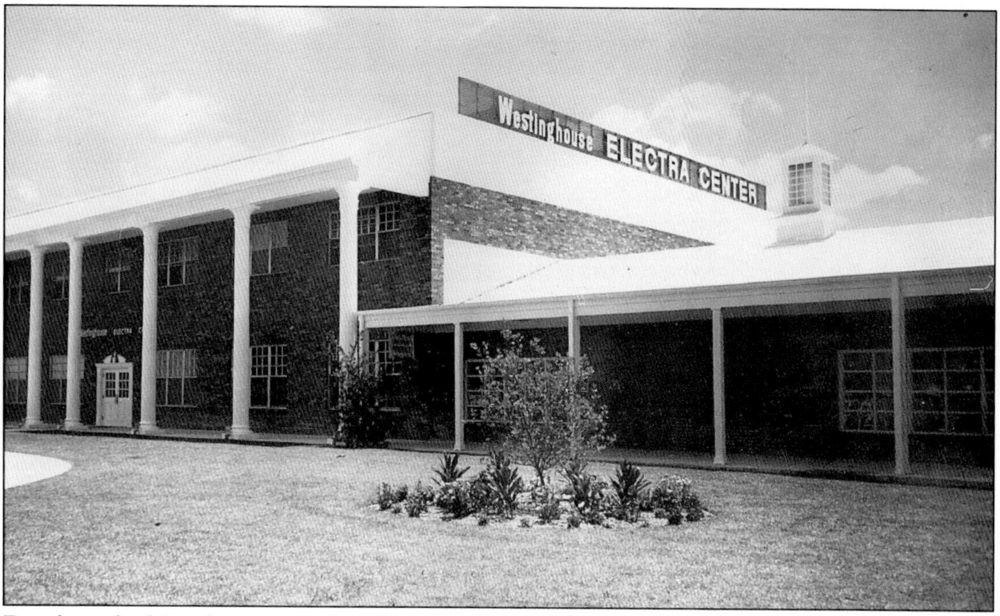

For those looking for a more familiar version of a dream house, the Westinghouse Electra Center, in the Village Green Shopping Plaza on University Drive at Sample Road, displayed every option available in the city. It also served as a movie theater, the meeting place for the city commission, and for Sunday services before there were churches. (Courtesy of Coral Ridge Properties.)

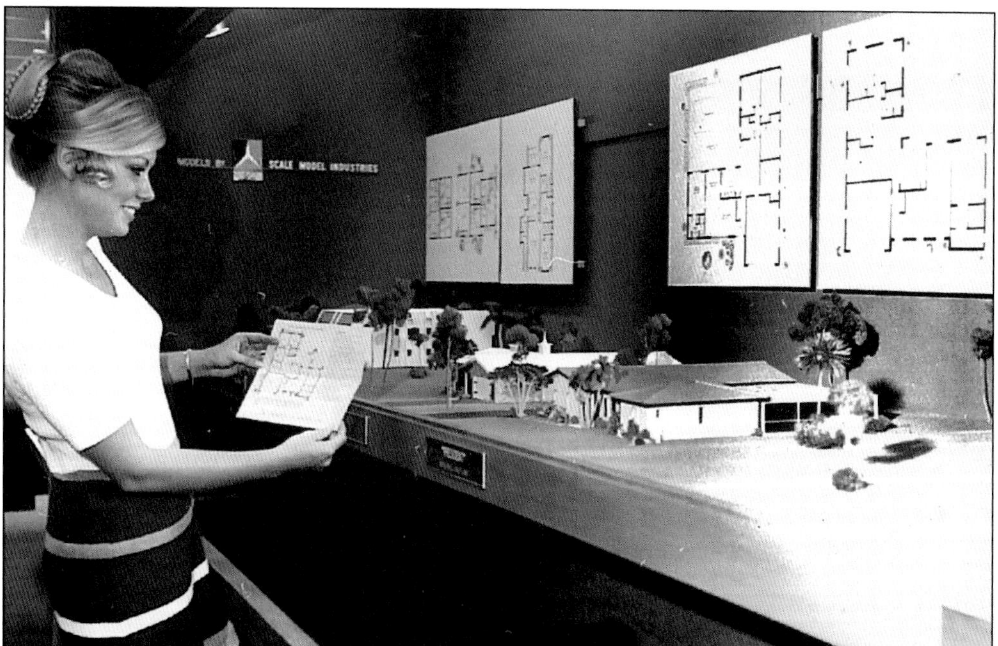

There were scale models from various builders, complete with landscaping. Debbie Smith, a home sales tour guide, provided floor plans of the models on display and of other houses in 1972. Westinghouse's on-site design center displayed its newest appliances in room settings for builders, architects, and the public. (Courtesy of Coral Ridge Properties.)

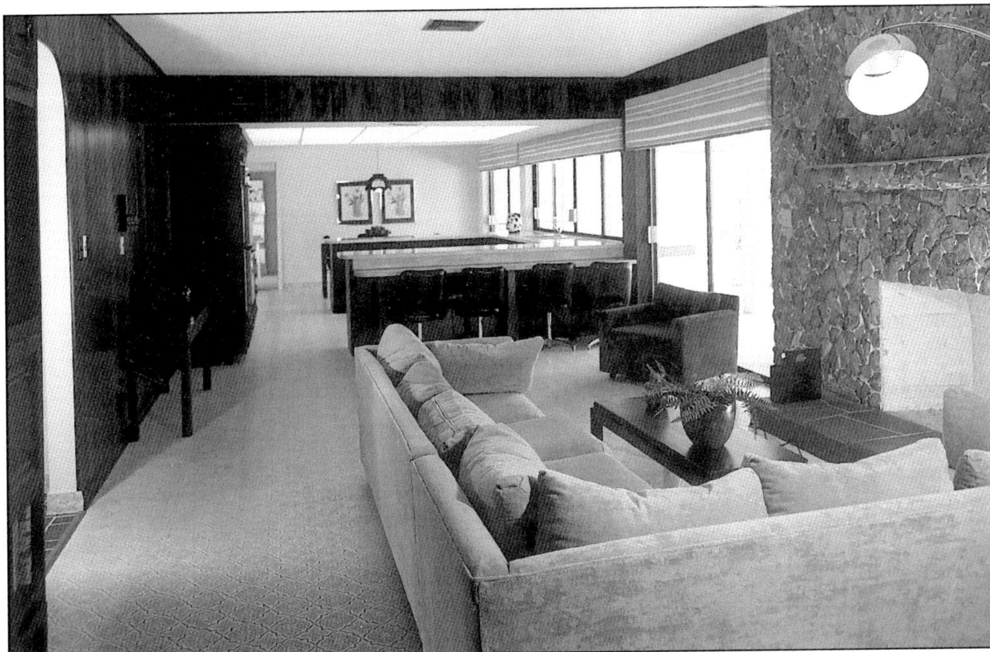

Model homes in the various subdivisions were furnished in the latest styles, including sectional sofas, chrome arc lamps, and cozy fieldstone fireplaces for people from Northern states who could not imagine a house without a hearth. (Courtesy of Coral Ridge Properties.)

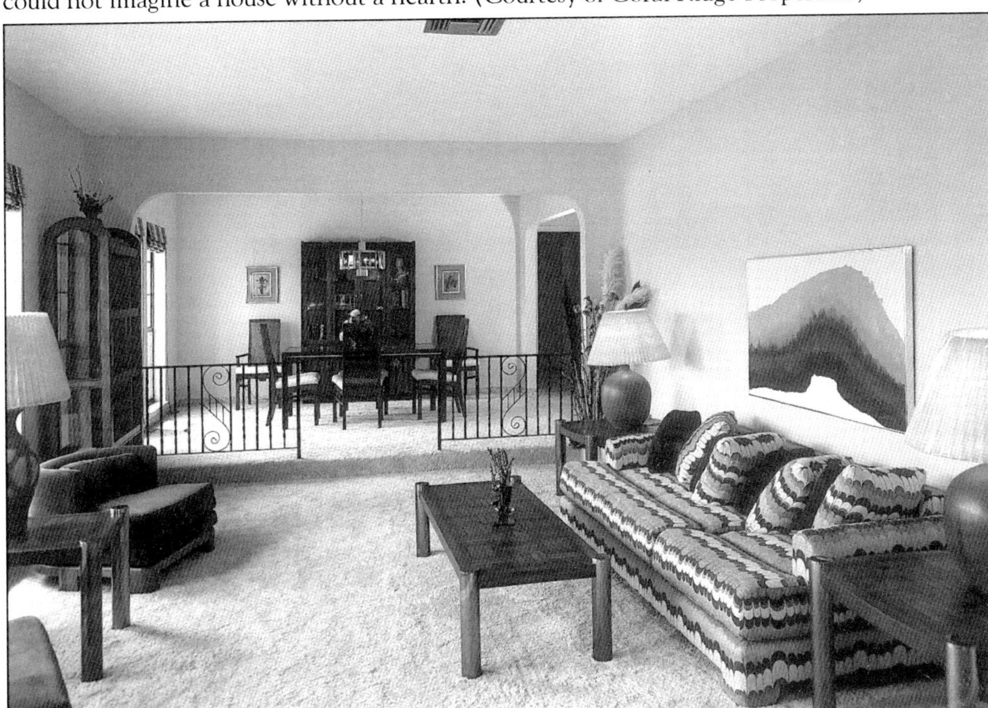

A sunken living room, tubular furniture, bold patterns, shag carpeting, and a wrought iron room divider were considered the height of elegance in the 1970s. (Courtesy of Coral Ridge Properties.)

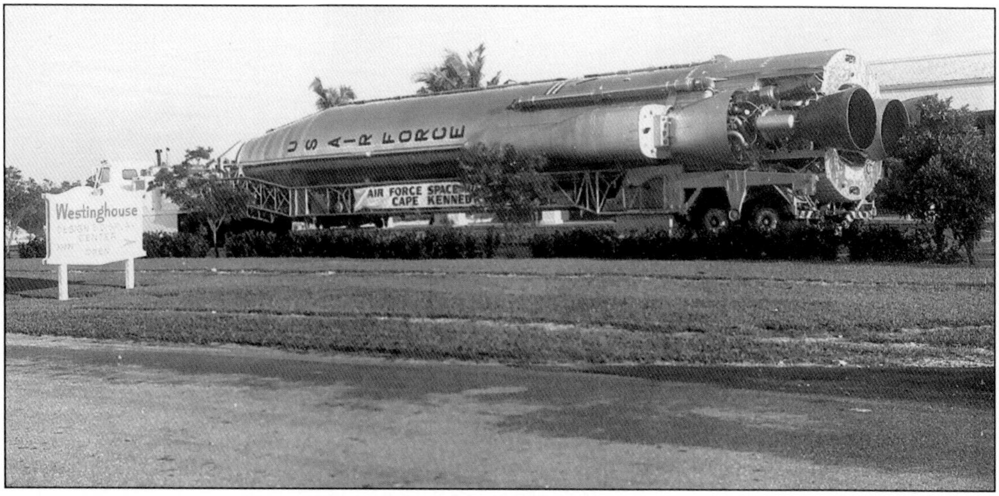

Westinghouse built more than Electra Lab houses in Coral Springs. The company was a major defense contractor and built the first plant in the Industrial Park. It also designed the camera that went to the surface of the moon with astronauts from 1969 to 1972. Replicas of the camera and other items from the missions were put on display at the Design and Display Center. To attract an audience, a NASA Redstone rocket was parked in front of the adjacent Village Green. (Courtesy of Coral Ridge Properties.)

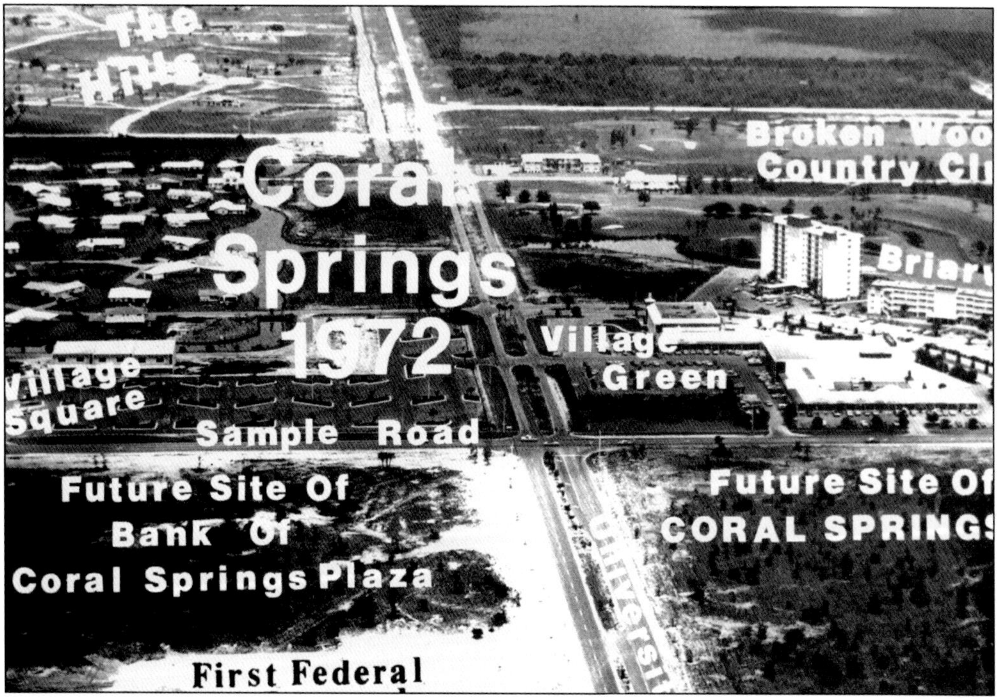

This 1972 aerial view of University Drive and Sample Road leaves much to the imagination. South of Sample are the future sites for the Bank of Coral Springs Plaza and the Coral Springs Mall. The areas not covered with vegetation appear white because of the sand. The red clay or loamy soils of the North did not exist in south Florida. Sweeping sand, rather than black dirt, from their entryways was a surprise to new residents from earthier climes. (Courtesy of Coral Ridge Properties.)

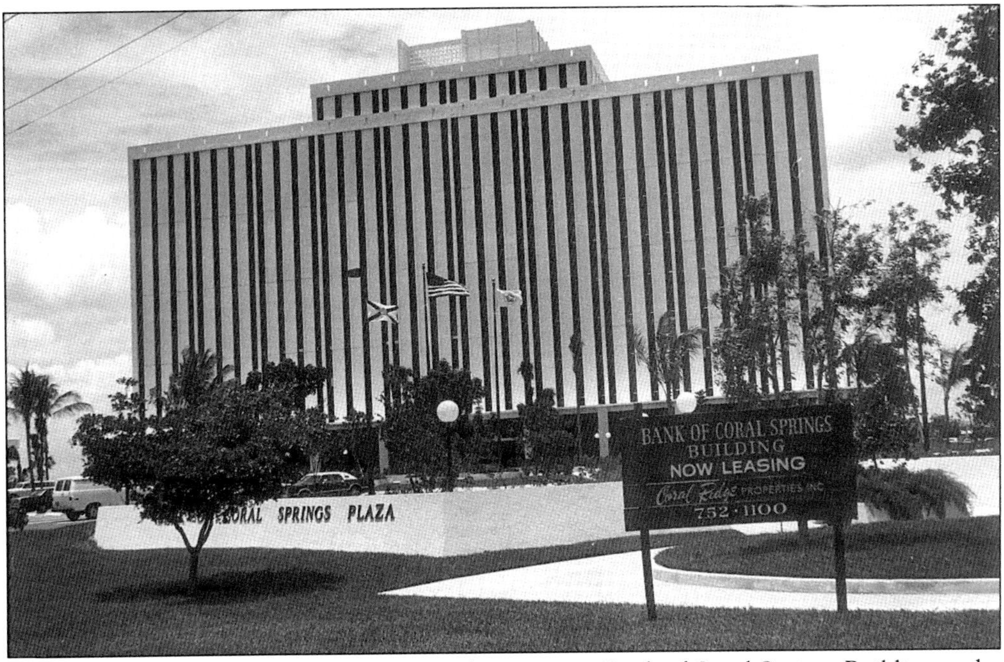

By 1976, the city had its first "skyscraper": the ten-story Bank of Coral Springs Building at the southwest corner of University Drive and Sample Road. Coral Ridge Properties built it as its new headquarters, leaving the Administration Building on Sample Road open for immediate use and eventual purchase by the City of Coral Springs. (Courtesy of Coral Ridge Properties.)

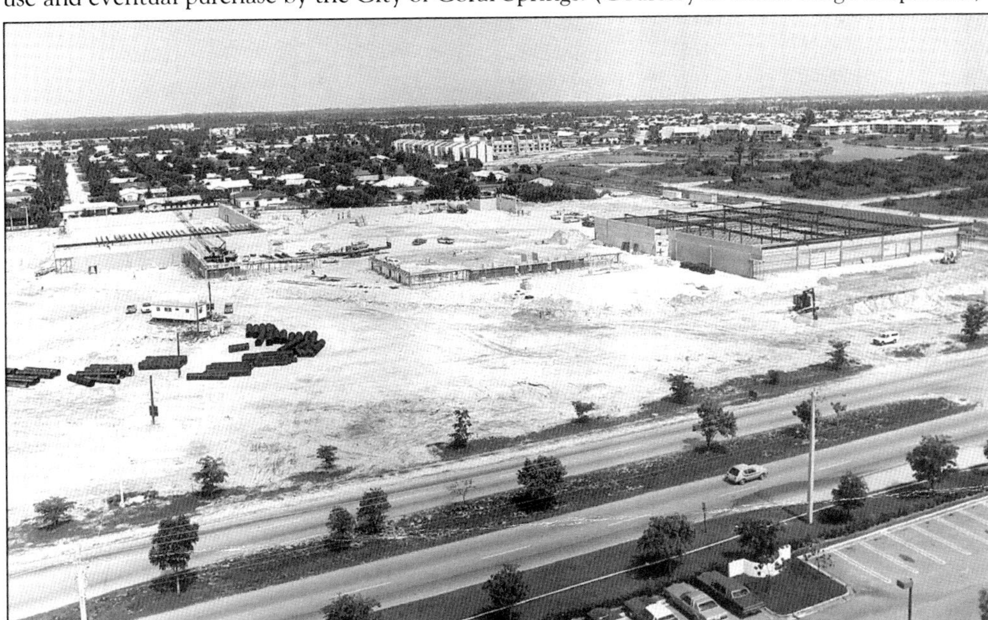

The southeast corner of University Drive and Sample Road is under development in 1978 as an enclosed shopping mall, in accordance with the master plan. A J. Byrons Department Store and a movie theater anchored the Coral Springs Mall, with many small shops inside and outside, including Eckerd's. Today it is the site of the Coral Springs Charter School and the Broward County Northwest Regional Library. (Courtesy of Coral Ridge Properties.)

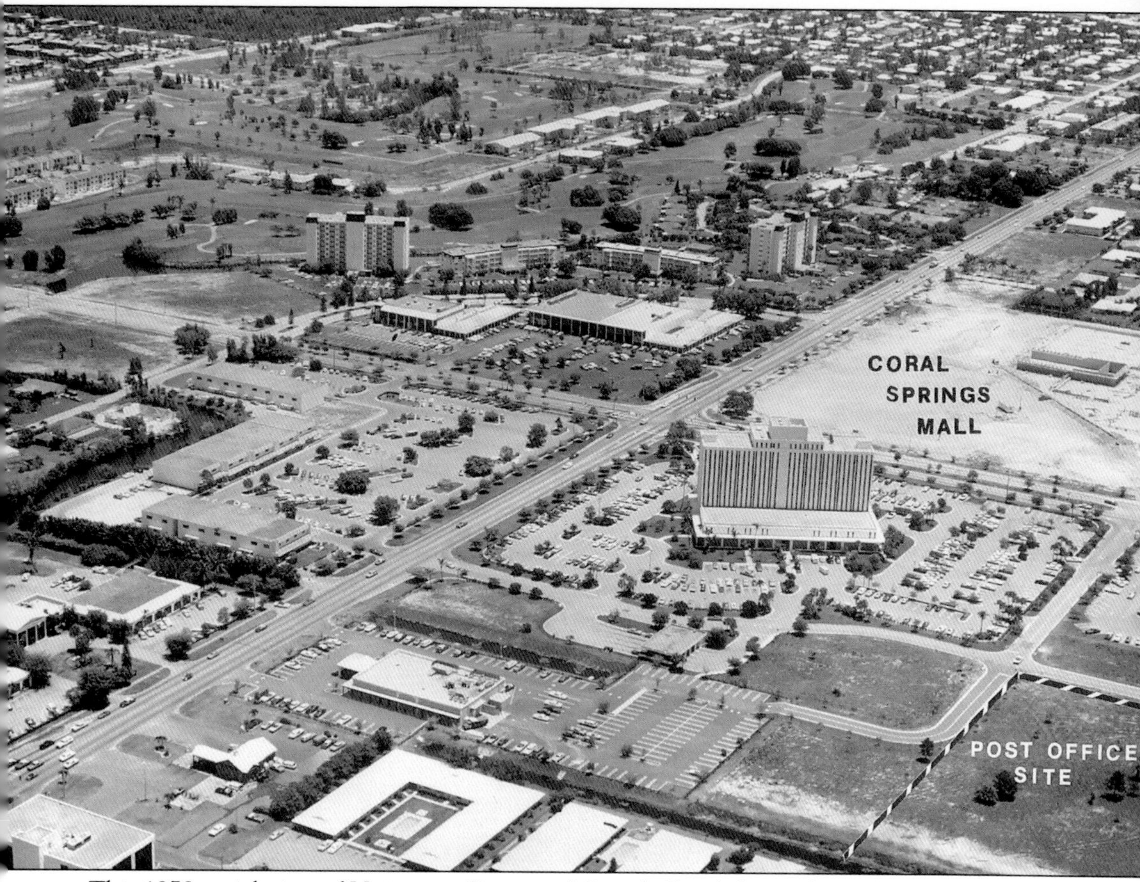

This 1978 aerial view of University Drive and Sample Road shows the mall nearly completed as well as territory plotted out for a new post office. On the far left is Coral Springs City Hall. Before Coral Ridge Properties moved to the Bank of Coral Springs Building in 1976, the City government leased space on the second floor of the Village Square Shopping Center, directly east of City Hall. (Courtesy of Coral Ridge Properties.)

Five

"The Premier City in Which to Live, Work and Raise a Family"

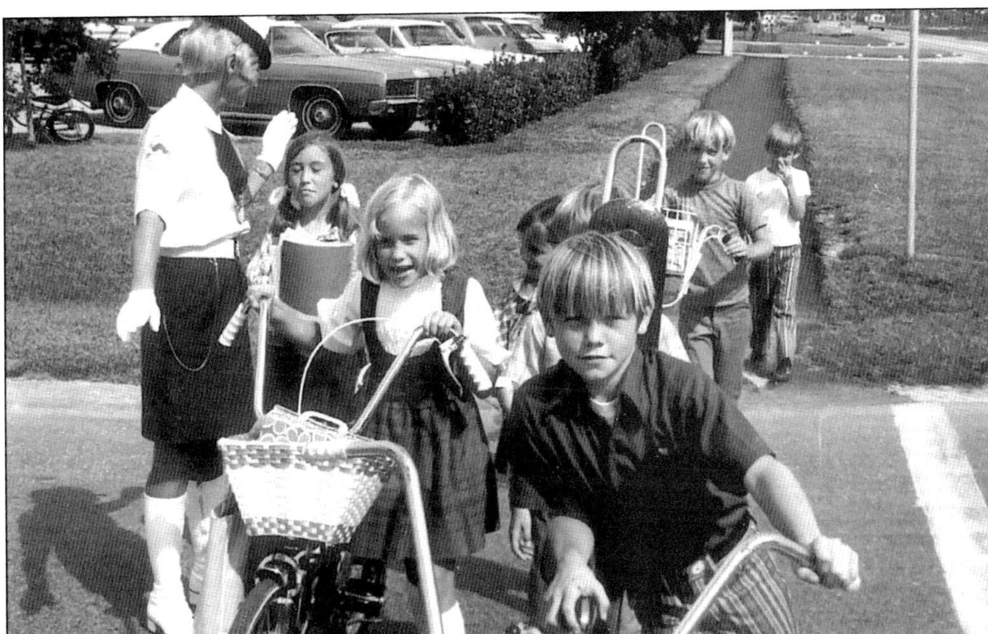

School days began and ended under the watchful eyes of crossing guards who wore these Coral Ridge Properties–issued uniforms, inspired by Christian Dior. This photograph was taken in 1971 in front of the west wing of City Hall at Coral Hills Drive. Prepared for 300 students, 600 showed up and had to attend double sessions in 18 portable trailers at the current location of the Coral Springs Medical Center. Before that they were bused to Margate Elementary School, and then Coconut Creek Elementary School. (Courtesy of Coral Ridge Properties.)

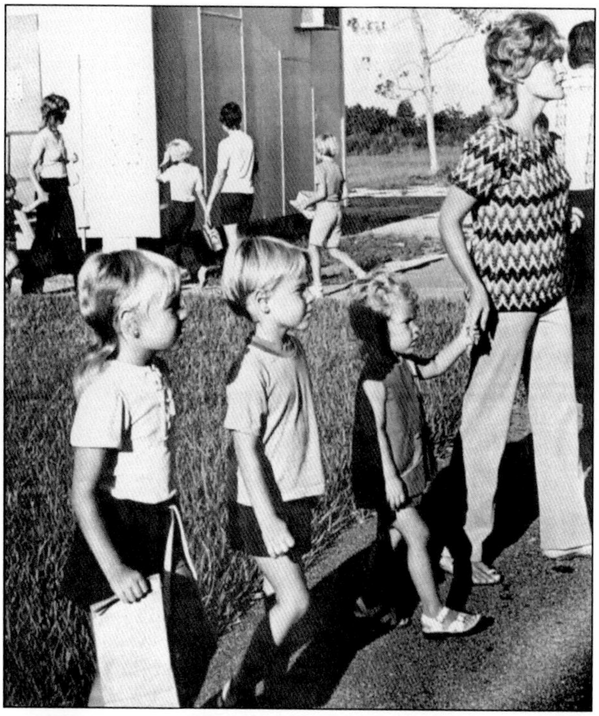

On the first day of school in 1972, the portables were nothing new to the returning students. The units were arranged in a circle like covered wagons rather than in rows. Assemblies were held in the center after a check for any rattlesnakes that might be sleeping on the trailer steps in the sun. Here Mrs. Charles Haaf is pictured, accompanying Nicole, Michael, and Shelley Haaf to classes. (Courtesy of *The Forum*.)

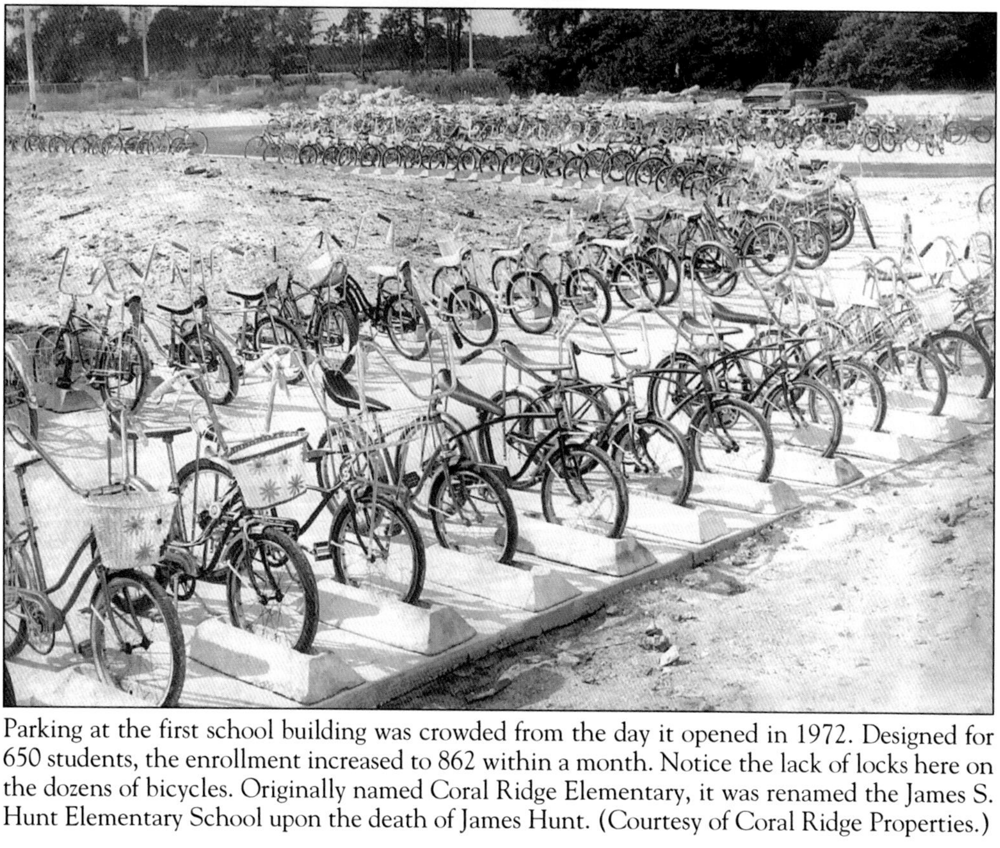

Parking at the first school building was crowded from the day it opened in 1972. Designed for 650 students, the enrollment increased to 862 within a month. Notice the lack of locks here on the dozens of bicycles. Originally named Coral Ridge Elementary, it was renamed the James S. Hunt Elementary School upon the death of James Hunt. (Courtesy of Coral Ridge Properties.)

This collage shows all the schools in session by 1977. Coral Springs Elementary School also opened in 1972, followed by Forest Hills Elementary School in 1974. Westchester Elementary School opened in 1974, then Coral Springs Middle School opened in 1975. Coral Springs High School and Ramblewood Middle School opened in 1976, and Ramblewood Elementary School opened in 1977. (Courtesy of Kenneth Waddell.)

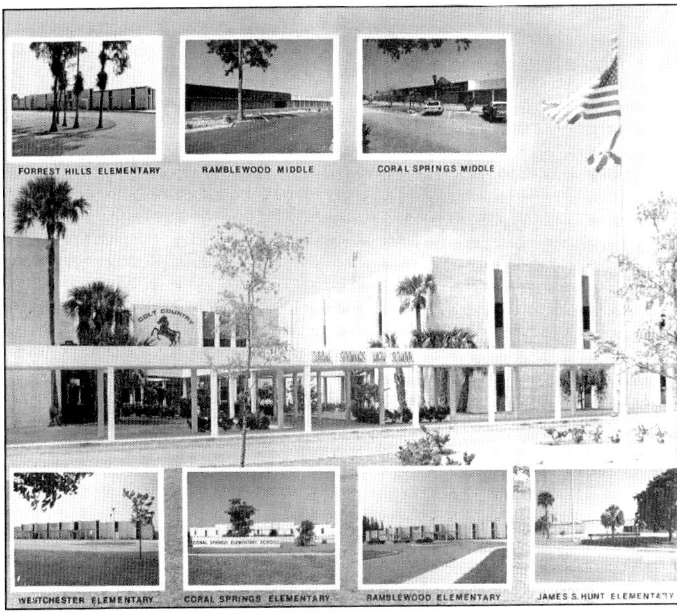

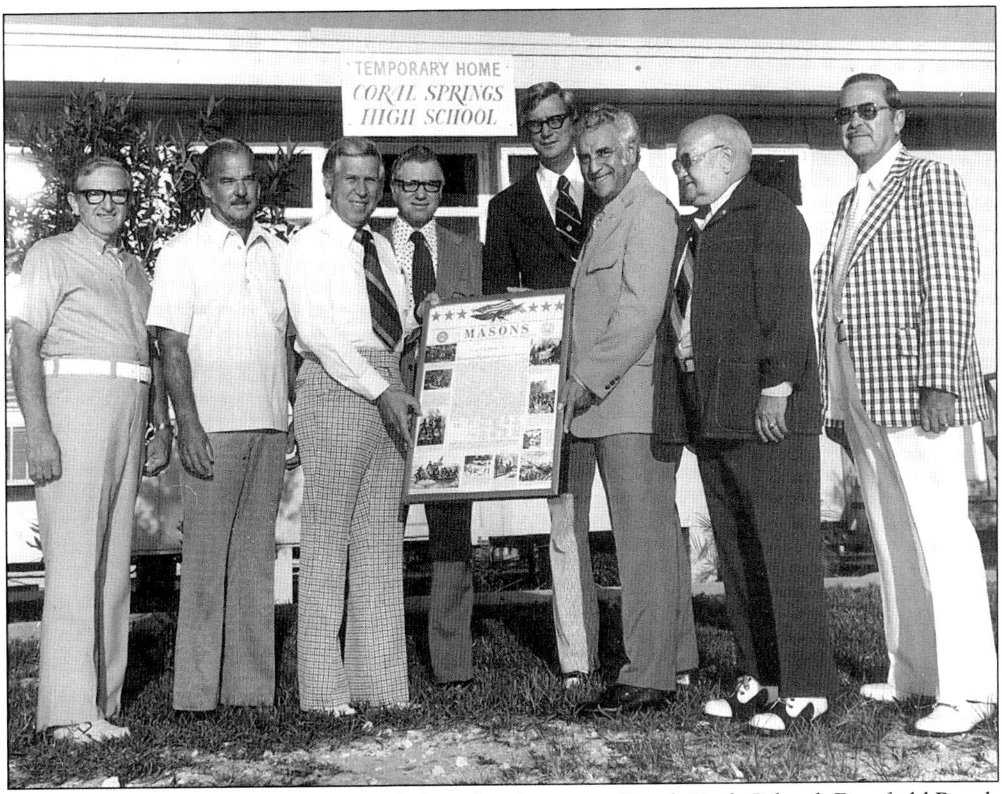

High School students were successively bused to Pompano Beach High School, Deerfield Beach High School, then to double sessions at Coconut Creek High. When Coral Springs High School was finally begun, portable trailers were used. Members of the Masons officiated at the laying of the cornerstone, and here, they surround the first principal, Russell Rowe (left of the plaque) and Mayor Ben Geiger (fifth from the left). (Courtesy of Coral Ridge Properties.)

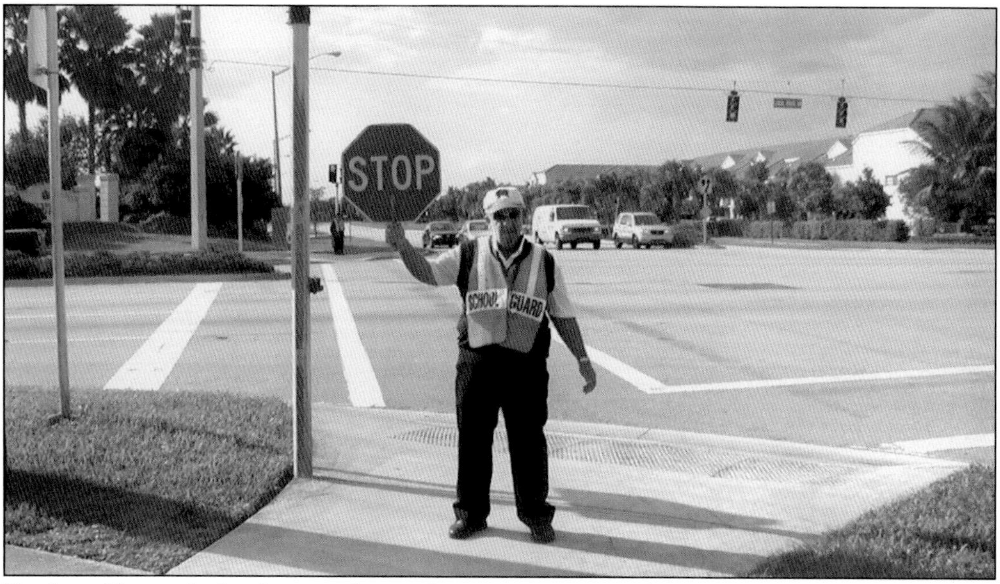

Twelve additional schools opened over the next 20 years and portables are still in use because of the burgeoning population, but now crossing guards wear different uniforms. (Courtesy of the City of Coral Springs.)

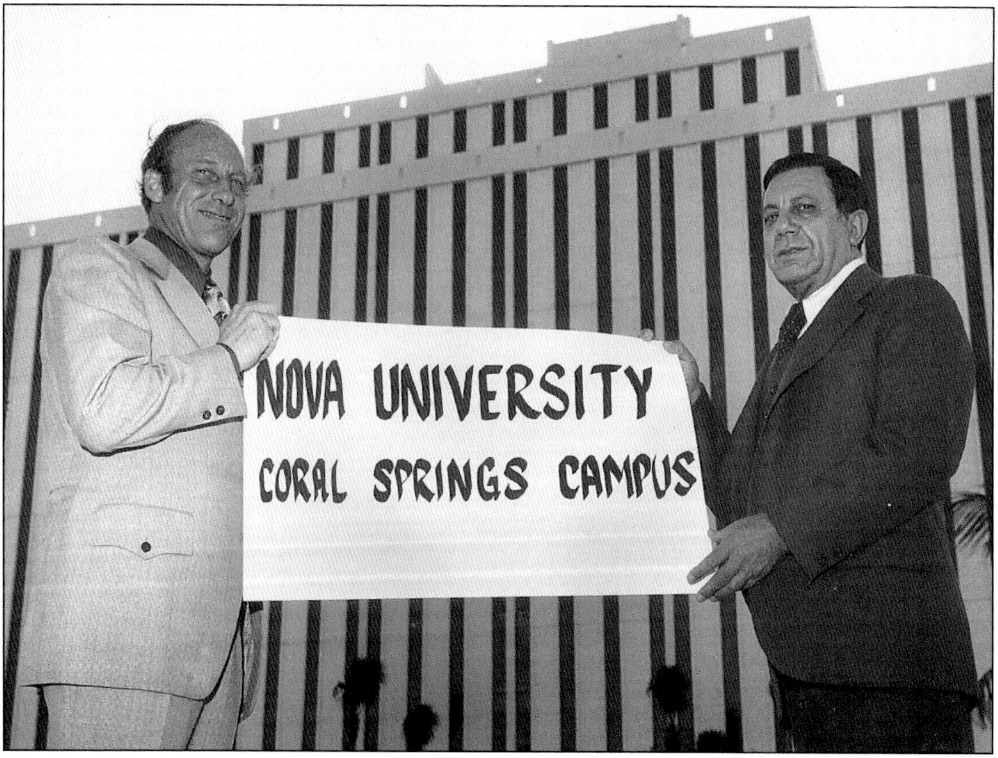

The Coral Springs campus of Nova University was open from 1976 until 1992, originally holding classes at the Westinghouse Design Center in Village Green. This is one part of the master plan that did not last. Joseph Taravella is on the right in front of the Bank of Coral Springs Building. (Courtesy of Coral Ridge Properties.)

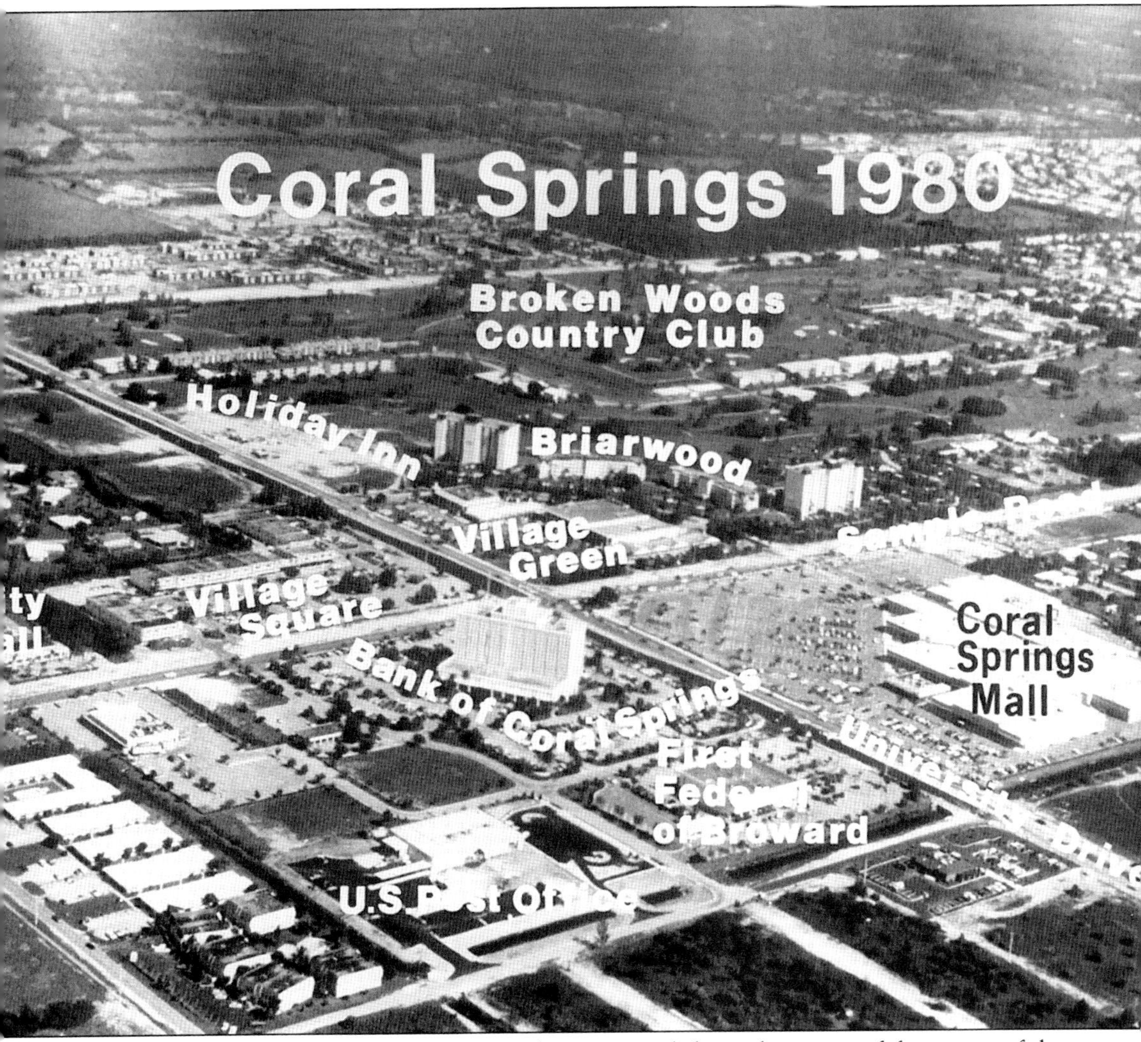

Finally, enough pieces of the puzzle are in place to reveal the architecture of the center of the city as we now know it, but the landscape is still pretty barren a block or two beyond. Some business names have changed but the buildings remain. (Courtesy of Coral Ridge Properties.)

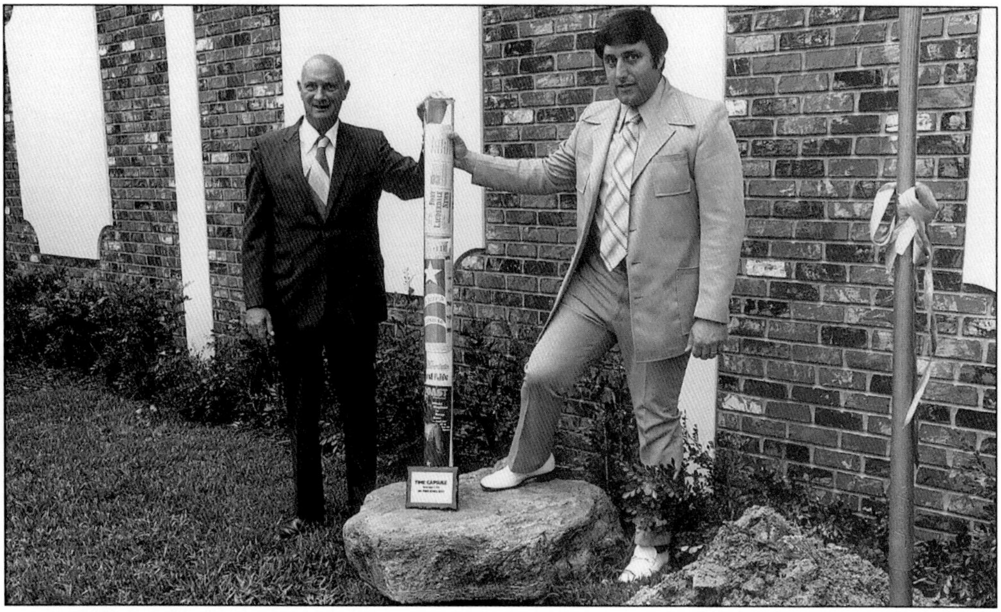

Time capsules are a tradition in Coral Springs. The bicentennial time capsule was buried at 3001 University Drive (then the Florida Coast Bank) in 1976. It was a plastic tube containing several newspapers, magazines, a July calendar of events, Olympic prints and stamps (it was an "Olympic year"), and a $2 bill. The participants are unknown. (Courtesy of Coral Ridge Properties.)

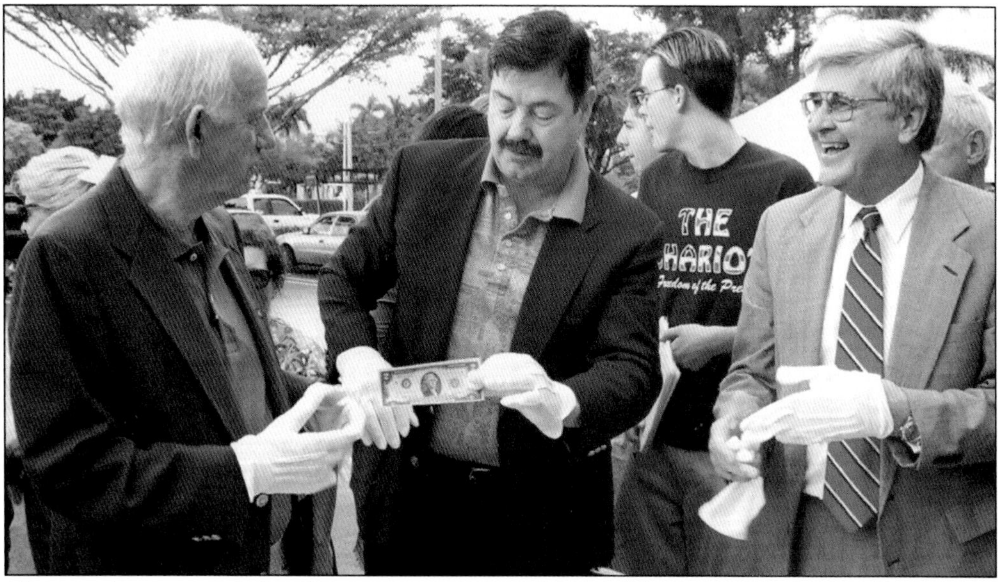

The capsule was unsealed in 2001 in the presence of three of the city's mayors, including former Mayor Edward Heafy, Mayor John Sommerer, and former Mayor Walter Blake (all wearing white archival gloves). The seal had broken and water had begun to destroy the papers. It will be reburied with the original contents and current newspapers, small portrait currency in all denominations (which are now "history"), and 34¢ Olympic stamps (2001 was another "Olympic year"). It is to be reopened on July 4, 2026, when the citizens of Coral Springs will again discover "time in a bottle." (Courtesy of the City of Coral Springs.)

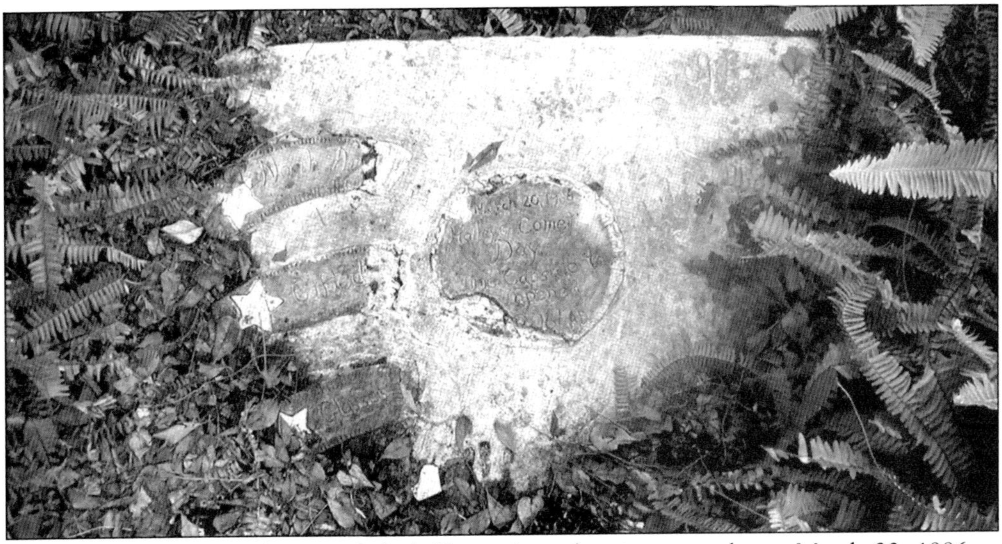

Students from the North Area Gifted Classes buried a time capsule on March 20, 1986 to commemorate the visit of Halley's Comet. The capsule is to be reopened in 2061 at the next flyby and is filled with drawings and essays. The concrete cover stone can be seen in Mullins Park behind Sartory Senior Center. Additional time capsules were buried for the opening of Coral Springs High School, the Charter School, Parkside Elementary School, and North Community Park. (Courtesy of the City of Coral Springs.)

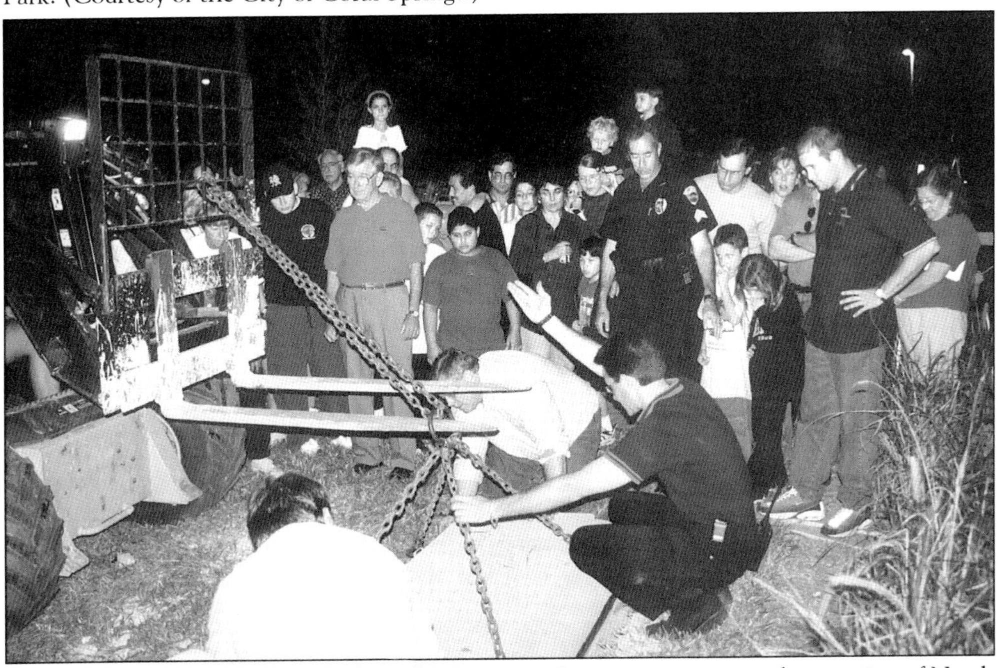

On December 31, 1999, the city buried a time capsule to commemorate the opening of North Community Park and the Millennium. Using a small coffin, it includes the master plan of the city, Stuart McIver's book *Coral Springs, The First 25 Years*, school year books and T-shirts, newspapers, a video of *Birth of a City*, a business plan, annual budget, city department directories, police and fire department rosters and patches, and letters to the future. It will be reopened in 2050. (Courtesy of the City of Coral Springs.)

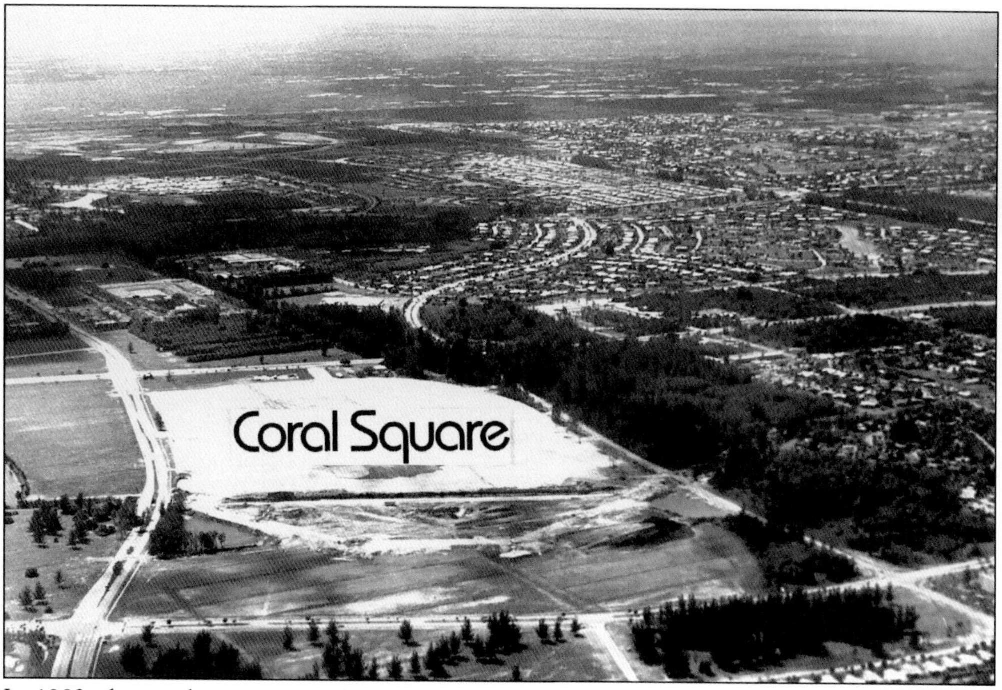

In 1983, the northeast corner of University Drive and Atlantic Boulevard, looking west, was relatively empty and in reserve for a large shopping mall, also part of the master plan. (Courtesy of Coral Ridge Properties.)

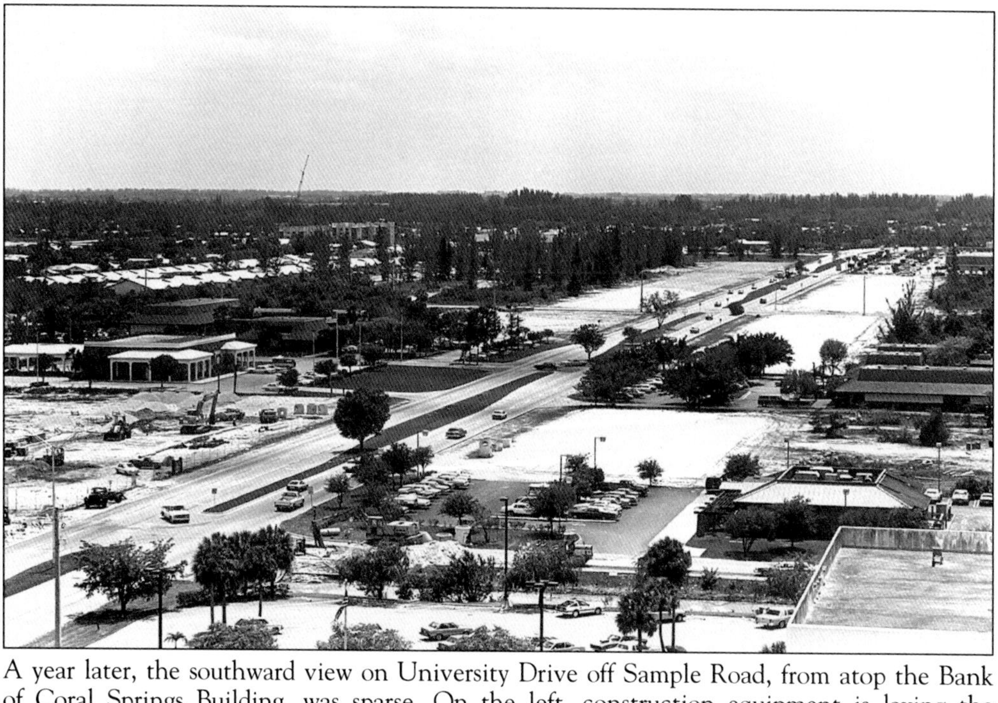

A year later, the southward view on University Drive off Sample Road, from atop the Bank of Coral Springs Building, was sparse. On the left, construction equipment is laying the foundation for the Coral Springs Sunrise Towers at 3111 University Drive. South of that is the Florida Coast Bank, now Amtrust. (Courtesy of Coral Ridge Properties.)

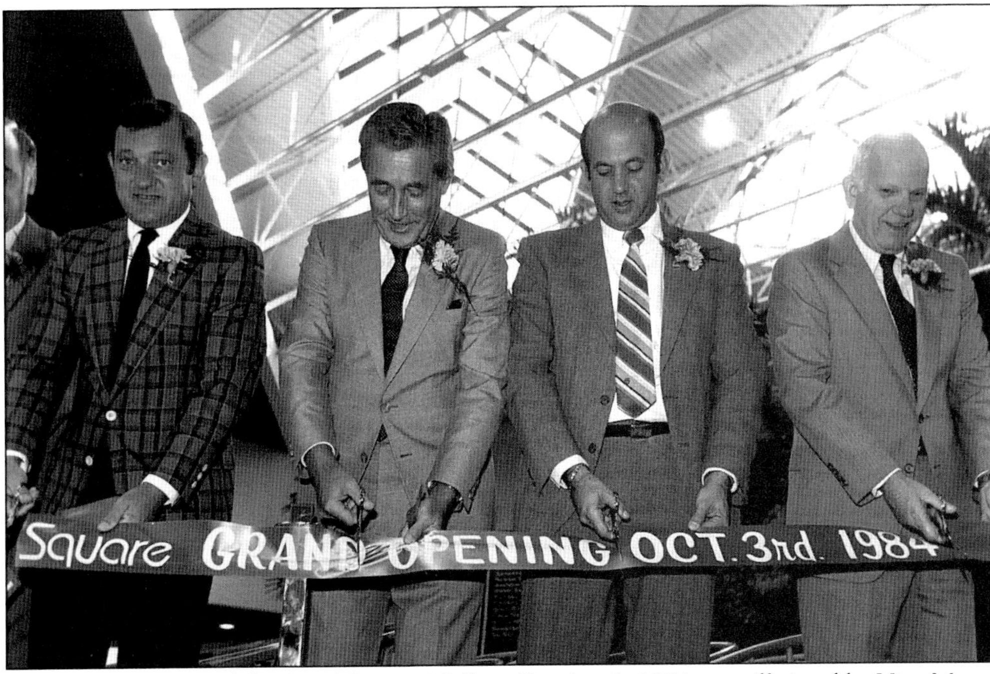

The grand opening of the Coral Square Mall on October 3, 1984 was officiated by Vice Mayor Don Sanders; Werner Buntemeyer, president of Coral Ridge Properties; and Commissioners Jim Gordon and Edward Heafy, among other dignitaries. (Courtesy of Coral Ridge Properties.)

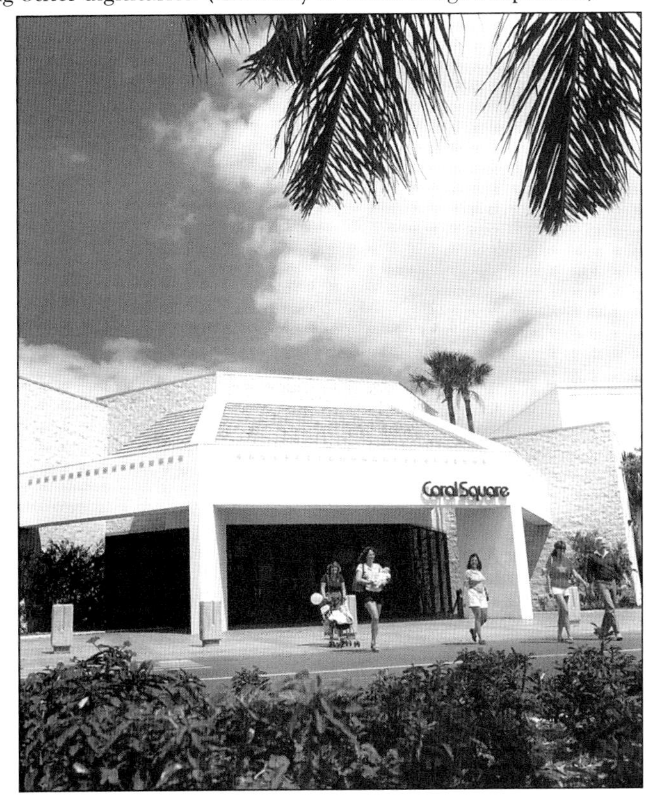

The Coral Square Mall became a major shopping venue for the county, covering 1.2 million square feet of space. The original anchor stores were Lord and Taylor's, Jordan Marsh, J.C. Penney's, and Burdines. (Courtesy of Coral Ridge Properties.)

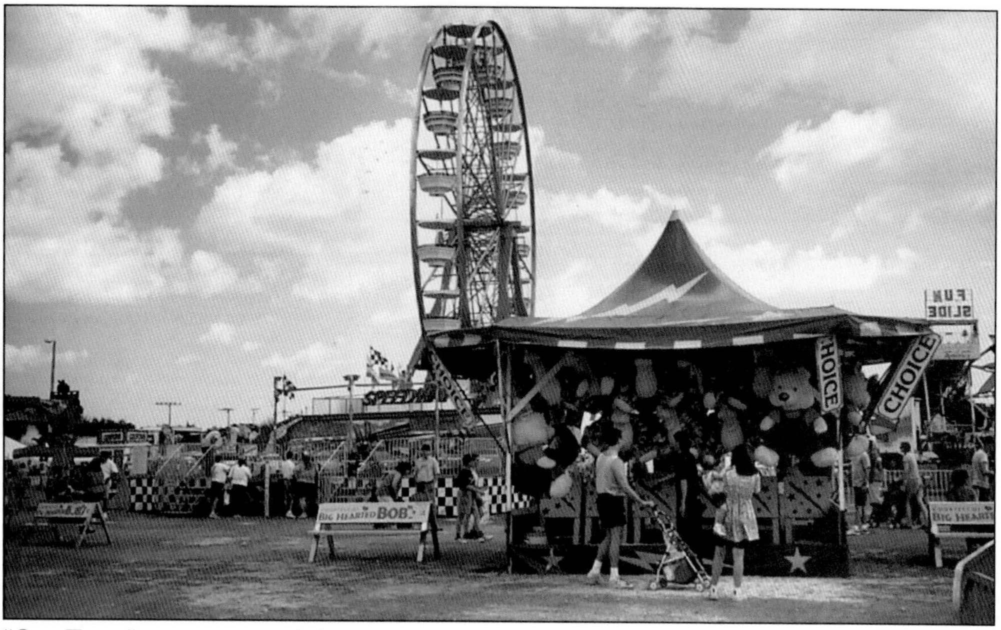

"Our Town" was an annual festival that began in October 1979 to assist merchants along Sample Road who were impacted by the construction to widen the thoroughfare. The Chamber of Commerce teamed up with the city's parks and recreation department to provide a venue that allowed them to advertise their businesses at booths in Mullins Park. There was a stage on one end for programs and entertainment, including the annual children's Halloween costume contest and the Kiwanis October Fest. When Our Town America Inc. was formed in 1996, it became an annual March event at Sportsplex. (Courtesy of the City of Coral Springs.)

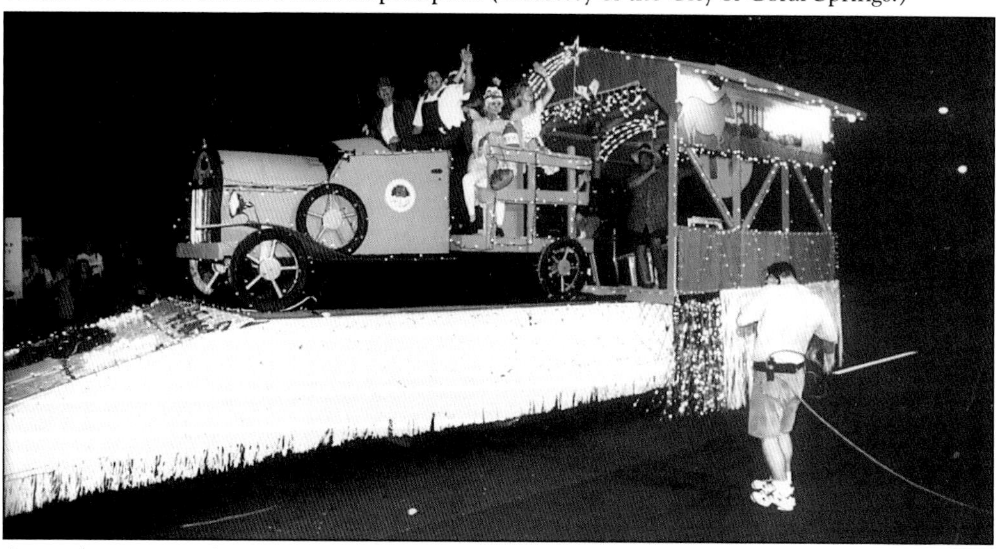

A parade was part of "Our Town" until 1994, when it was rescheduled for December because of rain. It was then changed to the "Light Up Coral Springs Holiday Parade" and has been held in December ever since. Early parades had hundreds of Scouts and Little Leaguers in tow. Floats progressed from simple trailers to theme-based creations, such as the 1998 City employee entry of the Beverly Hillbillies. On board, just pulling out of the covered bridge replica, are Robert Glenn, Peter Elmo, Janis Humpage, and Judy Zingale. (Courtesy of the City of Coral Springs.)

Six

Public Buildings

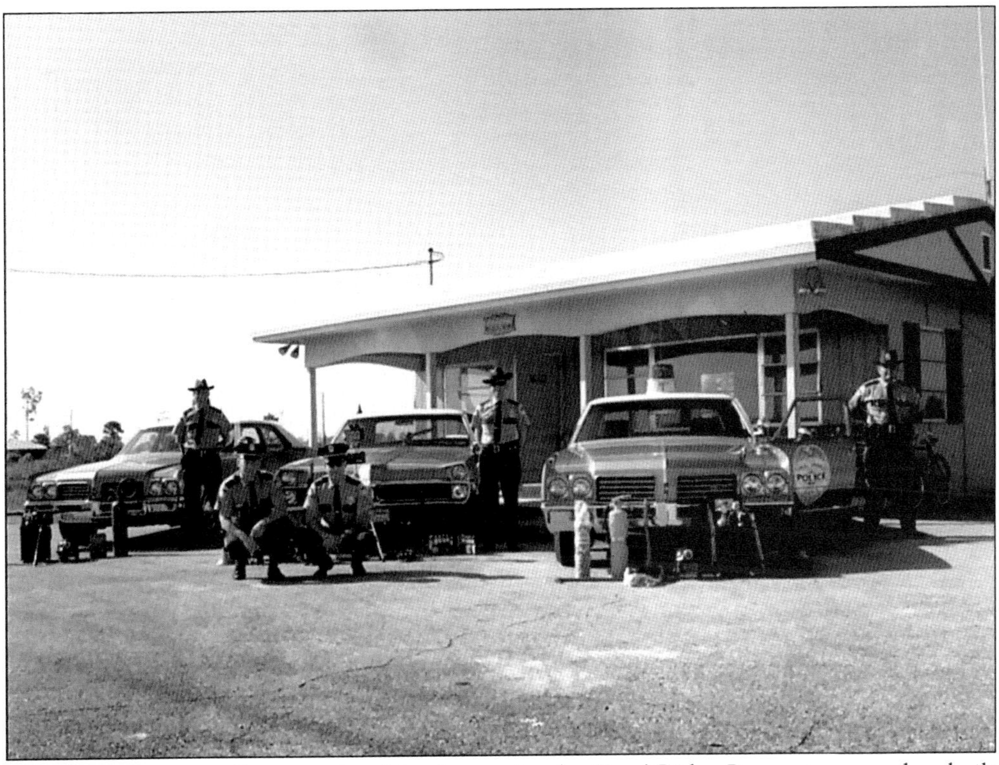

The first real estate office was slated for destruction by Coral Ridge Properties once they built their administration building in 1966. The city had it moved to 4500 Woodside Drive off Wiles Road to use as their administration building and later as the first police station. Pictured are all the officers, cars, and equipment of the time. When the police moved out in 1972, it became a clubhouse for the Jaycees. (Courtesy of Coral Ridge Properties.)

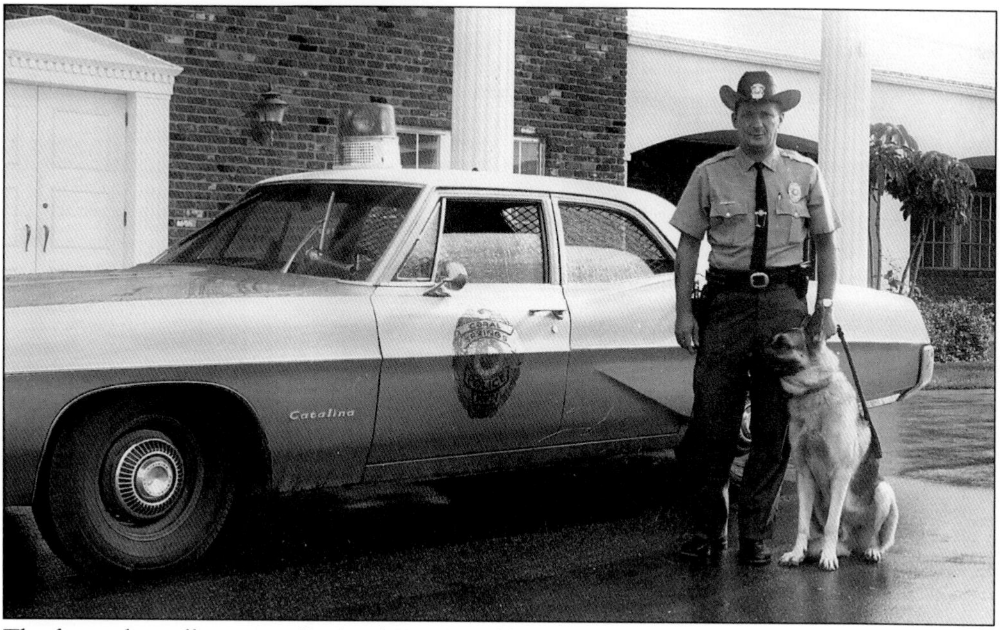

The first police officers were Richard "Vic" Vedilago and Sergeant Satan, his K-9. During their off-hours, the Margate Police were on call. Once, when Chief Vedilago was bragging to someone at the Red Fox Inn about Satan's skills, he gave the dog the order to attack. Satan obediently bit Vedilago on the hand. (Courtesy of Coral Ridge Properties.)

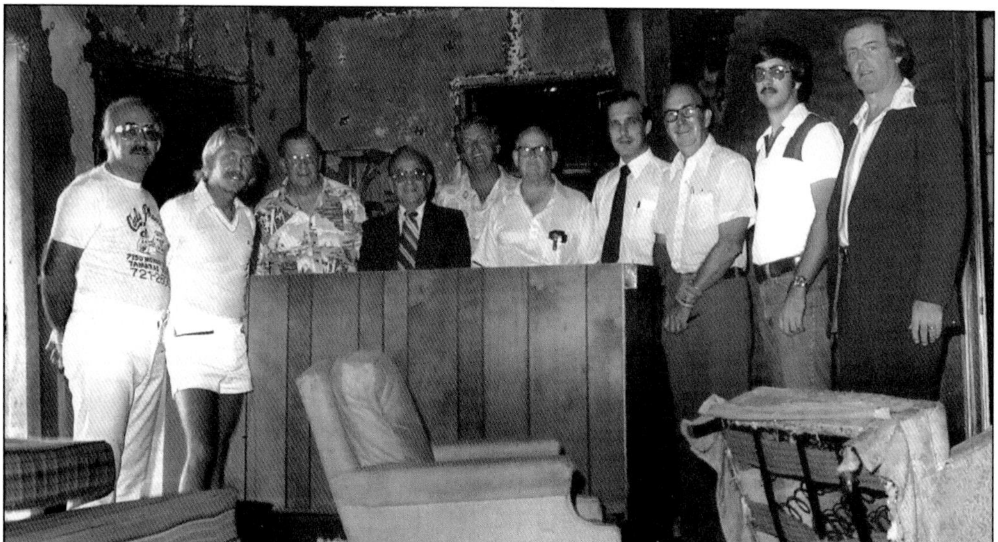

When the owner of the property wanted the former Police Station building moved in 1976, the Coral Springs Historical Society tried to find funds to move it to a new location. That having failed, the fire department had it towed to the city dump in the industrial park area to use for smoke drills, sometimes setting it alight. The Landmark Restoration Committee took notice of the destruction in 1977 and raised funds to have it moved. Some of the members of the restoration committee, pictured from left to right, are Vice Mayor Carl Zeytoonian, Brian Hansen, John Cassidy, Sandy Cugno, unidentified, John Trout, John Lynch, Jack Lotsey, Bill Sayers, and Chuck Connor. (Courtesy of Sandy Cugno.)

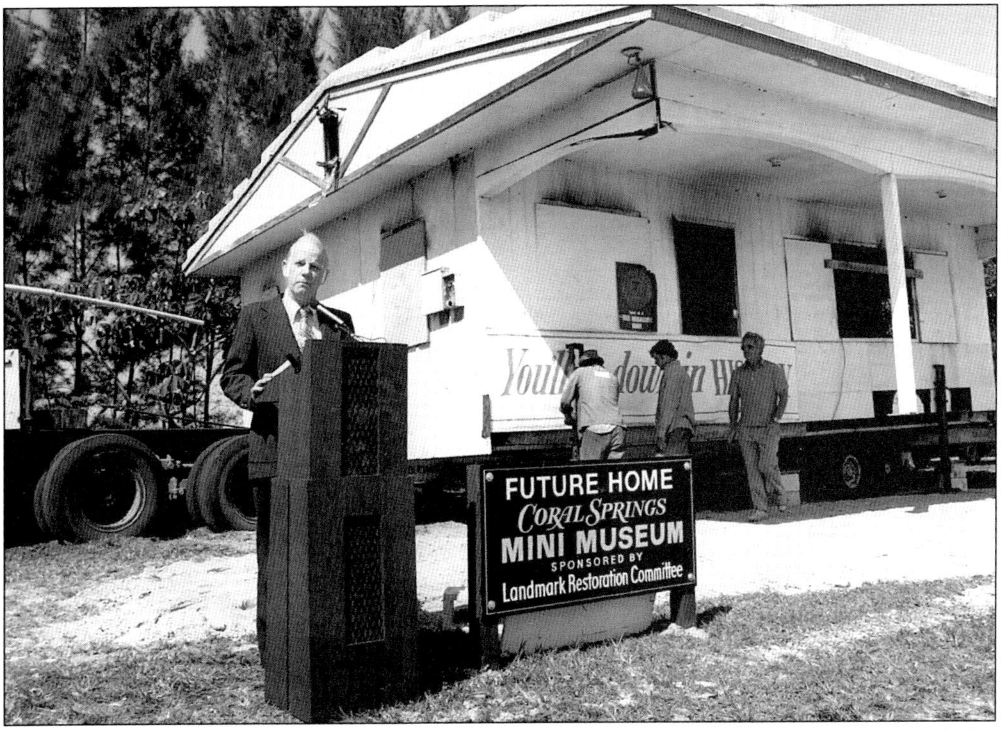

On October 20, 1977, a parade, complete with bands and city officials, accompanied the building as it was towed on a flat bed truck along Sample Road to University Drive and finally to Mullins Park. People lined the route cheering it on, and Mayor Edward Heafy welcomed it to its new home. It was placed west of the swimming pool by the park's entrance. (Courtesy of Coral Ridge Properties.)

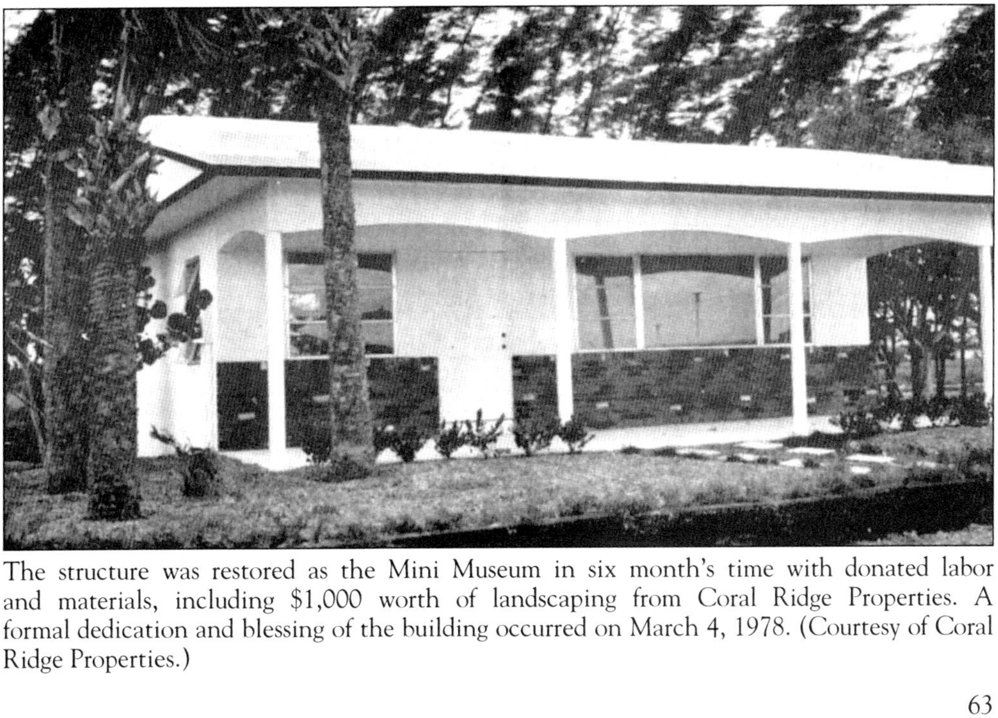

The structure was restored as the Mini Museum in six month's time with donated labor and materials, including $1,000 worth of landscaping from Coral Ridge Properties. A formal dedication and blessing of the building occurred on March 4, 1978. (Courtesy of Coral Ridge Properties.)

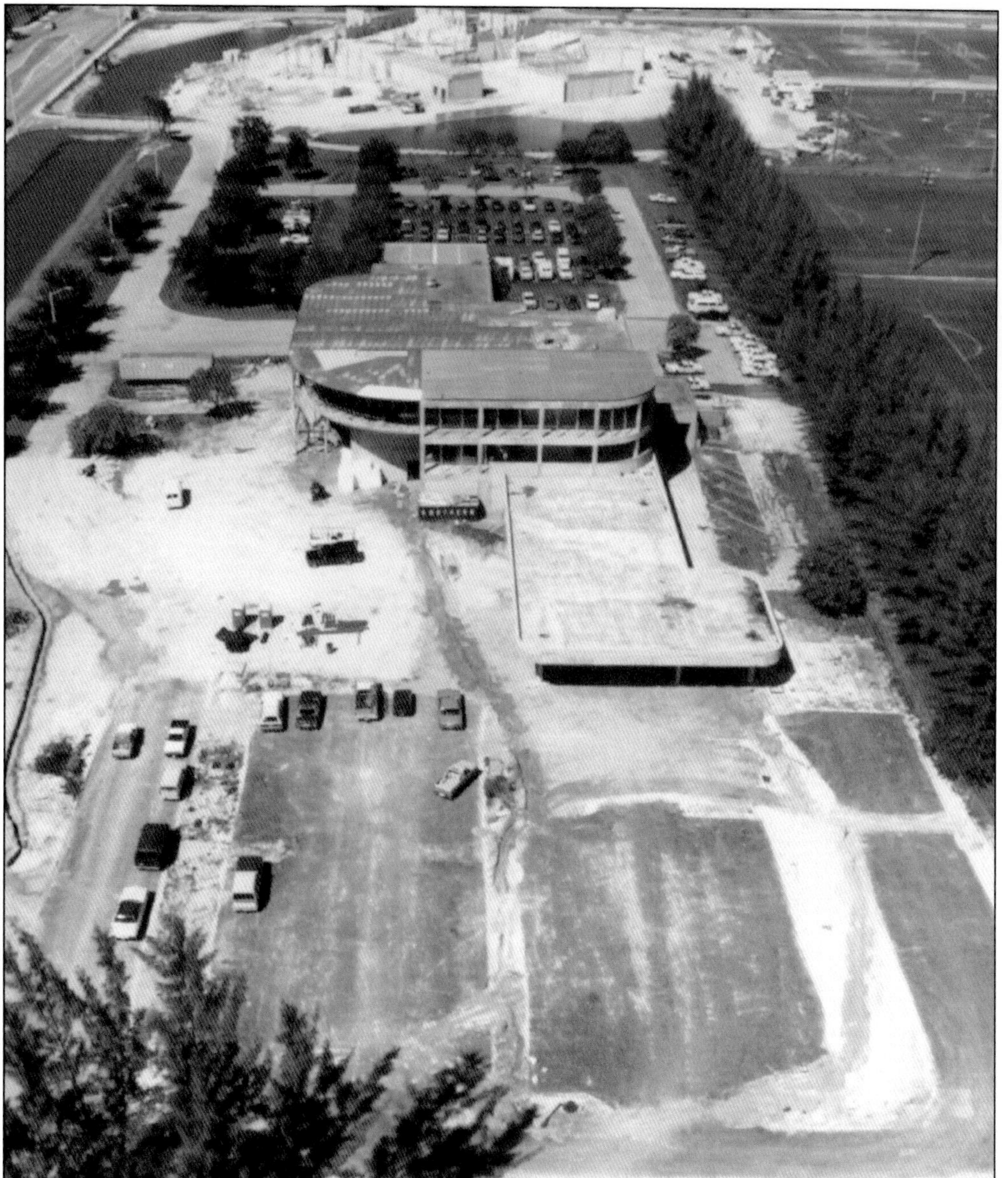

This aerial photograph shows the result of the city's first major General Obligation Bonds issued in 1986, for a total of $16 million. In the foreground, the Public Safety Building's shell is mostly completed. Behind it, the Coral Springs City Centre's walls are rising. Bond proceeds also developed parts of Cypress Park, additional facilities at Mullins Park, and other infrastructure projects. (Courtesy of the City of Coral Springs.)

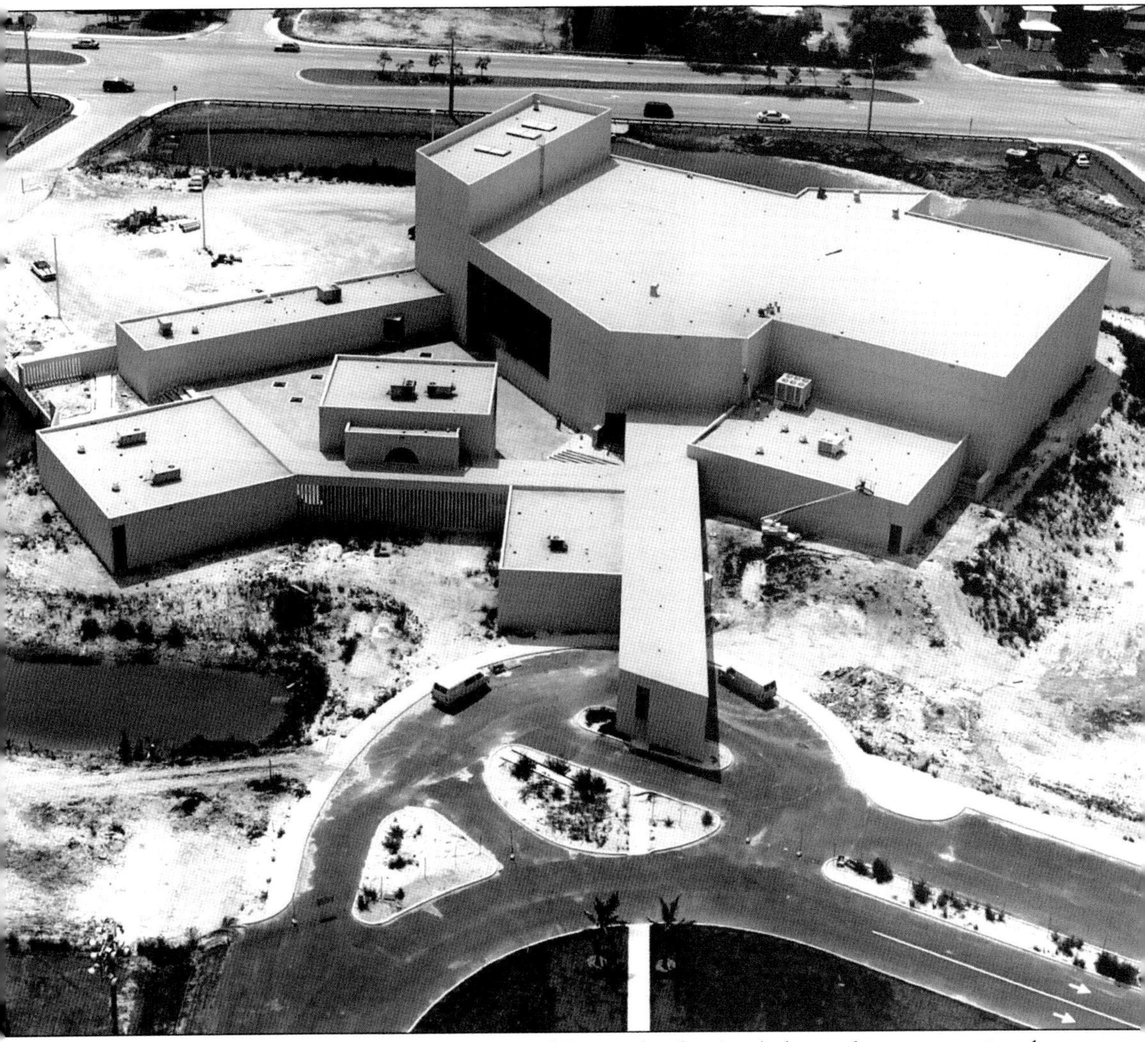

This 1990 bird's-eye view of the City Centre (Center for the Arts) shows the water setting that has welcomed everything from the Florida Philharmonic to the latest Broadway hits, such as *Rent*. In 1996 the Coral Springs Museum of Art was added to the complex. (Courtesy of Coral Ridge Properties.)

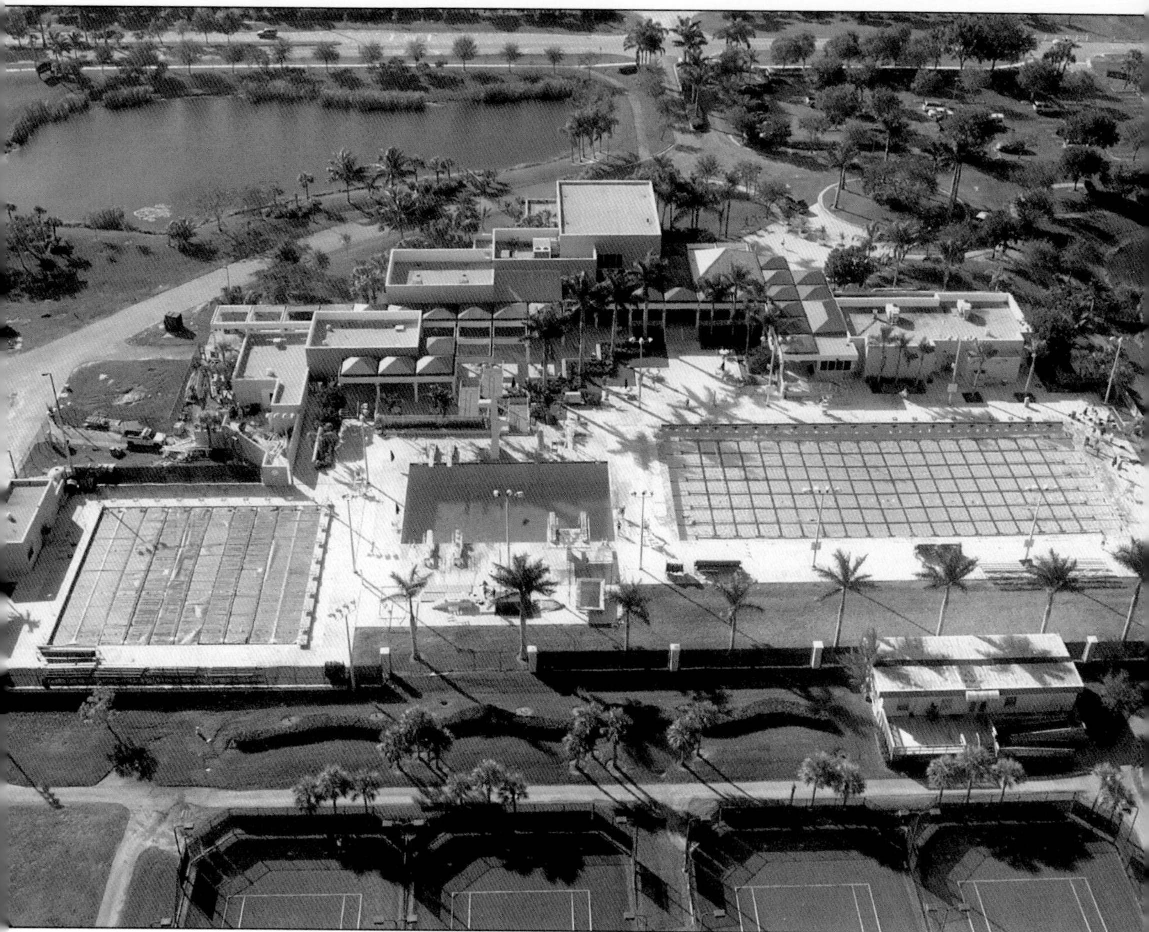

This aerial view shows the Aquatics Complex as it looked in 2000. At the time, the facility was less than five years old and was preparing to undergo an expansion that would provide a fitness center and an additional teaching pool. (Courtesy of the City of Coral Springs.)

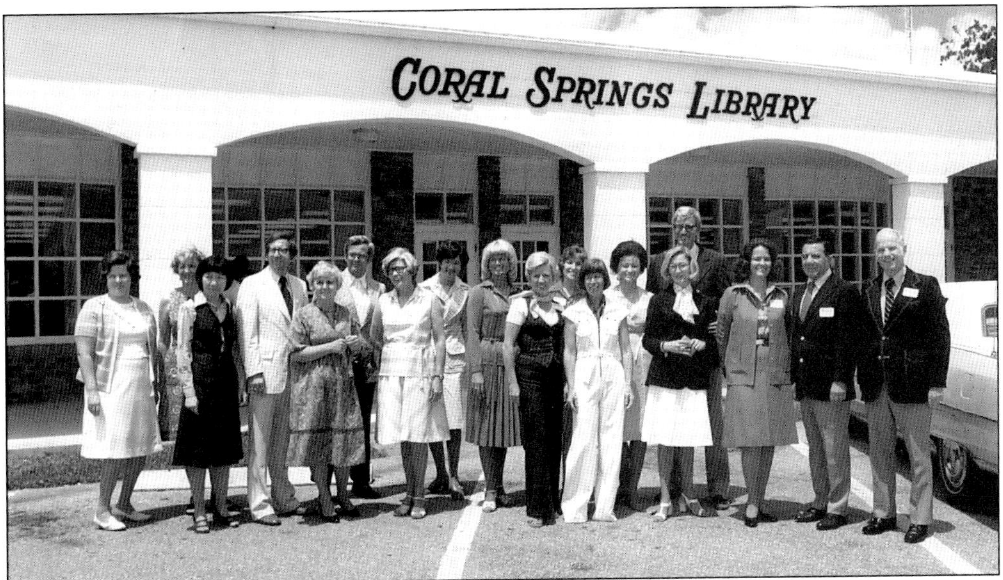

Through the efforts of the Welcome Wagon of Coral Springs, the first library opened in Village Square in early 1971 with 1,100 mostly donated books, shelves, and office supplies. It moved later that year with 1,600 books to the west wing of what is now City Hall and was dedicated on the Fourth of July. Pictured from left to right are three unidentified supporters, Broward County Director of Libraries Cecil Beach, Ann Kalb, two unidentified people, Marcia Beach, four more unidentified friends, P. Nicholson, Mayor Ben Geiger, unidentified, Joseph Taravella (president of Coral Ridge Properties), and Commissioner Edward Heafy. (Courtesy of Coral Ridge Properties.)

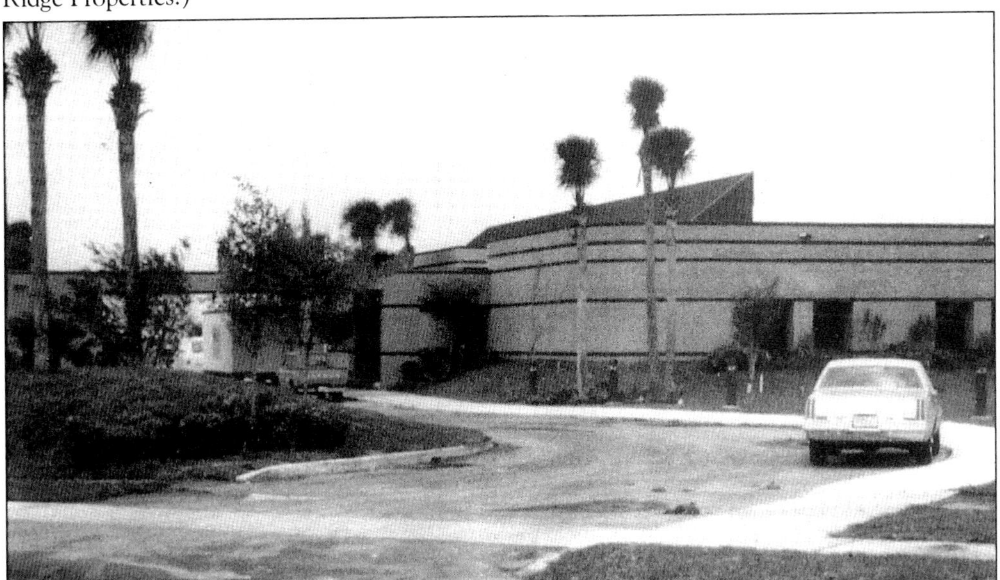

This library site was opened on April 25, 1978 (during National Library Week) across from Mullins Park on NW 29th Street. Built as the result of the 1978 Broward County bond issue, it cost $1.2 million, covered 13,900 square feet, and had the capacity for 50,000 books. The park-like setting encouraged patrons to read outdoors and feed the resident ducks in the nearby canal. (Courtesy of the Broward County Library.)

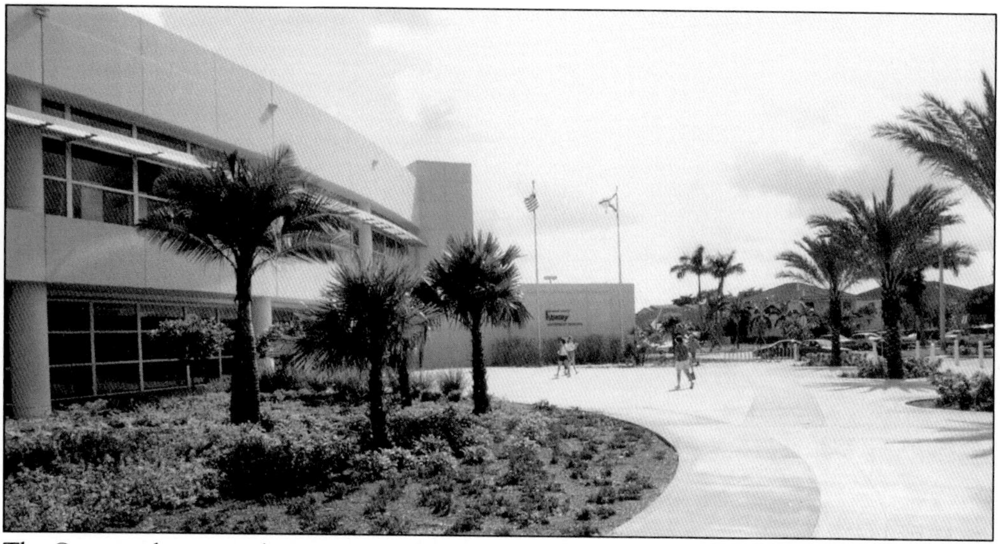

The City acted as general contractor for the renovation of the Coral Springs Mall, for both the City and Broward County. The project was completed on time and under budget, creating Coral Springs Charter School and the County's newest regional library, which opened on February 15, 2001. (Courtesy of the City of Coral Springs.)

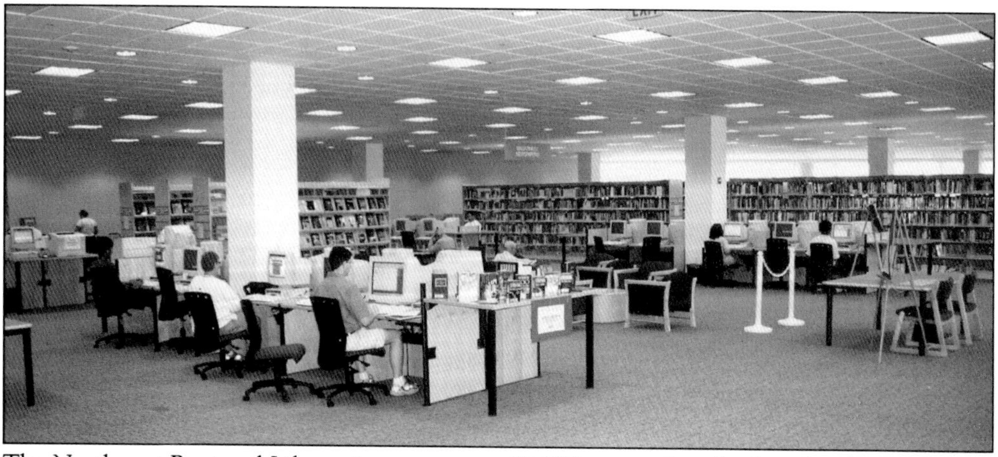

The Northwest Regional Library is a two-story, 72,000-square-foot facility that houses a large audio-visual collection, an extensive children's book room, a teen activity room, a community technology center, and 110,000 books, magazines, videotapes, DVDs, compact discs, books-on-tape, and computer software—all with a collection expansion capacity of 150,000. (Courtesy of the City of Coral Springs.)

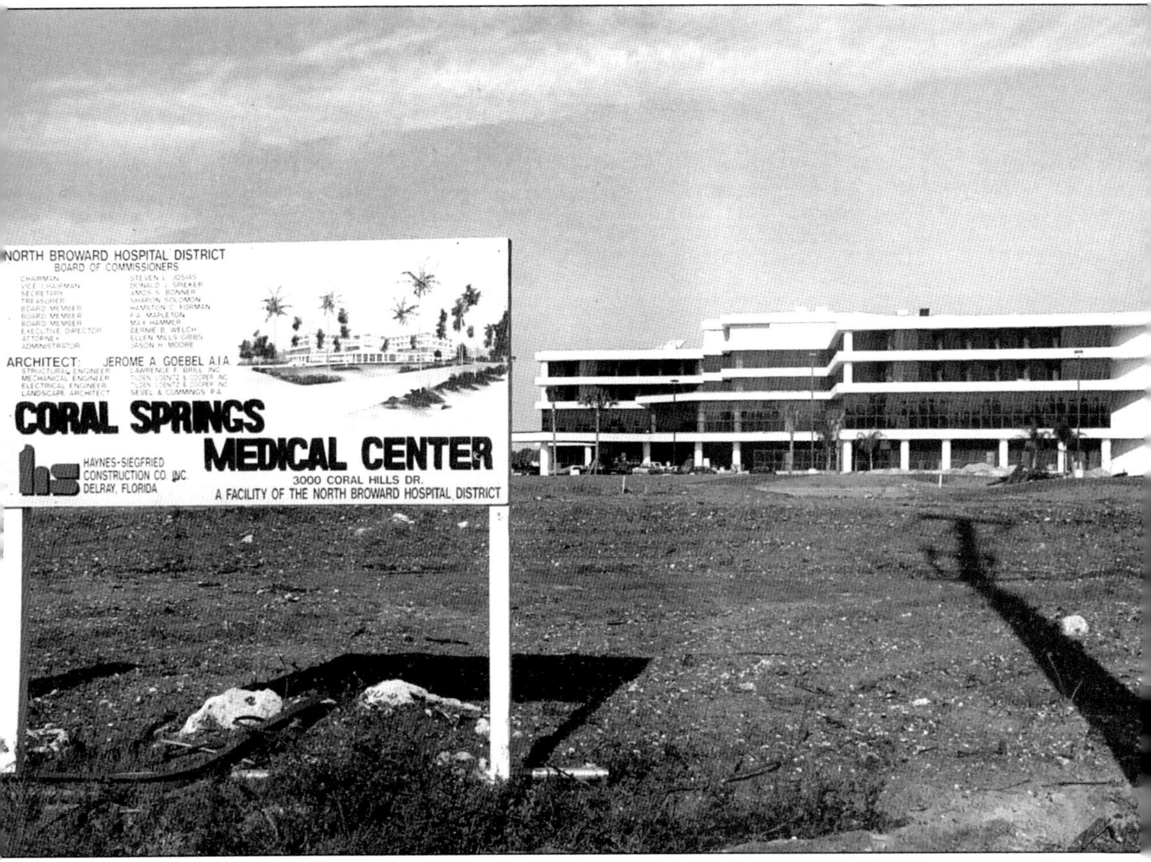

In the 1980s, Coral Springs' doctors wanted a hospital but the state felt there were enough hospital beds in the area. Robert Hofmann, executive vice president of Coral Ridge Properties, was also president of the Diabetes Foundation that owned 20 acres of property along Coral Hills Drive. He brought this to the attention of the North Broward hospital district, offering the acreage on which to build a hospital if it was built within two years. The district appealed to the state and the Coral Springs Medical Center was born on June 27, 1987. This "prenatal" photograph was taken December 3, 1986. (Courtesy of Coral Ridge Properties.)

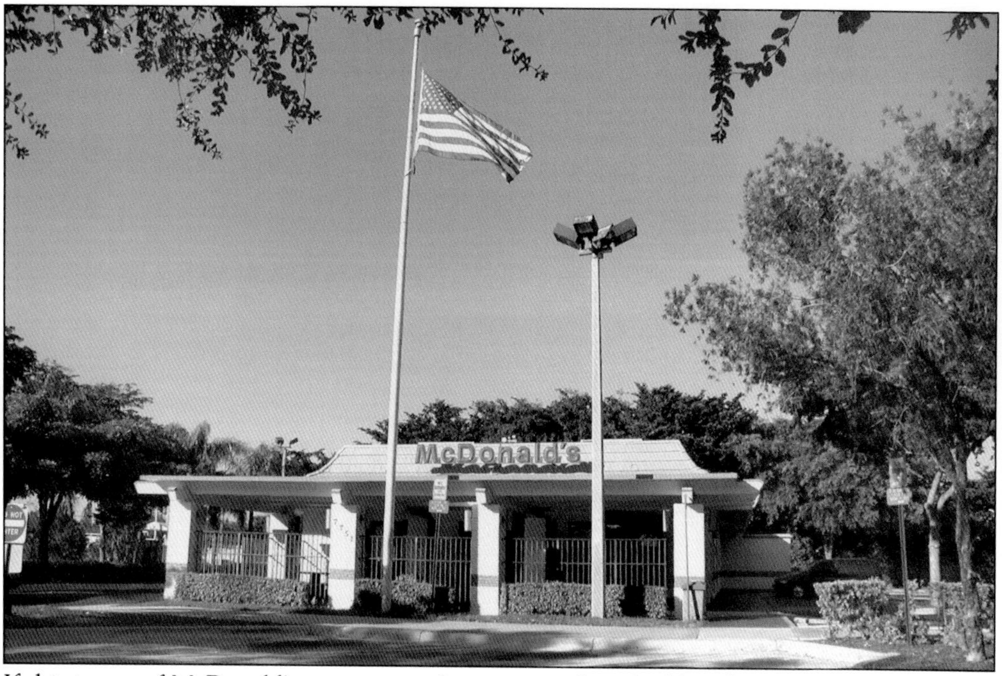

If this image of McDonald's causes out-of-towners to do a double-take, it is probably because there are no "golden arches." Coral Springs was the first city to reject the customary design as part of its restrictive advertising ordinances. Also, the code permits only the state and national flags to be flown, giving rise to a surprising number of patriotic displays throughout the city. (Courtesy of the City of Coral Springs.)

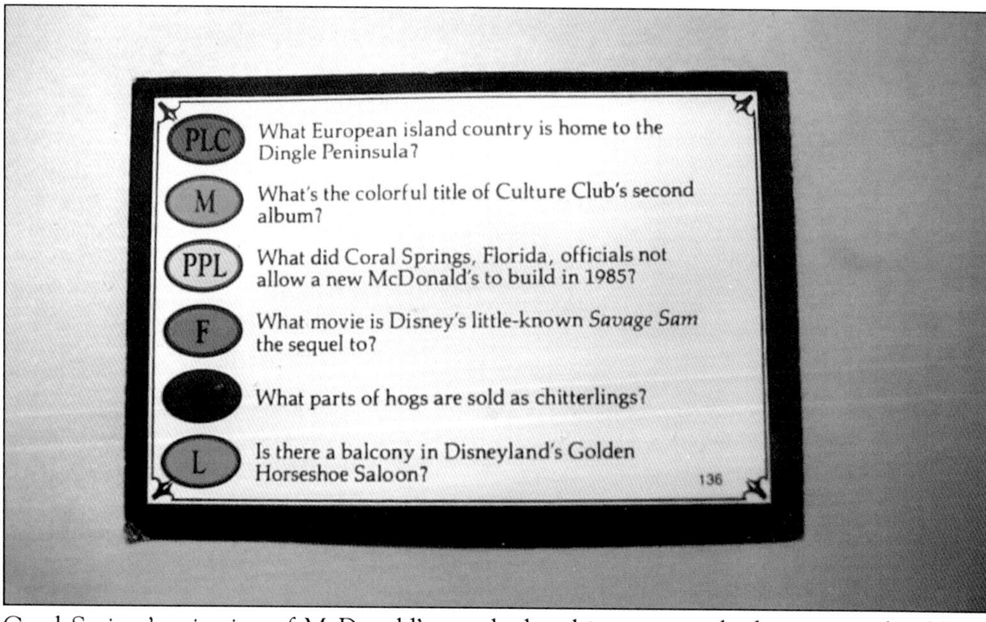

Coral Springs's rejection of McDonald's standard architecture resulted in national publicity and even a question in the board game *Trivial Pursuit*. It asks, "What did Coral Springs, Florida, officials not allow a new McDonald's to build in 1985?" Answer: "Golden Arches." (Courtesy of the City of Coral Springs.)

Seven

The Sporting Life

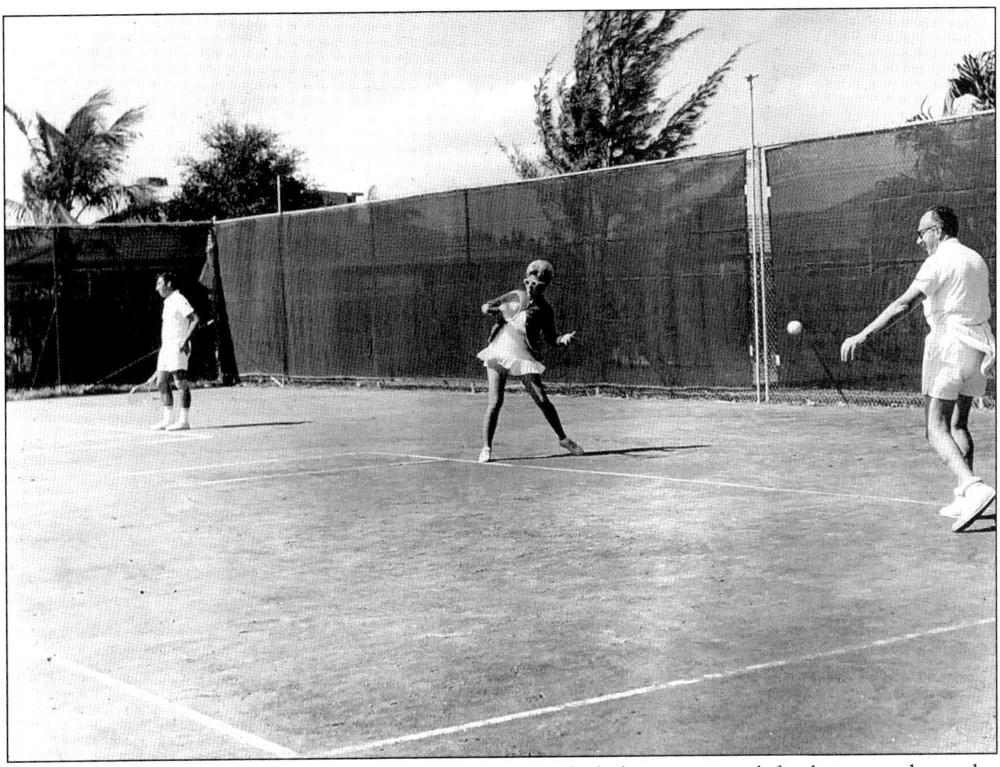

Some of the first construction in Coral Springs included recreational facilities, such as the Broken Woods Country Club, which opened in 1966. As the city's developers had planned, the earliest residents were given access to amenities on par with luxury developments in beach communities. Shown here from left to right are Guy Bono, unidentified, and Bret Cipes. (Courtesy of Coral Ridge Properties.)

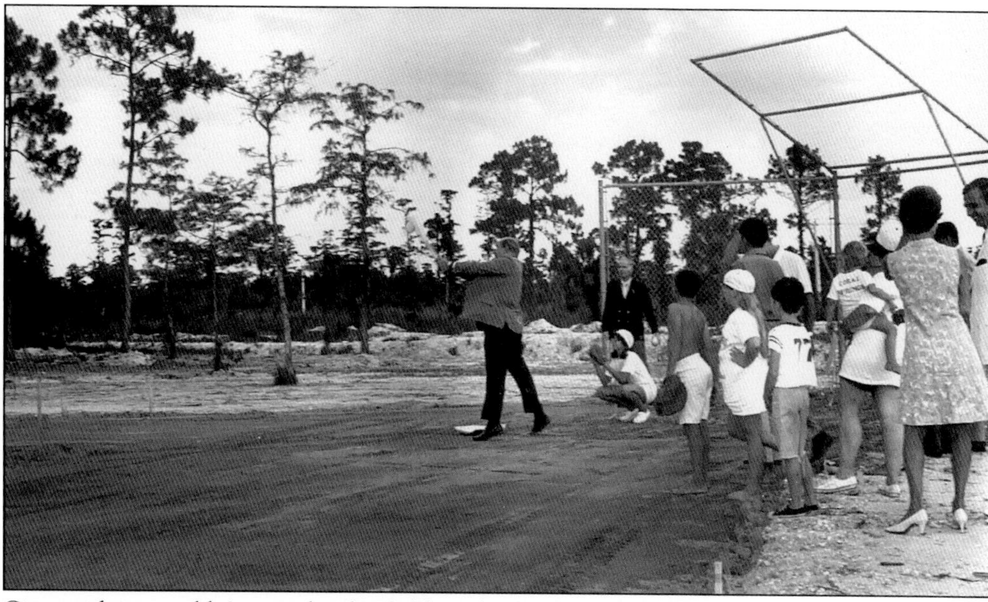

City residents couldn't wait for the fields to be finished so they could practice batting at the June 6, 1970 dedication of Lion's Park. It became the city's first Little League ballpark. Note the formal attire of some of the viewers and participants, including Mayor George MacGregor at bat. (Courtesy of Coral Ridge Properties.)

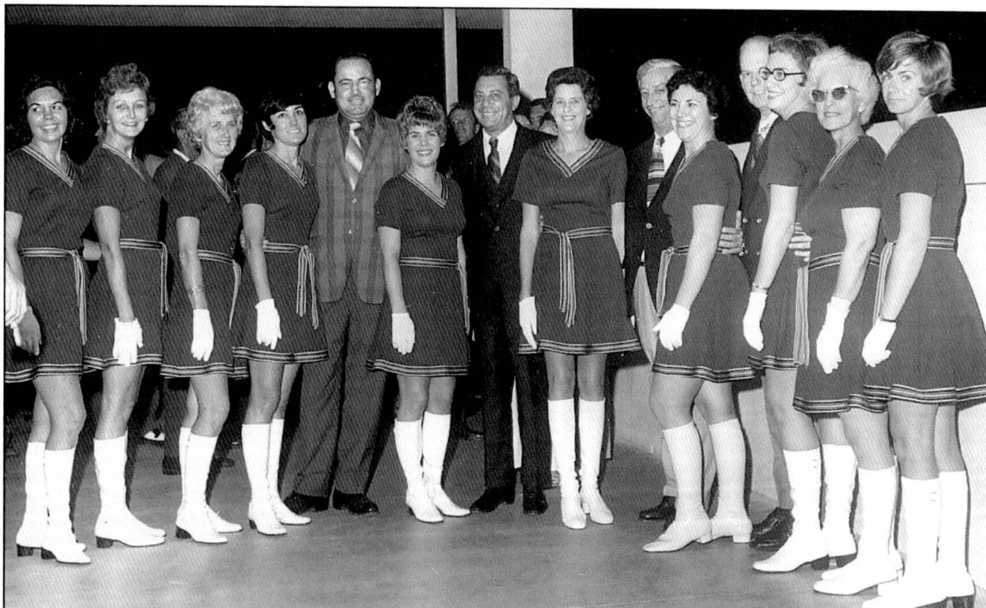

The Coral Springs Chamber of Commerce Women's Division was dispatched in uniform to the Ft. Lauderdale airport to greet golfers when they arrived to play in city tournaments and to chauffeur them to their hotel and country clubs. From left to right are Betty Larsen, Barbara Phillips, unidentified, Barbara Malone, Mayor George MacGregor, Marion Nolan, Joseph Taravella (president of Coral Ridge Properties), Helene Sullivan, County Commissioner William Stevens, Lucy Bono, City Commissioner Edward Heafy, Sue Tisdale, Carolyn Mullins, and Pat McCluskey. Not shown is Emily Heafy. (Courtesy of Coral Ridge Properties.)

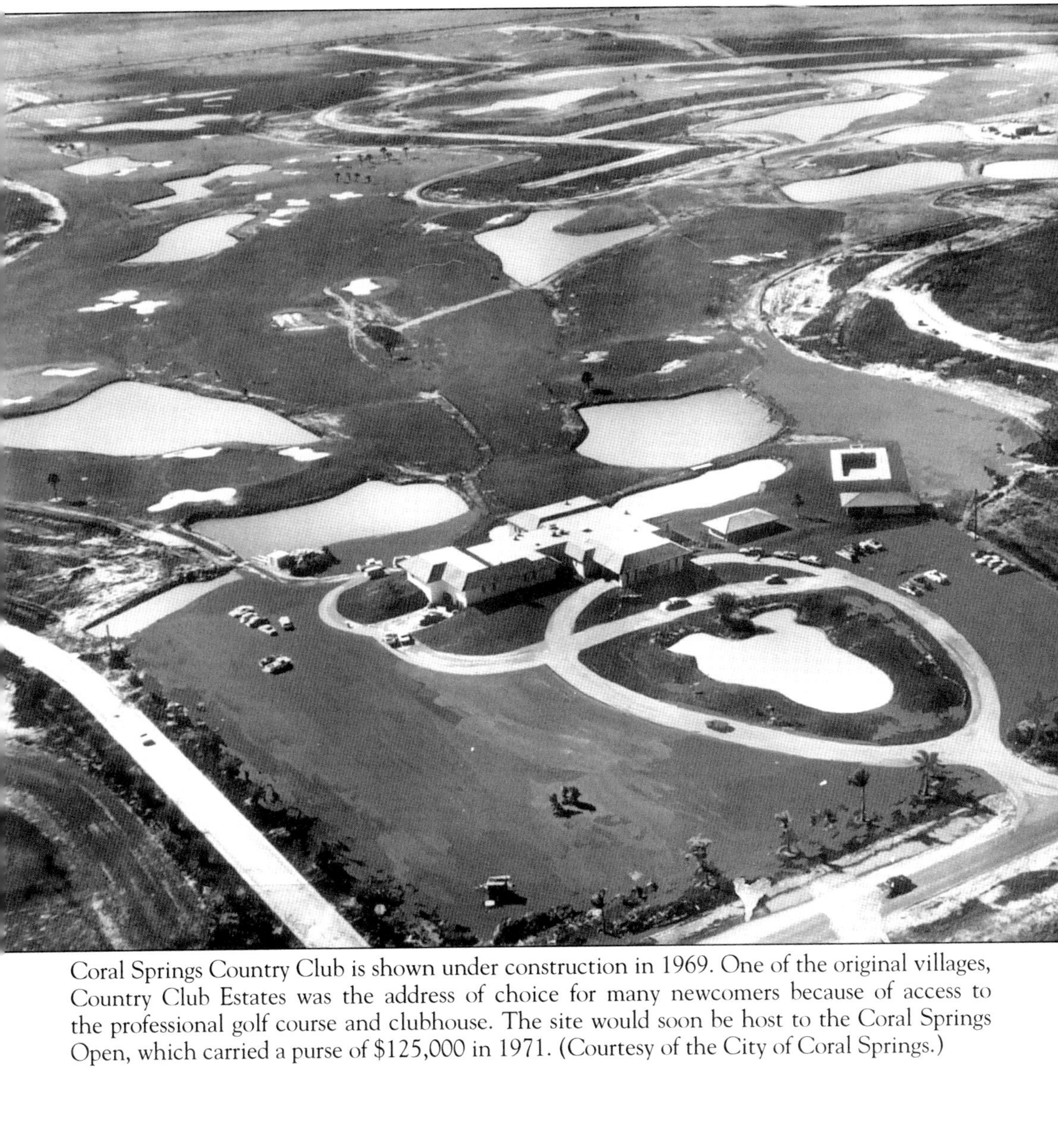

Coral Springs Country Club is shown under construction in 1969. One of the original villages, Country Club Estates was the address of choice for many newcomers because of access to the professional golf course and clubhouse. The site would soon be host to the Coral Springs Open, which carried a purse of $125,000 in 1971. (Courtesy of the City of Coral Springs.)

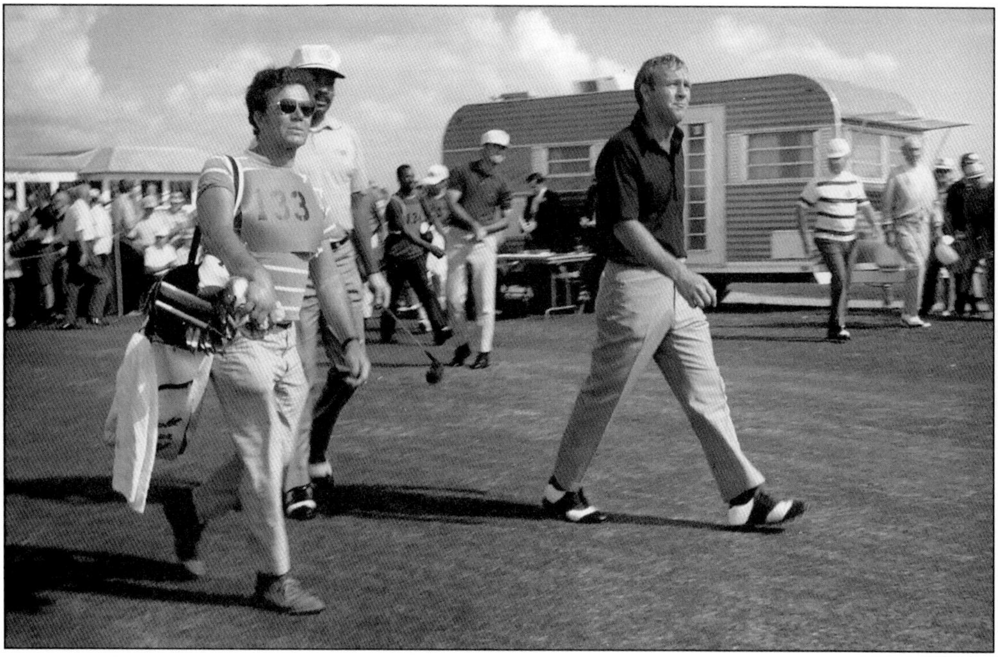

Arnold Palmer strides across the fairways at the Coral Springs Country Club during the 1971 PGA Open Tour. The two-year-old course proved to be a popular stop for professionals. Palmer finished 24th that year, with Lee Trevino and Jack Nicklaus taking first and second rank after an 18-hole tiebreaker. (Courtesy of Coral Ridge Properties.)

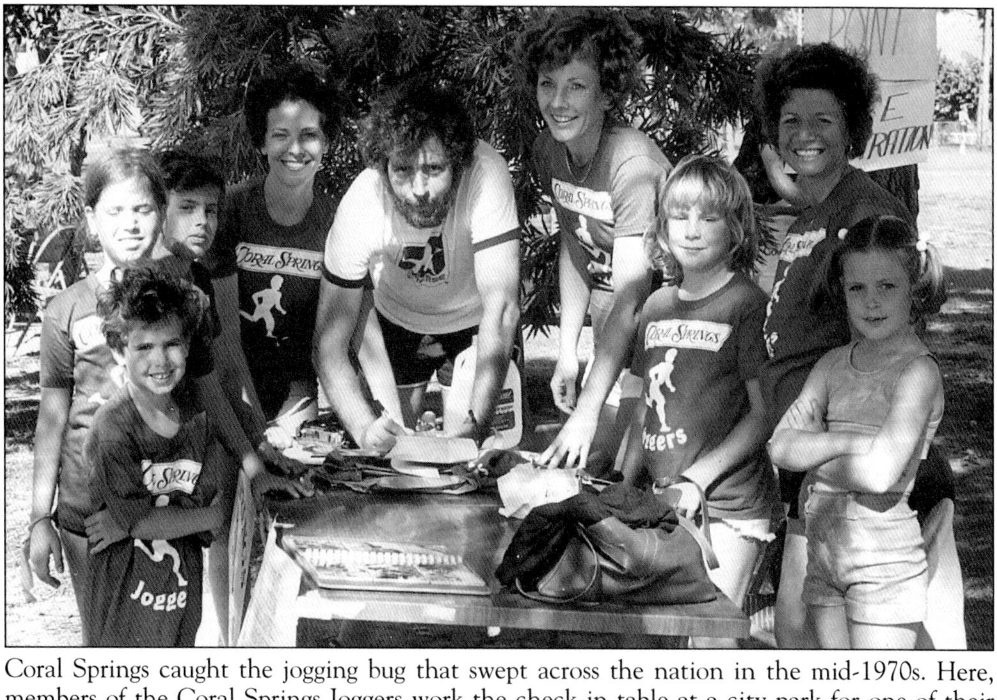

Coral Springs caught the jogging bug that swept across the nation in the mid-1970s. Here, members of the Coral Springs Joggers work the check-in table at a city park for one of their sponsored runs. Runners of all ages participated in weekly and monthly events. (Courtesy of Coral Ridge Properties.)

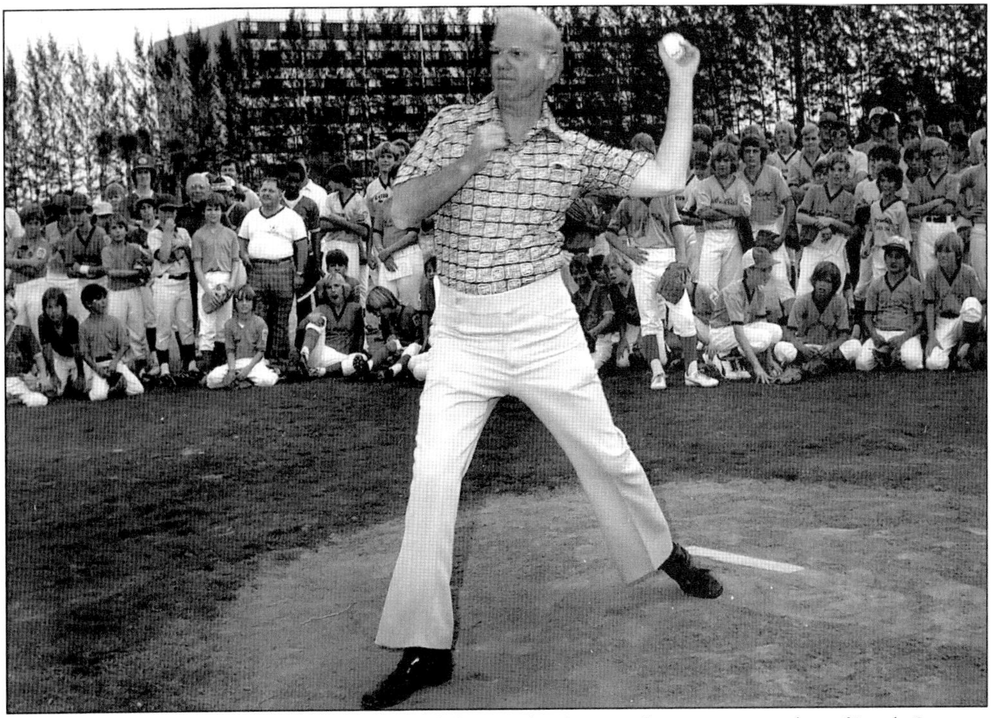

Mayor Edward Heafy takes the mound and throws the first pitch on opening day of Little League in Mullins Park. Several teams and their coaches look on. Behind the line of Australian Pines, the outline of St. Andrews Towers can be seen. (Courtesy of the City of Coral Springs.)

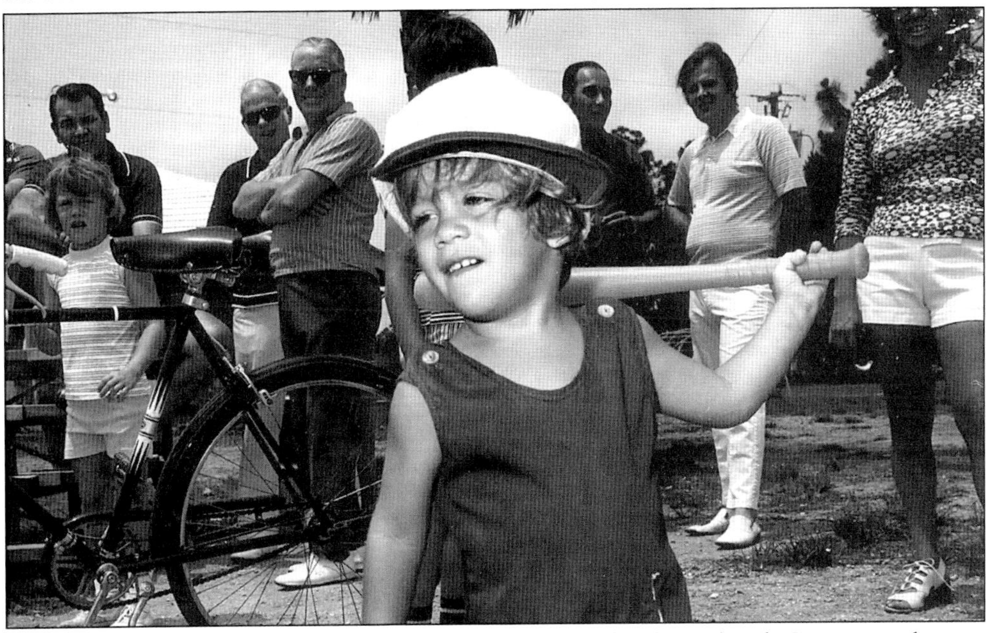

T-ball brought the whole family out for fun-filled South Florida weekends. Leagues and teams sprouted up all over the city as young families continued to move into town. In the background, from left to right, are Paul Singer, Edward Heafy, unidentified, Paul Angelo, and two other unidentified adults. (Courtesy of Coral Ridge Properties.)

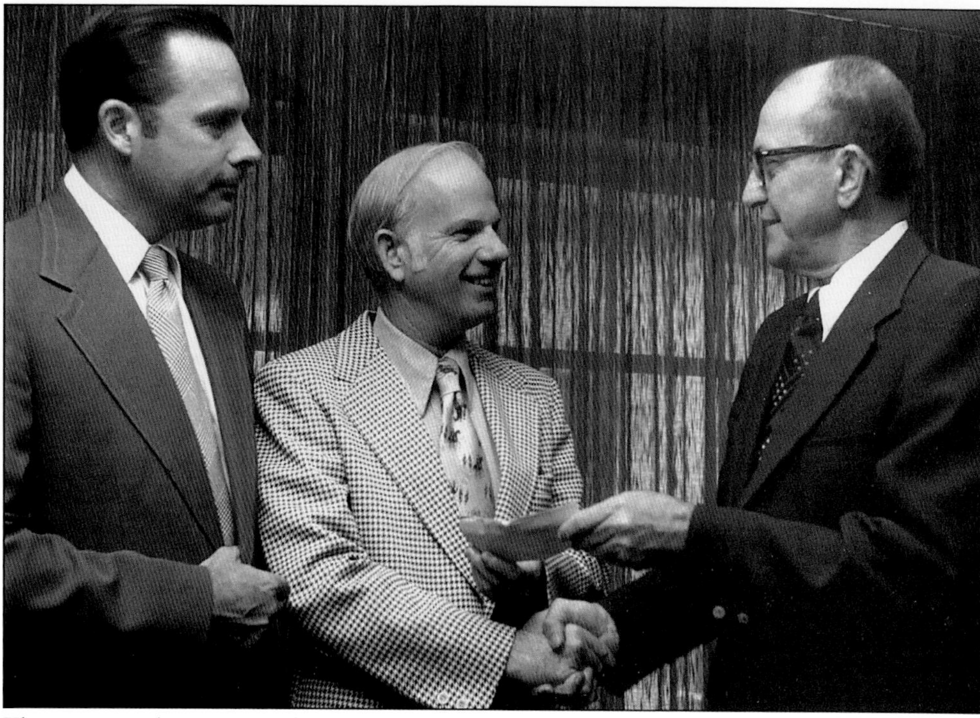

The new Coral Springs High School needed a stadium, so the public was enlisted to raise the necessary $175,000. Coral Ridge Properties donated the funds for the scoreboard in August 1976. From left to right are George Hodapp, chief engineer for Coral Ridge Properties, Commissioner Edward Heafy, and Robert Hofmann, president of Coral Ridge Properties. (Courtesy of the Heafy Collection.)

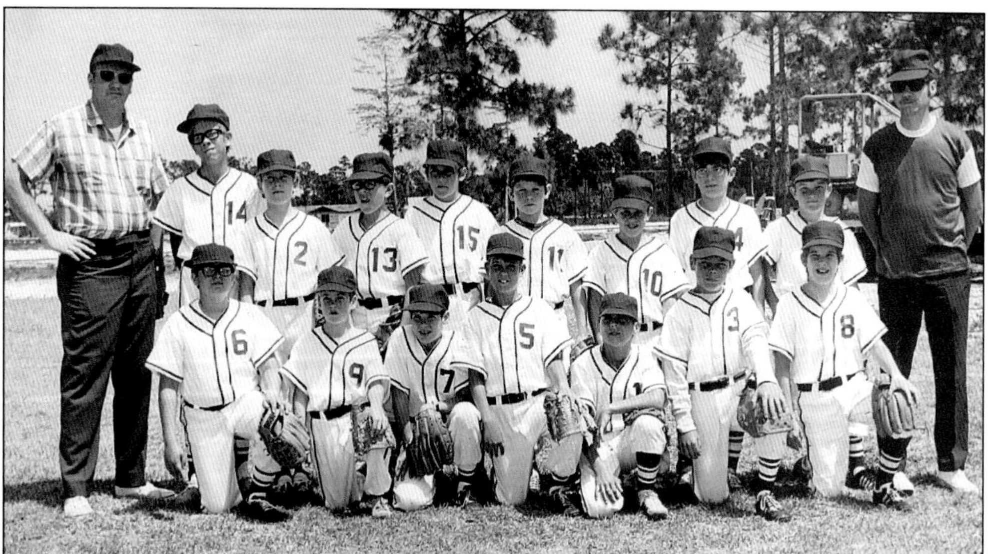

Little League baseball, sponsored by local businesses and coached by volunteer dads, soon became the most popular sport in town. Thousands of little sluggers filled the numerous ball fields in the city, creating a demand for more facilities like those in Lion's Park, where this photograph was taken. (Courtesy of Coral Ridge Properties.)

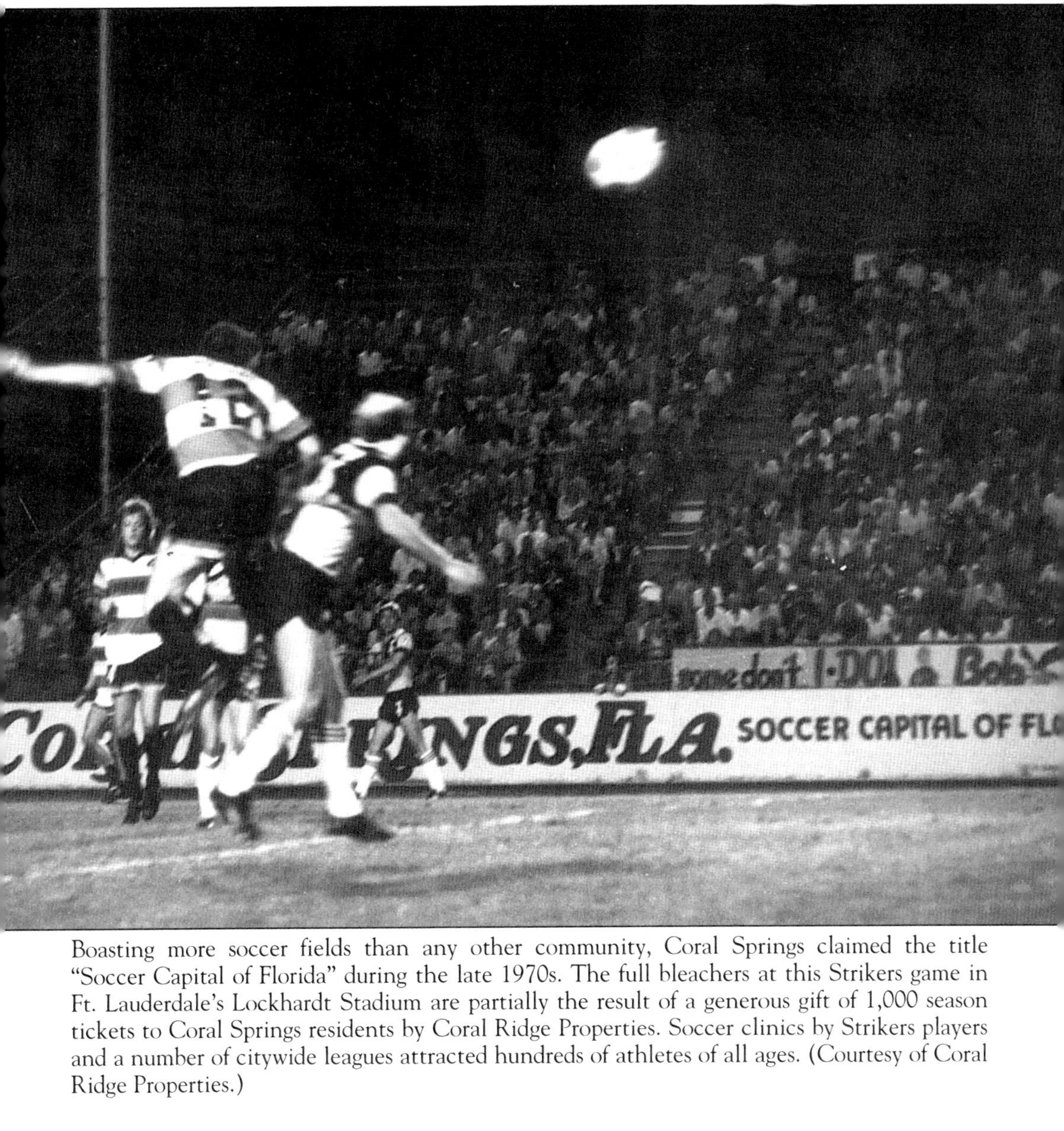

Boasting more soccer fields than any other community, Coral Springs claimed the title "Soccer Capital of Florida" during the late 1970s. The full bleachers at this Strikers game in Ft. Lauderdale's Lockhardt Stadium are partially the result of a generous gift of 1,000 season tickets to Coral Springs residents by Coral Ridge Properties. Soccer clinics by Strikers players and a number of citywide leagues attracted hundreds of athletes of all ages. (Courtesy of Coral Ridge Properties.)

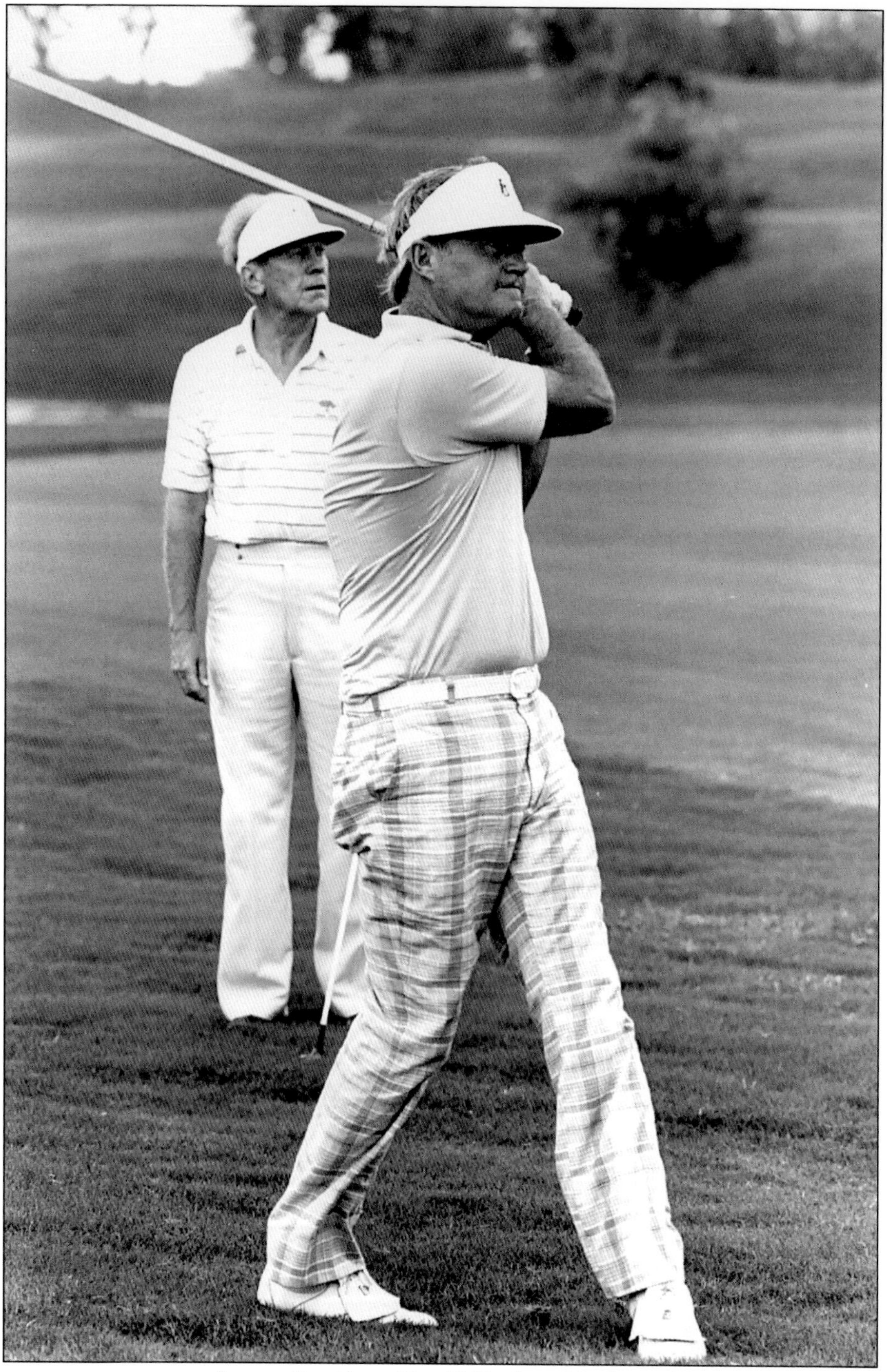

An awesome twosome—former President Gerald Ford and Jack Nicklaus—are pictured here at the 1984 pro-am golf tournament at Eagle Trace Country Club. The President first came to town in 1976 while campaigning and promised to return. Jack Nicklaus also returned to play in the Honda Classic, as did Ray Floyd, Tom Weiskopf, Tom Kite, Craig Stadler, Hale Irwin, Greg Norman, and Nick Faldo, among others. (Courtesy of the City of Coral Springs.)

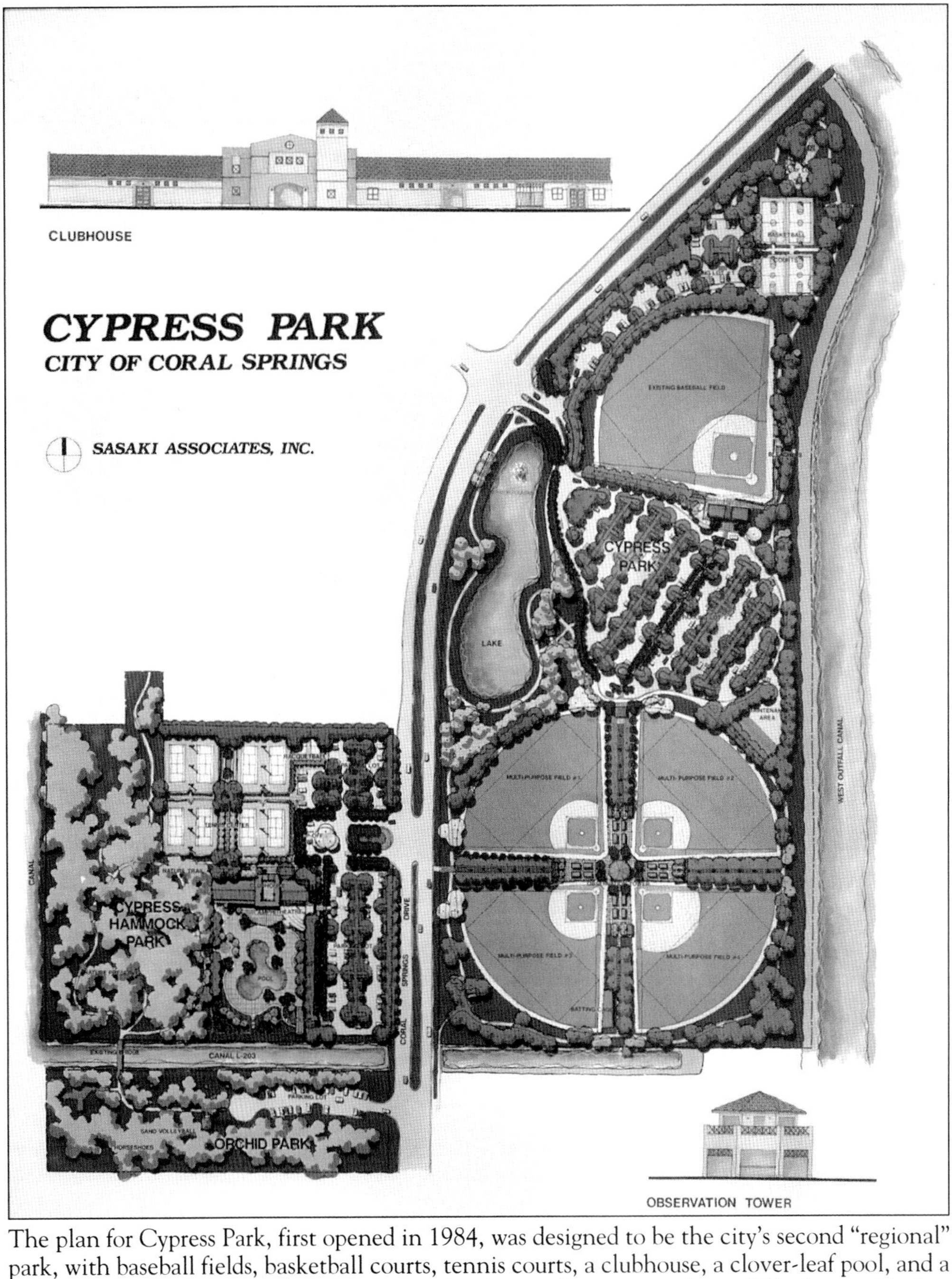

The plan for Cypress Park, first opened in 1984, was designed to be the city's second "regional" park, with baseball fields, basketball courts, tennis courts, a clubhouse, a clover-leaf pool, and a boardwalk through a natural cypress grove. As always, the entire park was fully designed before a single shovel struck the ground. (Courtesy of the City of Coral Springs.)

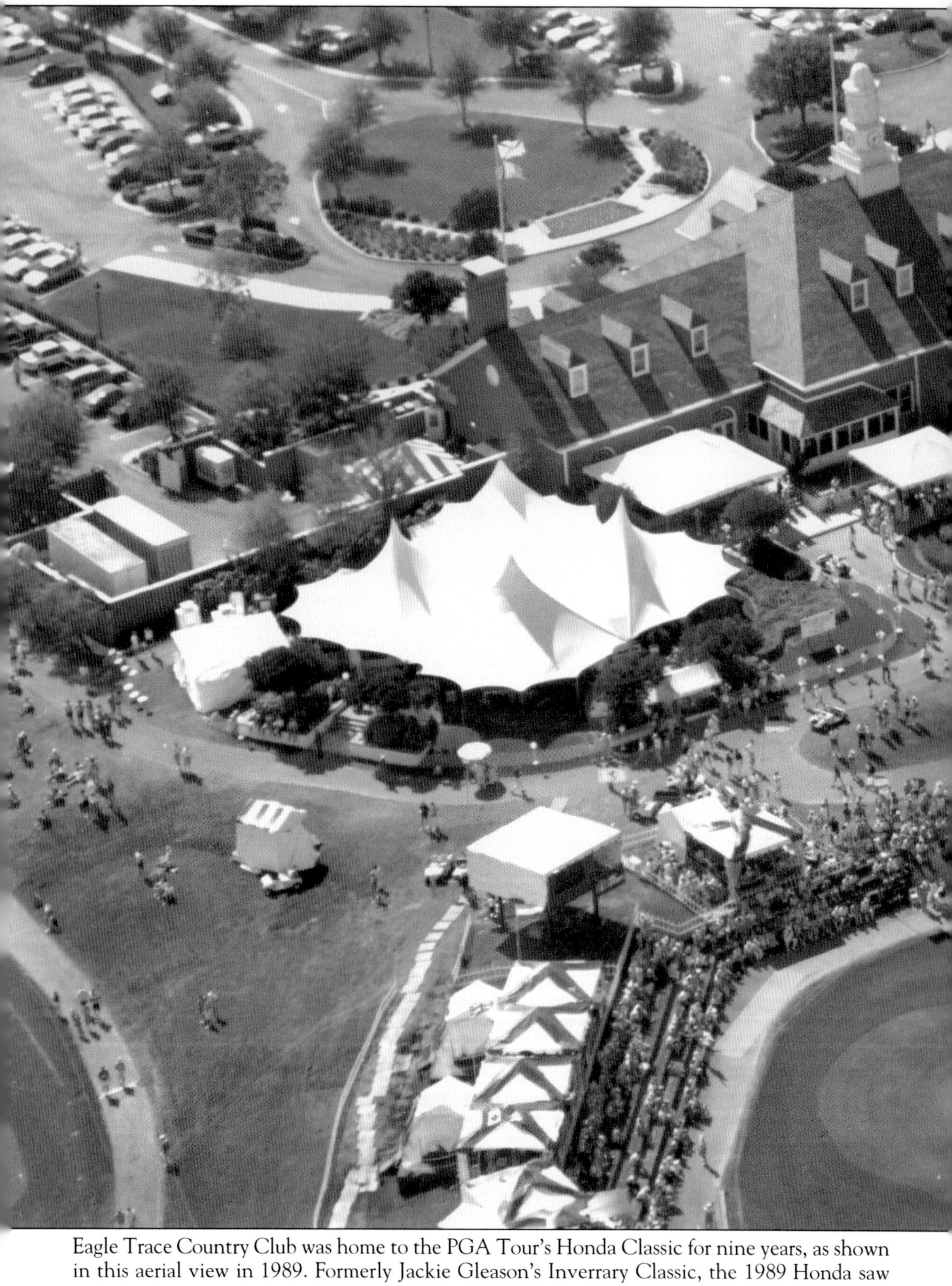

Eagle Trace Country Club was home to the PGA Tour's Honda Classic for nine years, as shown in this aerial view in 1989. Formerly Jackie Gleason's Inverrary Classic, the 1989 Honda saw

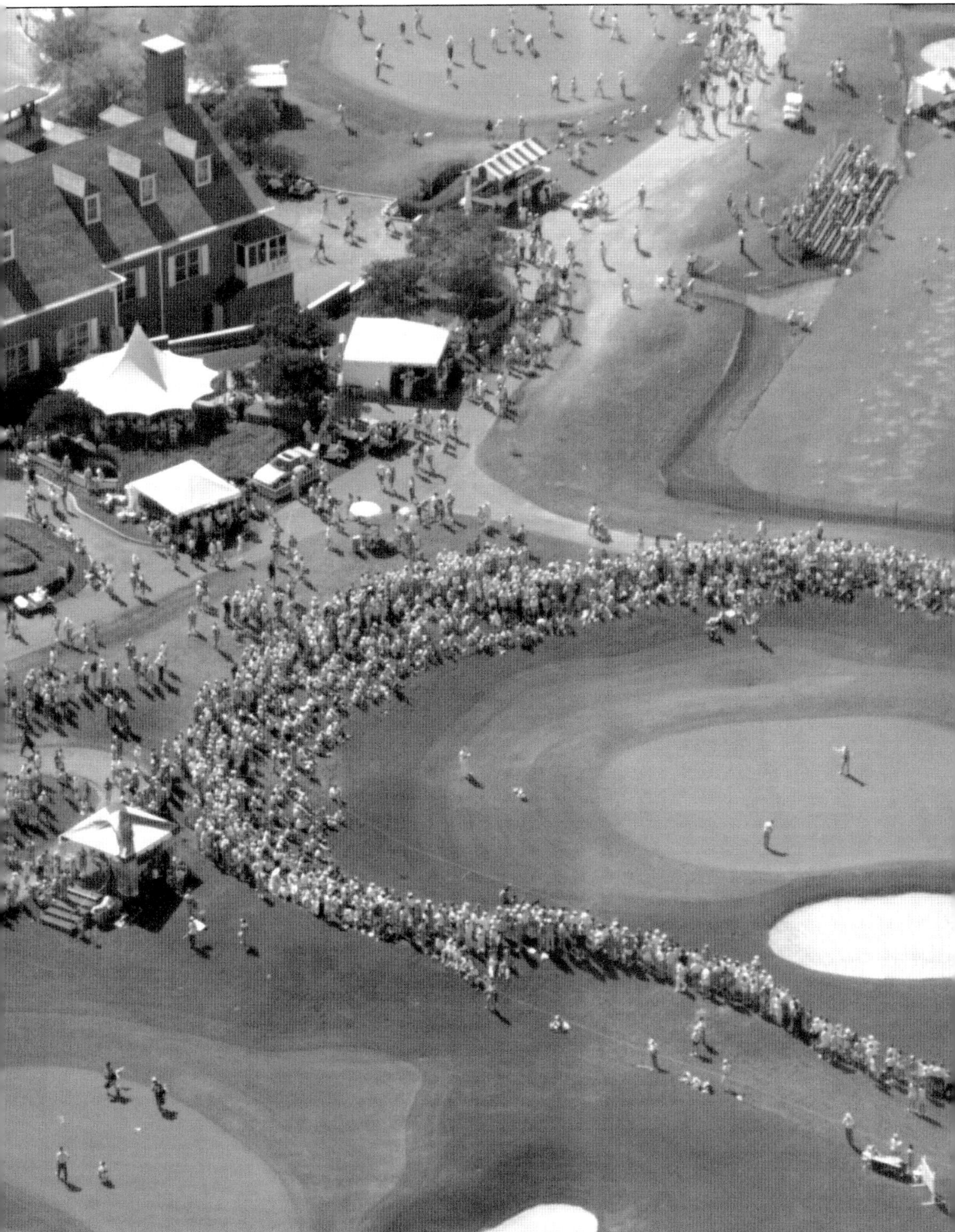

winner Blaine McCallister shoot 266, a tournament record. The 72-par course was ranked 20th in the state by *Golf Digest*. (Courtesy of the City of Coral Springs.)

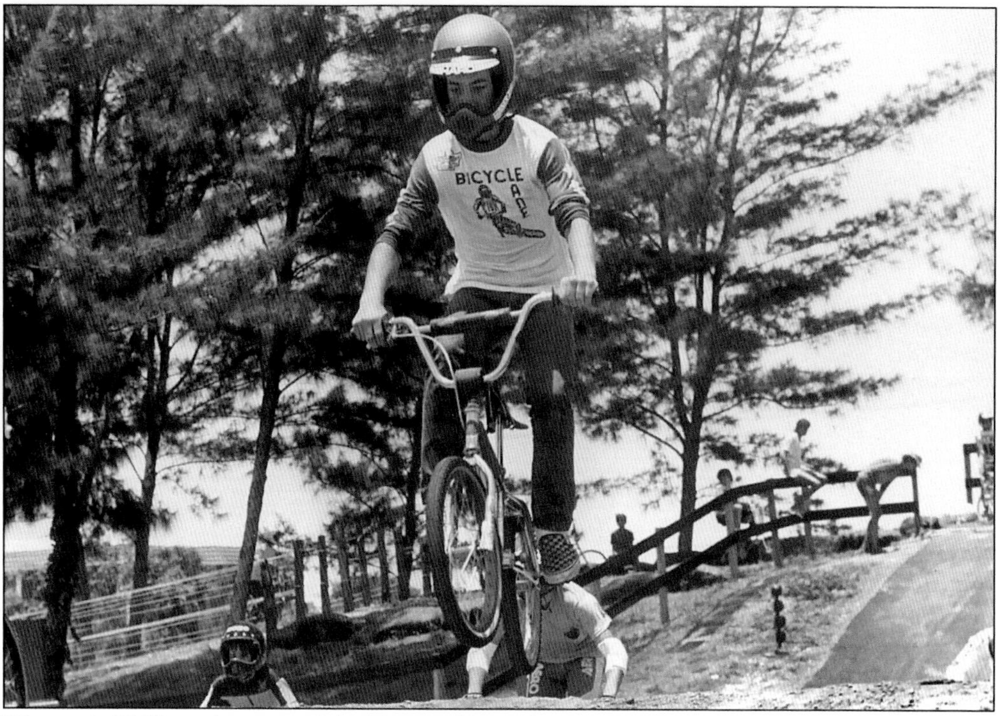

The city's BMX track is part of the National Bicycle League's national racing network. Built in the 1980s, the track was one of the first of its kind in South Florida, bringing professional-level facilities to local BMX buffs. (Courtesy of the City of Coral Springs.)

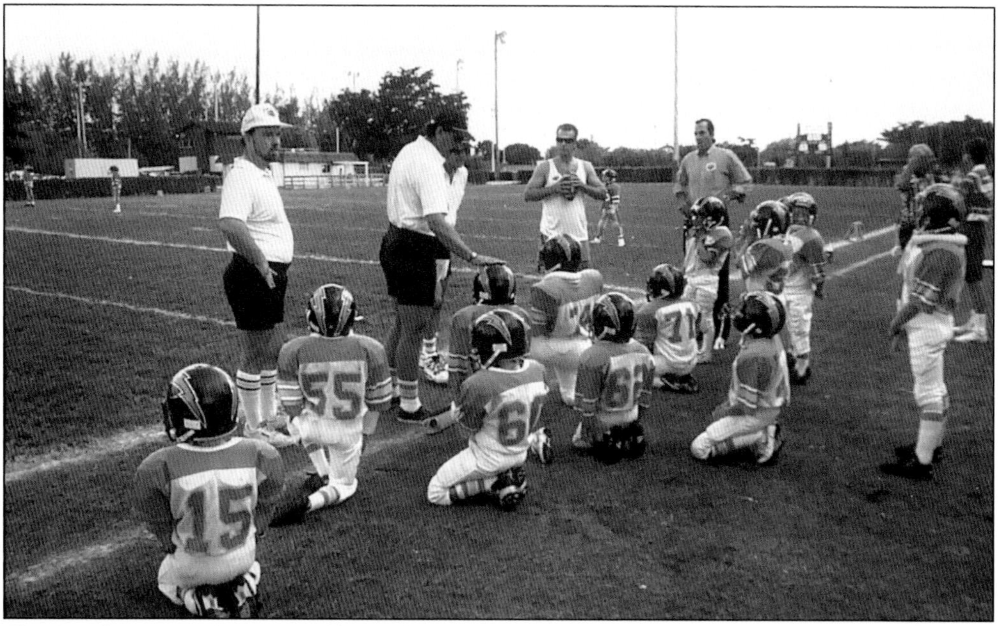

The Coral Springs Chargers tackle football team fielded seven teams by weight class, which were among the best in the American Youth Football League. In keeping with the city's technology-friendly and futuristic personality, earlier teams had names like "Electras" and "Dynamos." (Courtesy of the City of Coral Springs.)

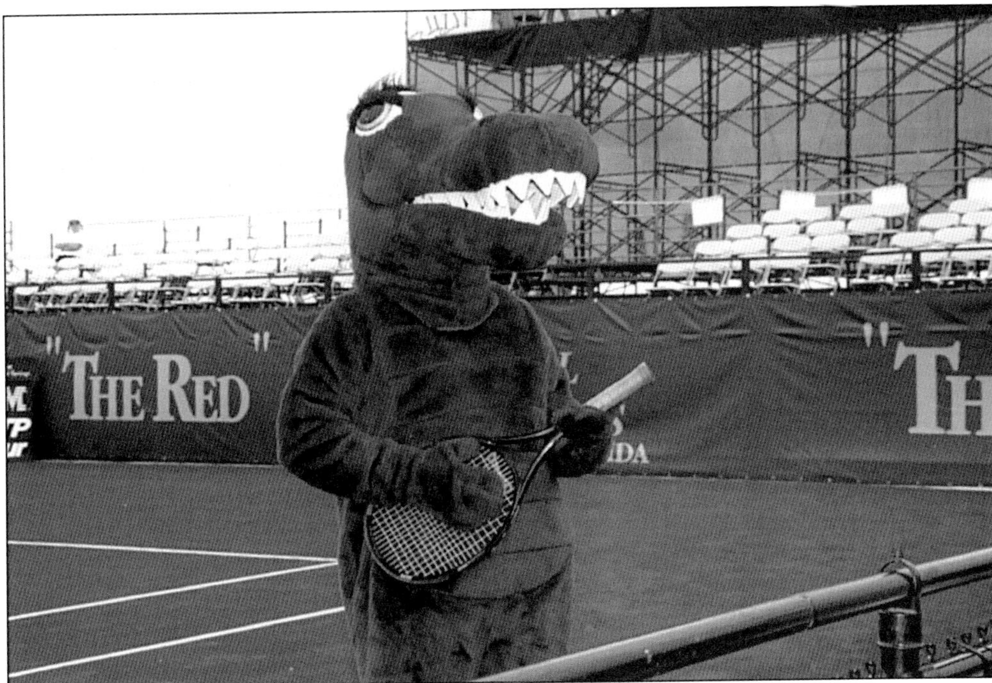

Completed in 1993, the Coral Springs Tennis Center hosted the first America's Red Clay Tennis Championship, affectionately known as "The Red," that same year. The tournament's mascot is shown playing air guitar on his racket in the stadium court. (Courtesy of the City of Coral Springs.)

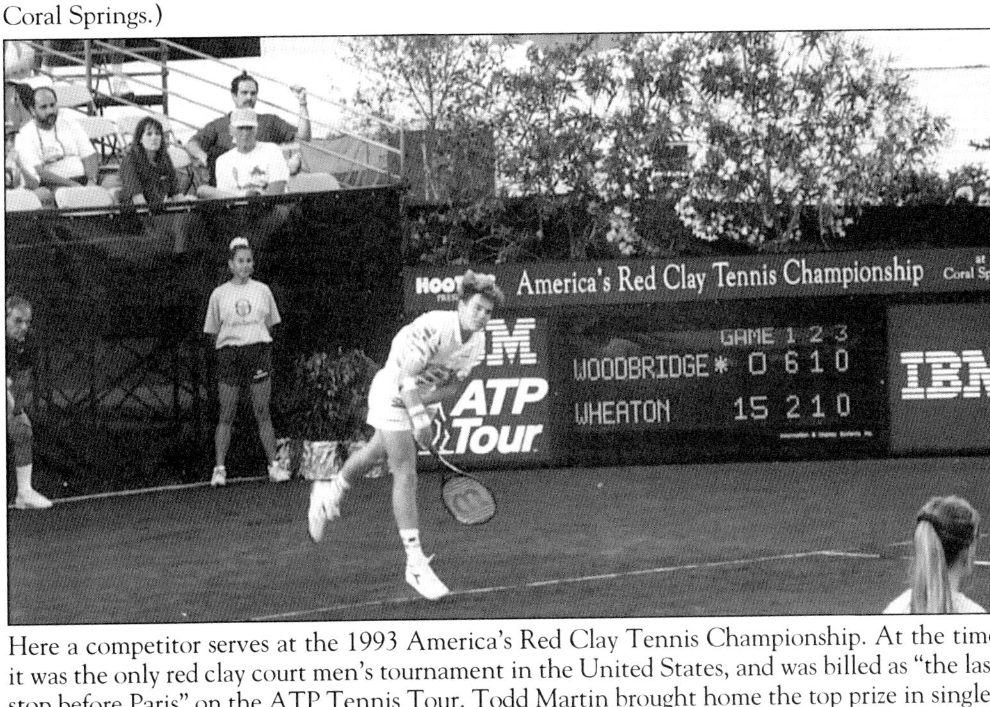

Here a competitor serves at the 1993 America's Red Clay Tennis Championship. At the time it was the only red clay court men's tournament in the United States, and was billed as "the last stop before Paris" on the ATP Tennis Tour. Todd Martin brought home the top prize in singles that year, with the team of Patrick McEnroe and Jonathan Stark winning doubles. (Courtesy of the City of Coral Springs.)

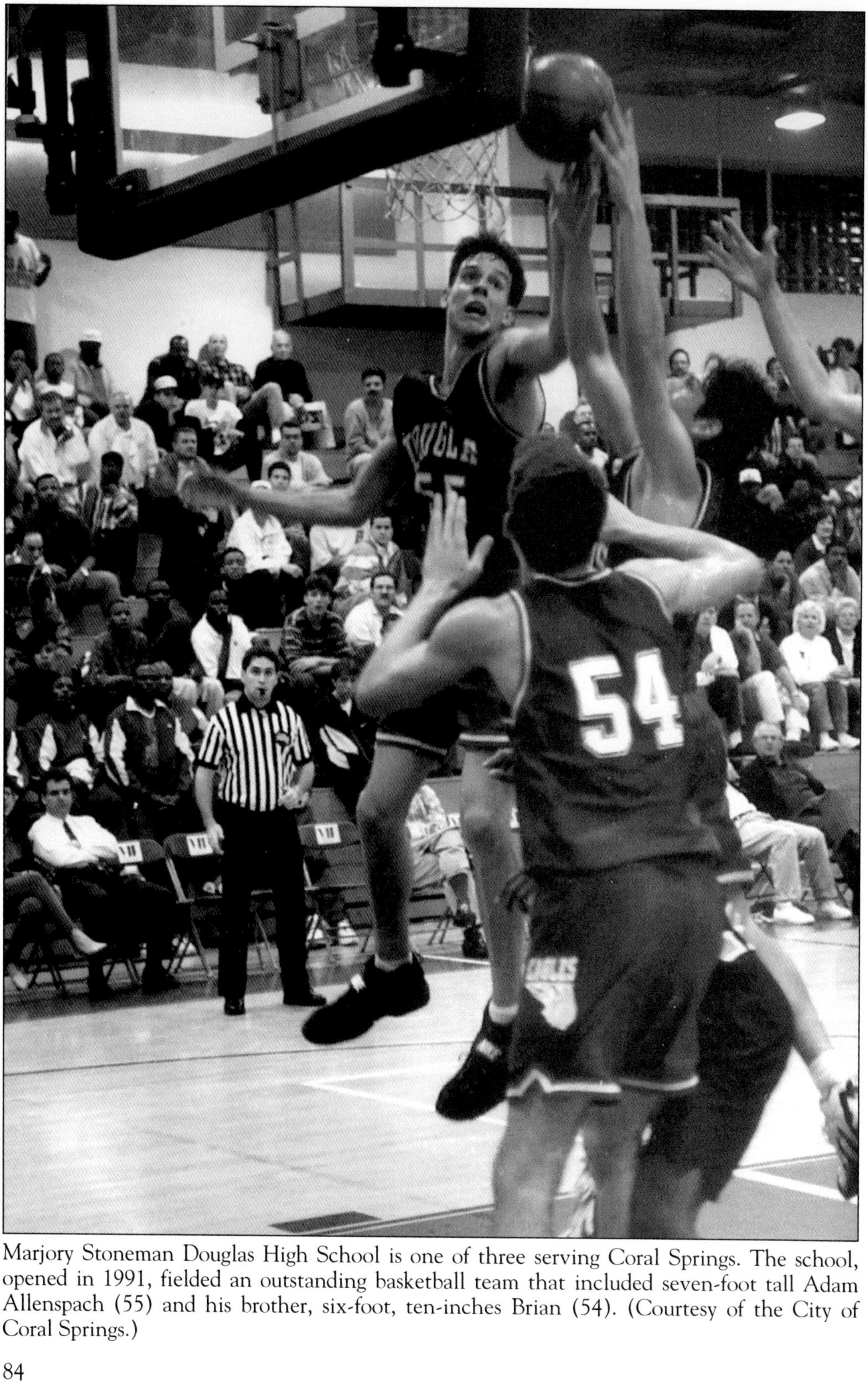

Marjory Stoneman Douglas High School is one of three serving Coral Springs. The school, opened in 1991, fielded an outstanding basketball team that included seven-foot tall Adam Allenspach (55) and his brother, six-foot, ten-inches Brian (54). (Courtesy of the City of Coral Springs.)

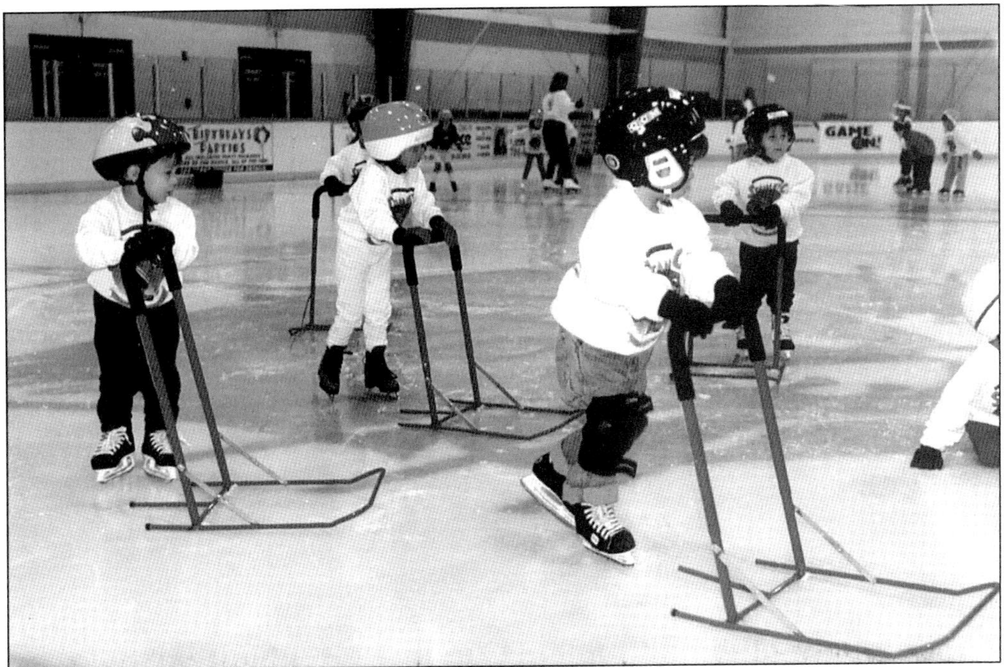

Incredible Ice, in the city's regional park "Sportsplex," trains future figure skaters and hockey champs and is the official training center for the NHL's Florida Panthers. (Courtesy of the City of Coral Springs.)

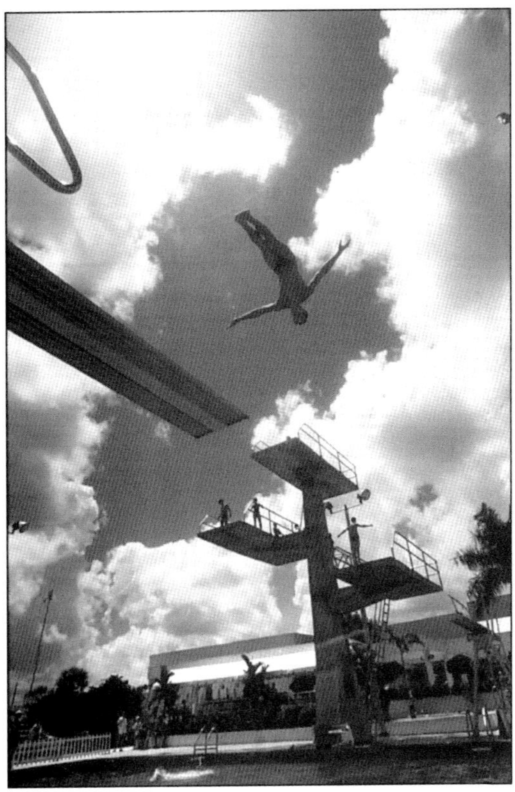

A diver leaps into the 25-yard pool from a three-meter springboard. In the background are the dive platforms at five, seven-and-a-half, and ten meters. The Aquatics Complex hosts the Junior National Diving Championships, and it served as a training site for the 1996 Summer Olympic Games. (Courtesy of the City of Coral Springs.)

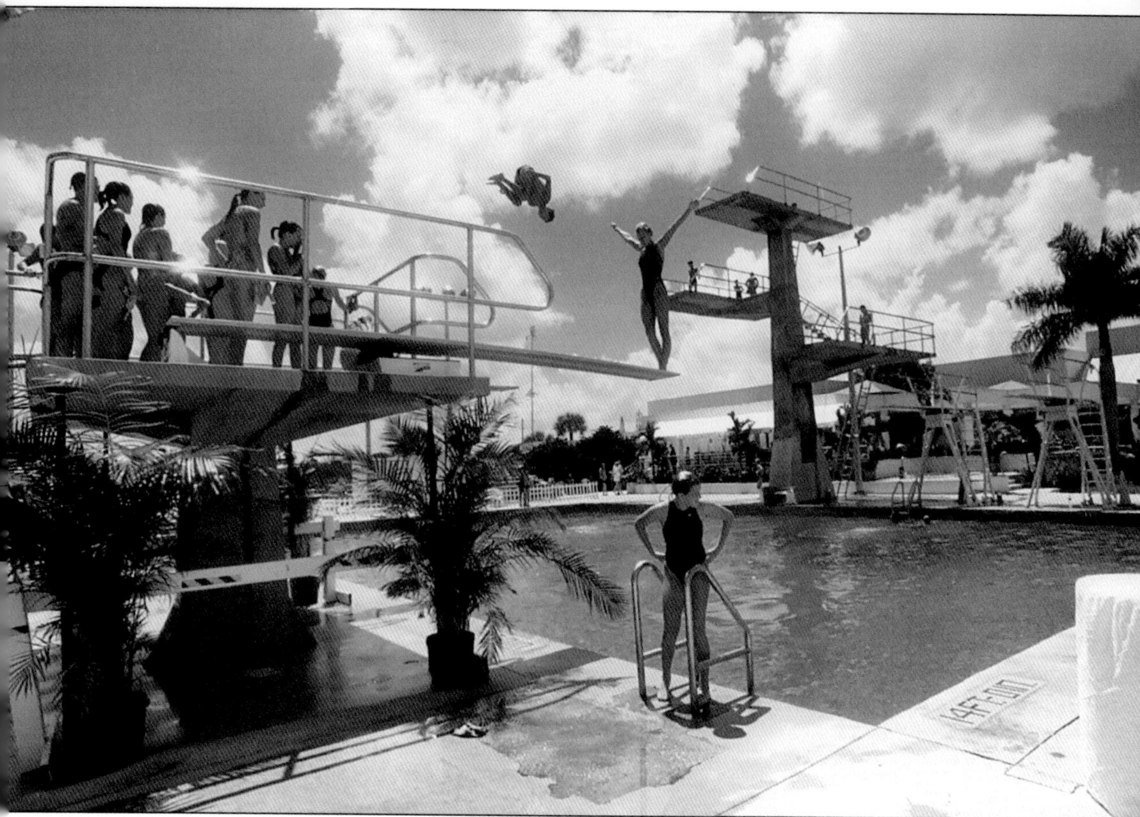

Olympic hopefuls crowd the diving platforms of the Aquatics Complex in August 1996 at the Speedo United States Junior National Diving Championship. (Courtesy of the City of Coral Springs.)

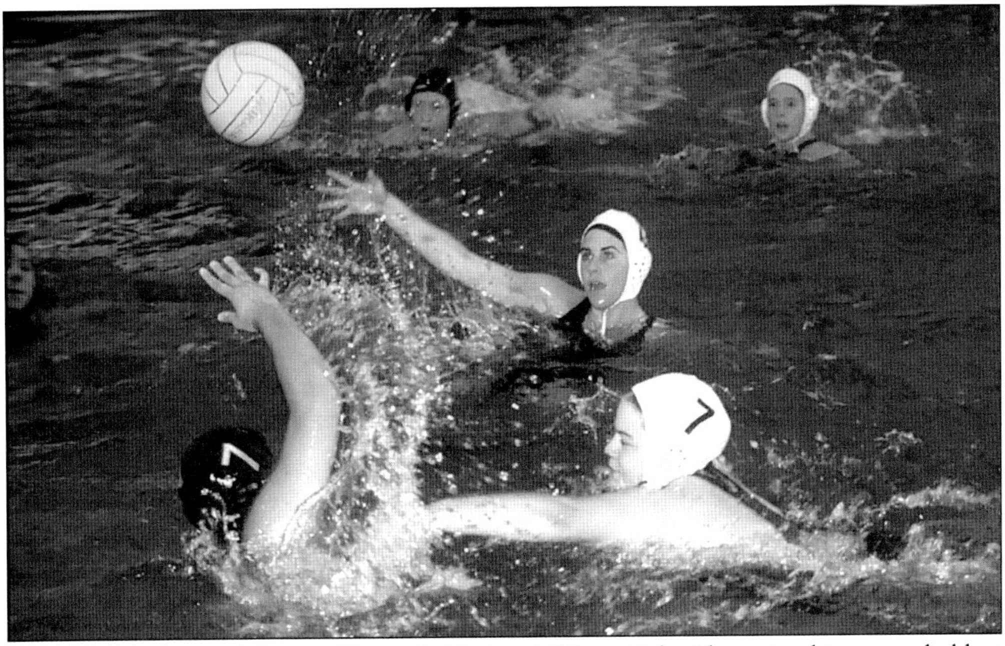

The 1999 Junior and Senior Women's National Water Polo Championships were held at the Aquatics Complex in July and August. In addition to fans and spectators, scouts for the 2000 Olympic women's water polo team came to check out the talent. (Courtesy of the City of Coral Springs.)

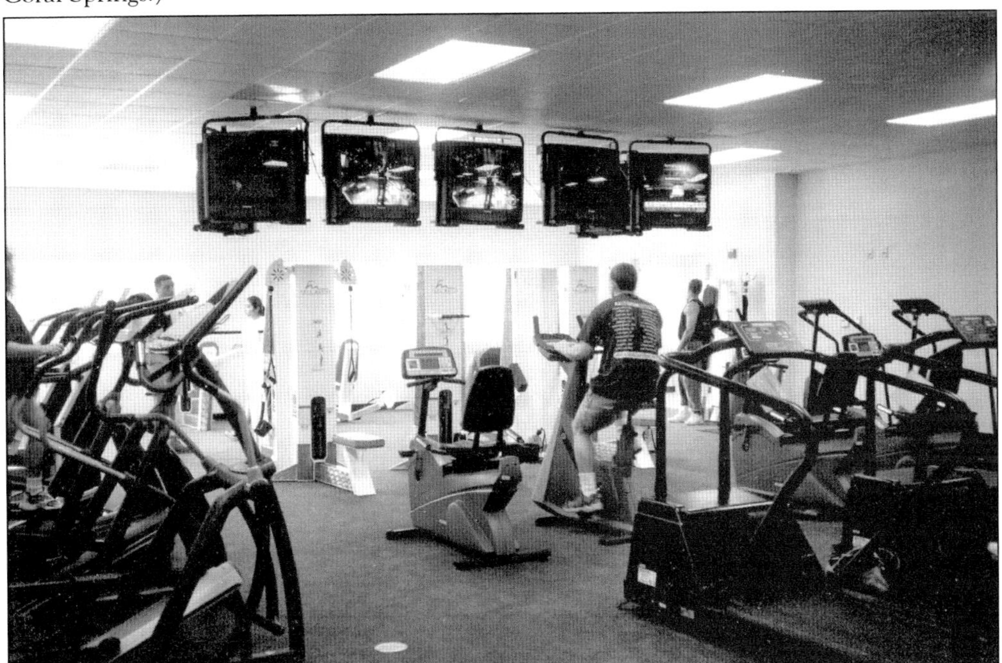

A recent renovation of the Aquatics Complex added state-of-the-art fitness equipment, from treadmills and Nautilus equipment to free weights. The new equipment was first requested for Olympic training, but has proven to be a popular addition with everyone. (Courtesy of the City of Coral Springs.)

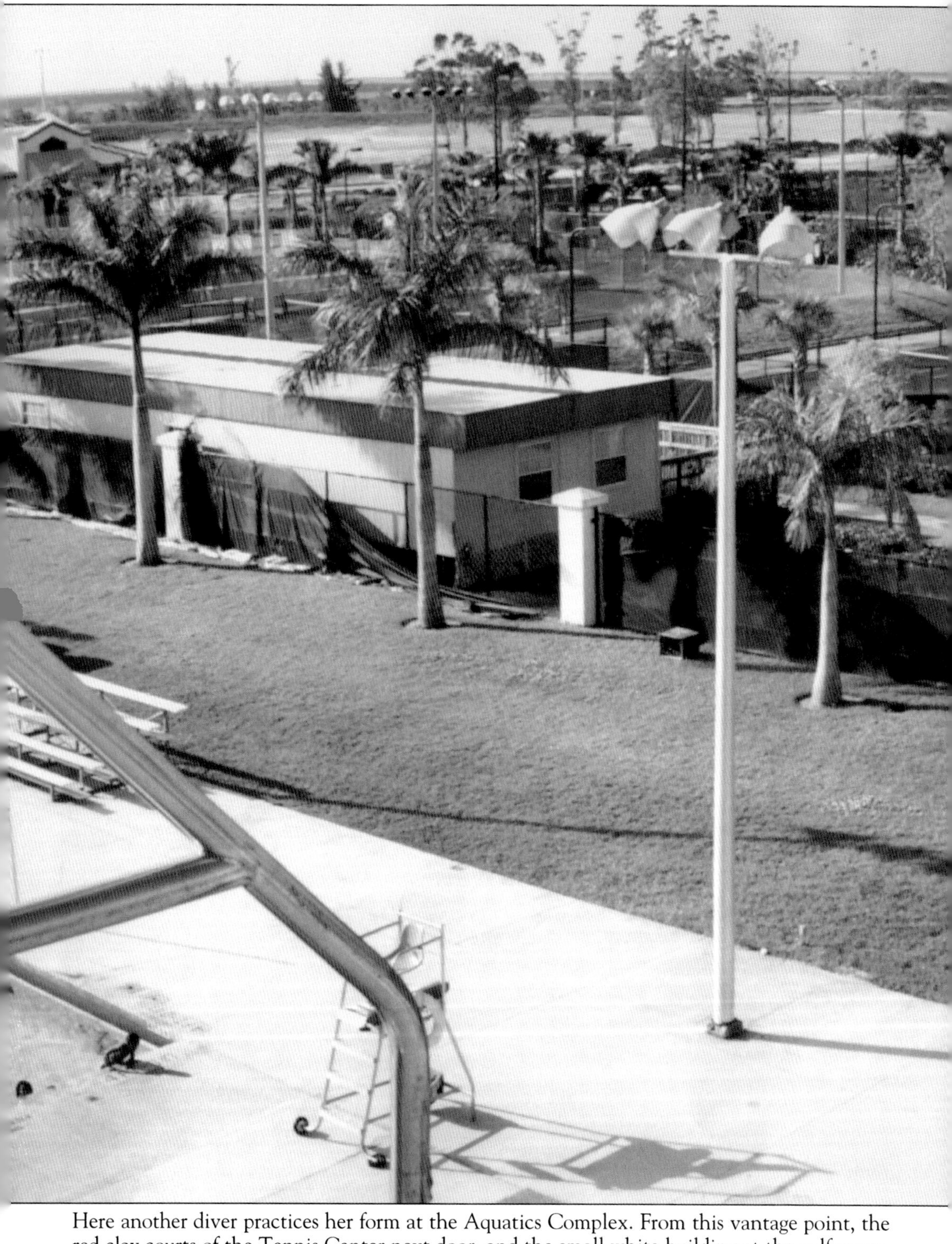

Here another diver practices her form at the Aquatics Complex. From this vantage point, the red clay courts of the Tennis Center next door, and the small white building at the golf range, can be seen at the top of the picture. The upper right portion of the photograph includes a

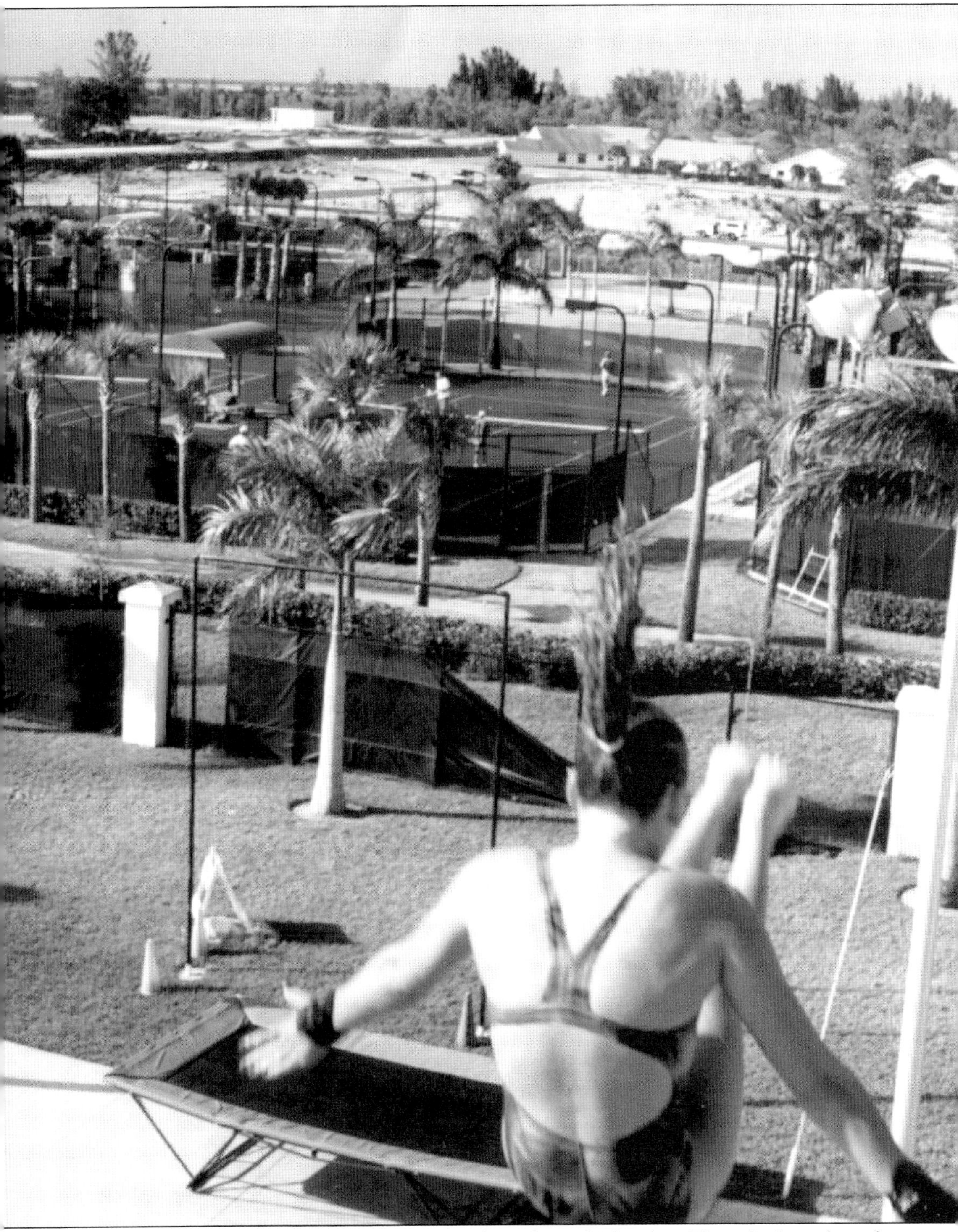

single-family development under construction along the park's borders. These facilities form the south end of Sportsplex. Incredible Ice and Sawgrass Springs Middle School are on the north end. (Courtesy of the City of Coral Springs.)

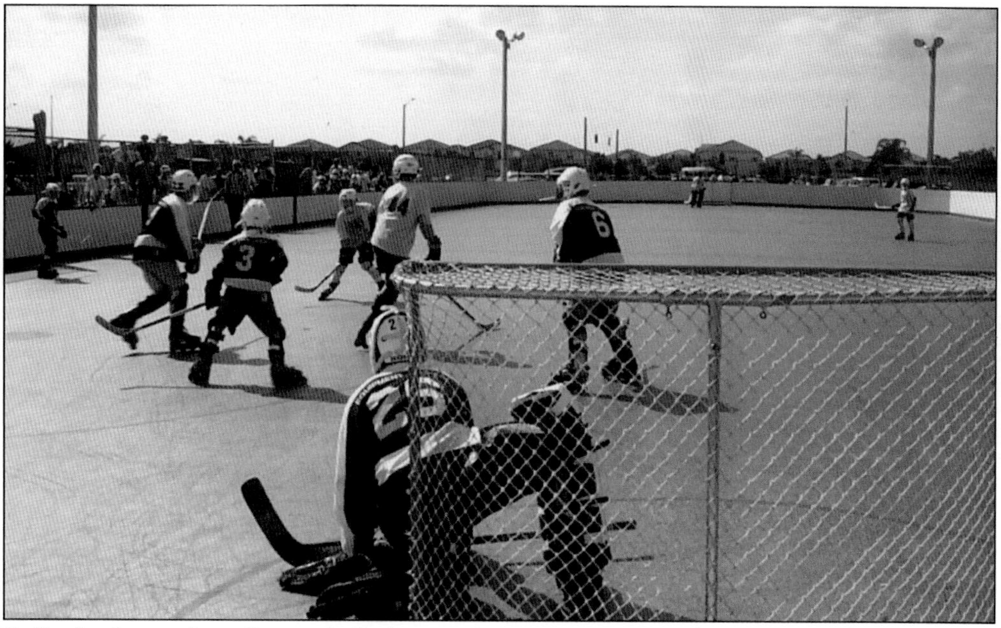

Roller hockey rinks at Riverside Park provide a warm open-air alternative to the ice hockey rinks. Many unusual sporting activities are available in the city, from field hockey and netball to the Coral Springs Road Runner's radio-controlled off-road racetrack. (Courtesy of the City of Coral Springs.)

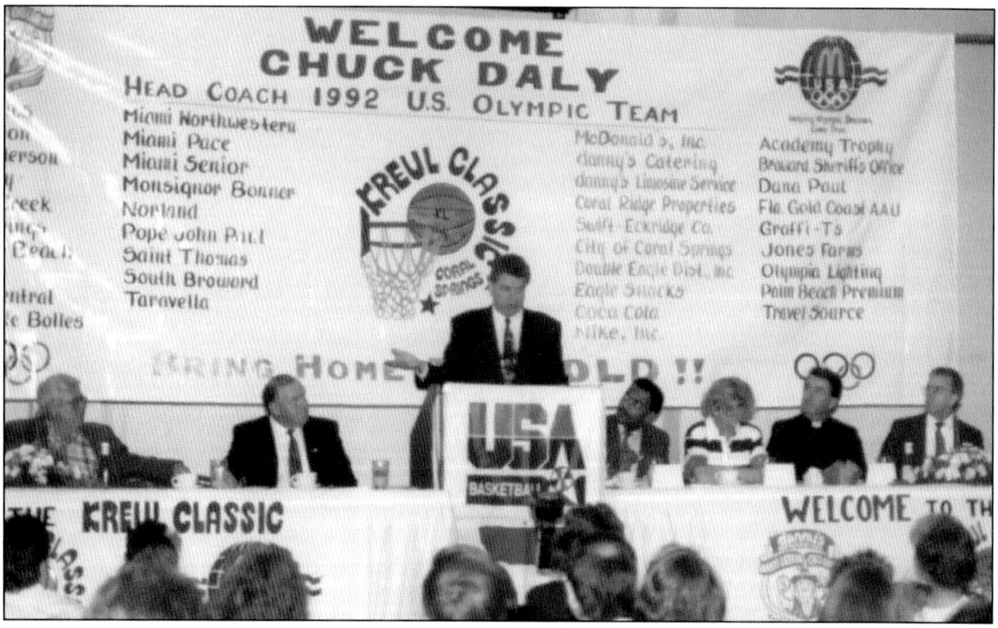

The Kreul Classic Basketball Tournament has called Coral Springs home since 1990. The tournament is the largest high school holiday basketball tournament in the country and is televised on Fox Sports Net and Florida's Sunshine Network. Founder Jim Reilly began the tournament as a memorial to James P. Kreul, a friend and fellow sports volunteer in the community. Here, 1992 Olympic basketball coach Chuck Daly gives a keynote address to the assembled players and volunteers. (Courtesy of the City of Coral Springs.)

Eight

Places of Repose

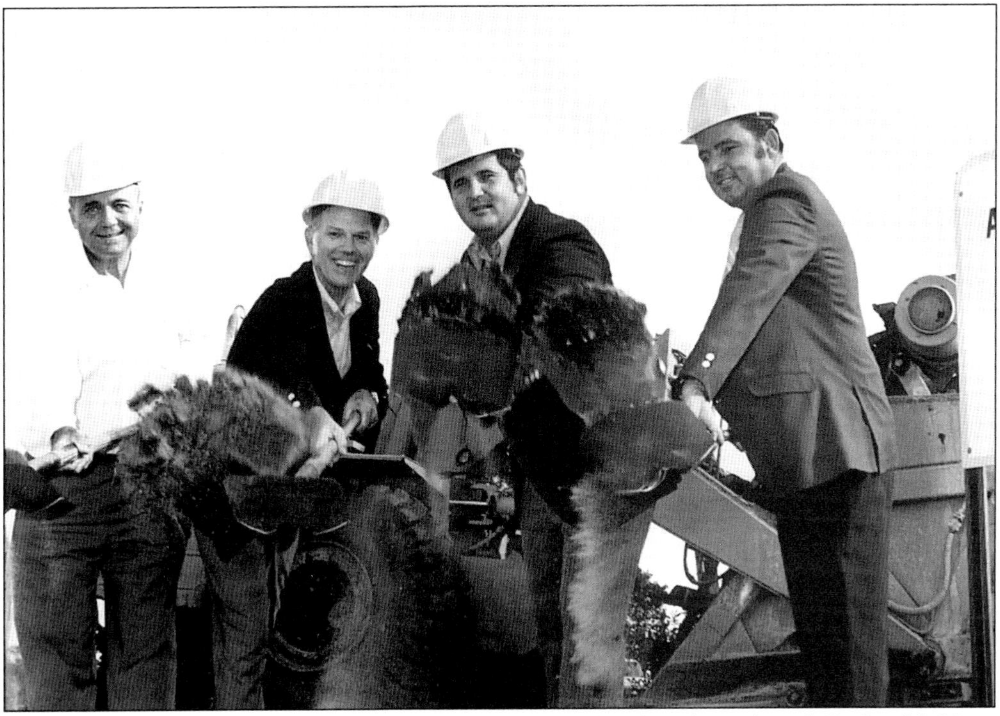

From left to right, City Commissioners James E. Edwards, Edward Heafy,and Richard J. Hunt and Mayor George MacGregor break ground on the first citywide park, which was later named Mullins Park in honor of the city's first elected mayor, Lewie Mullins. Formerly the assistant vice-president of construction for Coral Ridge Properties, Mullins died after only ten months in office. Located in the heart of the city, the site continues to be a community gathering place. It includes the Center for the Arts, the Public Safety Building, Sartory Senior Center, the Teen Center, the Gymnasium, and the Museum of Coral Springs History. (Courtesy of the City of Coral Springs.)

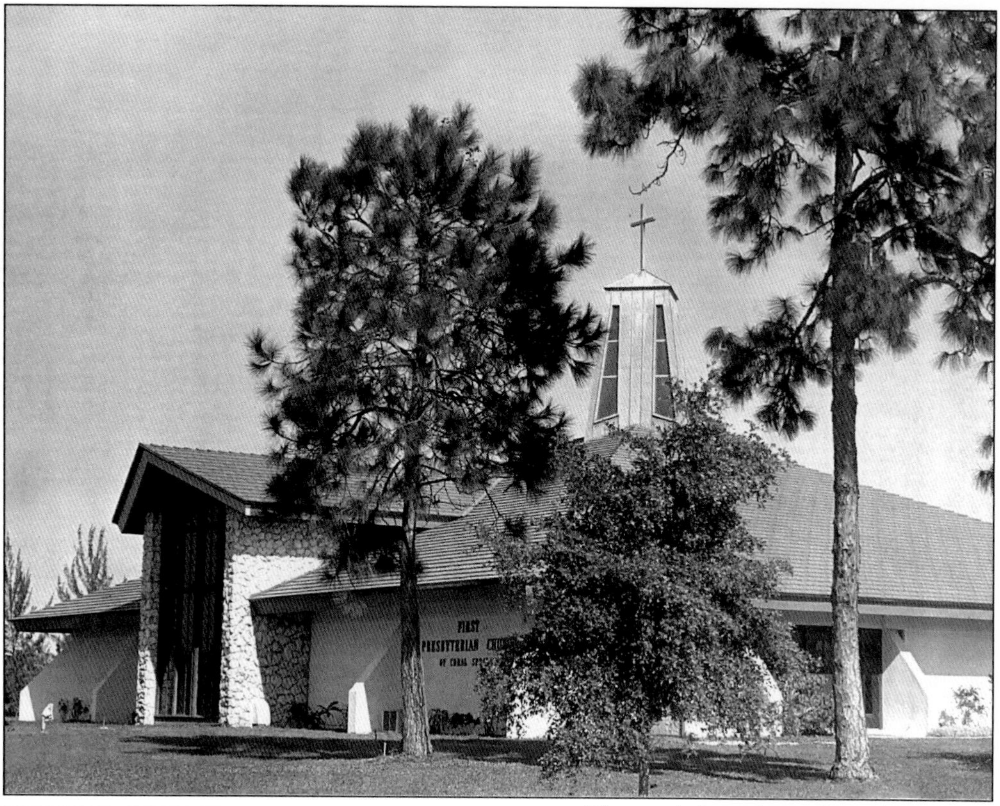

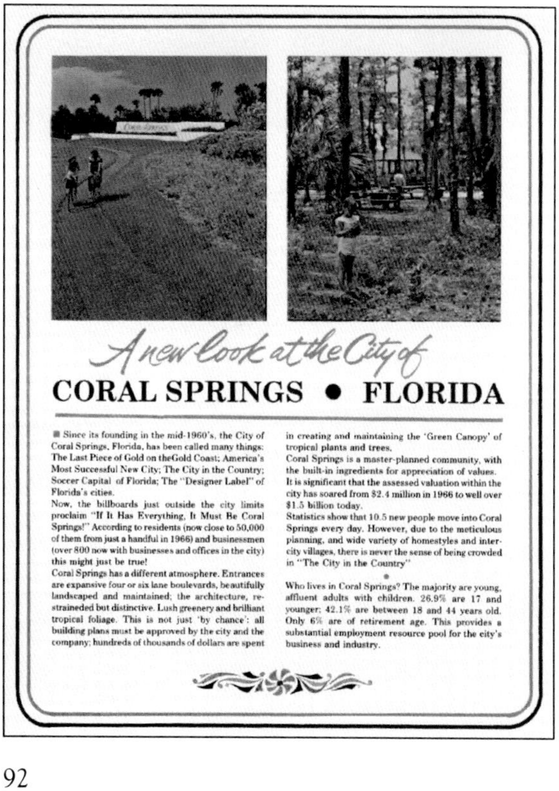

A new look at the City of

CORAL SPRINGS • FLORIDA

■ Since its founding in the mid-1960's, the City of Coral Springs, Florida, has been called many things: The Last Piece of Gold on theGold Coast; America's Most Successful New City; The City in the Country; Soccer Capital of Florida; The "Designer Label" of Florida's cities.

Now, the billboards just outside the city limits proclaim "If It Has Everything, It Must Be Coral Springs!" According to residents (now close to 50,000 of them from just a handful in 1966) and businessmen (over 800 now with businesses and offices in the city) this might just be true!

Coral Springs has a different atmosphere. Entrances are expansive four or six lane boulevards, beautifully landscaped and maintained; the architecture, restraineded but distinctive. Lush greenery and brilliant tropical foliage. This is not just 'by chance': all building plans must be approved by the city and the company; hundreds of thousands of dollars are spent in creating and maintaining the 'Green Canopy' of tropical plants and trees.

Coral Springs is a master-planned community, with the built-in ingredients for appreciation of values.

It is significant that the assessed valuation within the city has soared from \$2.4 million in 1966 to well over \$1.5 billion today.

Statistics show that 10.5 new people move into Coral Springs every day. However, due to the meticulous planning, and wide variety of homestyles and inter-city villages, there is never the sense of being crowded in "The City in the Country"

•

Who lives in Coral Springs? The majority are young, affluent adults with children. 26.9% are 17 and younger; 42.1% are between 18 and 44 years old. Only 6% are of retirement age. This provides a substantial employment resource pool for the city's business and industry.

The city's first place of worship was First Presbyterian Church of Coral Springs, at the corner of Riverside Drive and Royal Palm Boulevard. This building is now part of the Coral Springs Christian Academy, as the congregation has moved to a larger sanctuary further east on Royal Palm Boulevard. Over the years, more than 38 other churches and synagogues have been founded in the city. (Courtesy of the City of Coral Springs.)

A Coral Ridge Properties sales brochures from the 1980s emphasizes the natural look of the city, particularly the "green canopy of tropical plants and trees." The text goes on to point out that "this is not 'by chance,'" but rather planned every step of the way. It also boasts that ten-and-a-half people moved into town every day. (Courtesy of the Coral Ridge Properties.)

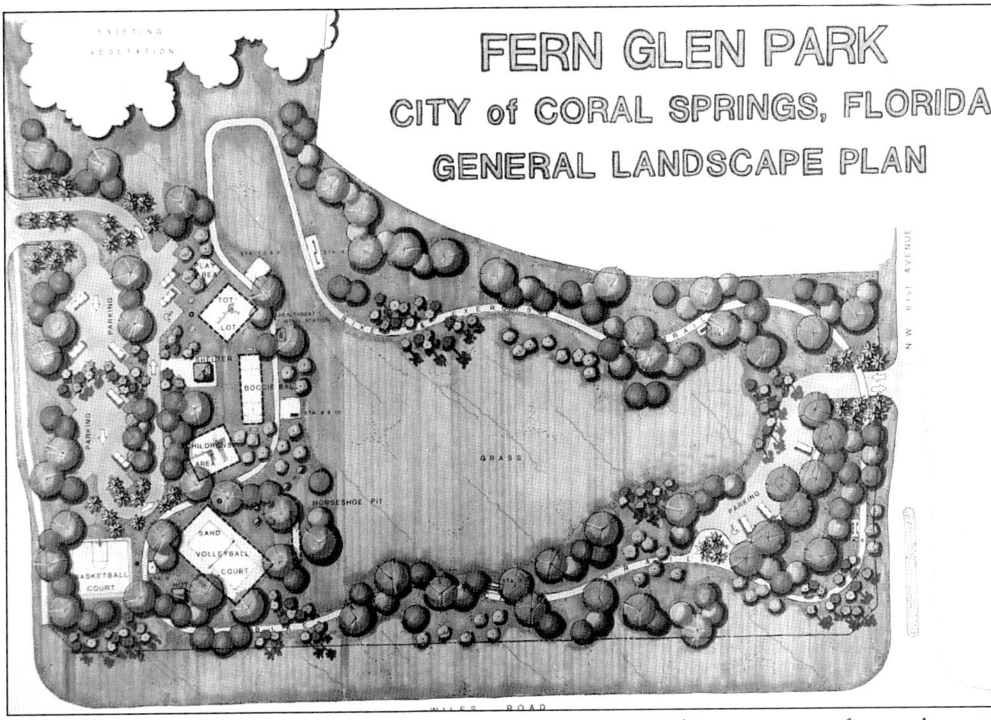

Fern Glen Park was designed to provide fitness and recreational opportunities for residents in a lush, natural setting. As with all of the city's 46 parks (totaling 732 acres), each detail was carefully planned and constructed. (Courtesy of the City of Coral Springs.)

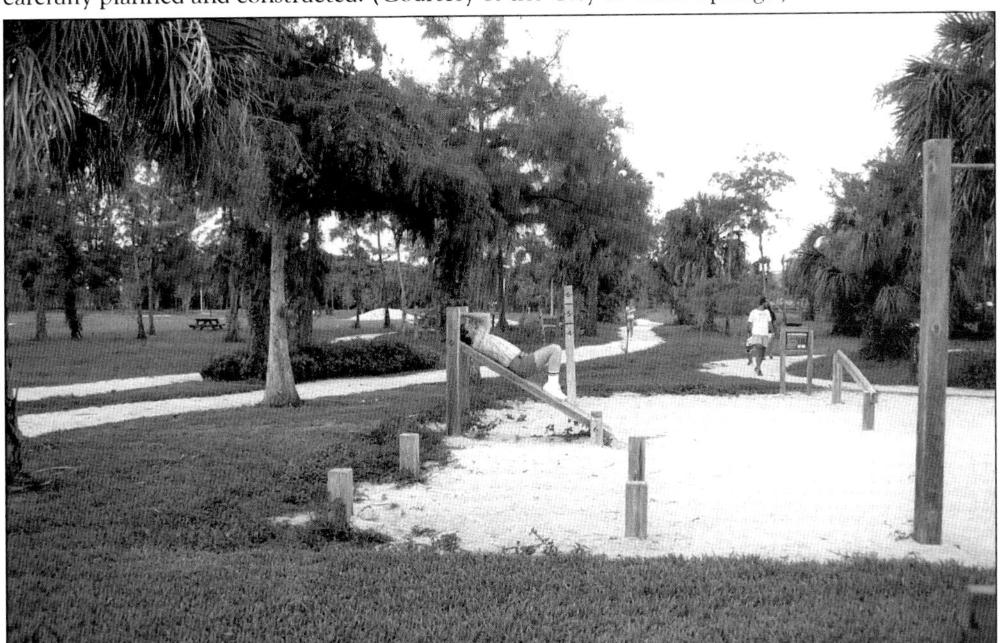

Residents keep in shape using fitness trails, like this one in Ralph Diaz Park. A jogging trail is dotted with stations that provide a variety of exercises designed to promote strength and flexibility. (Courtesy of the City of Coral Springs.)

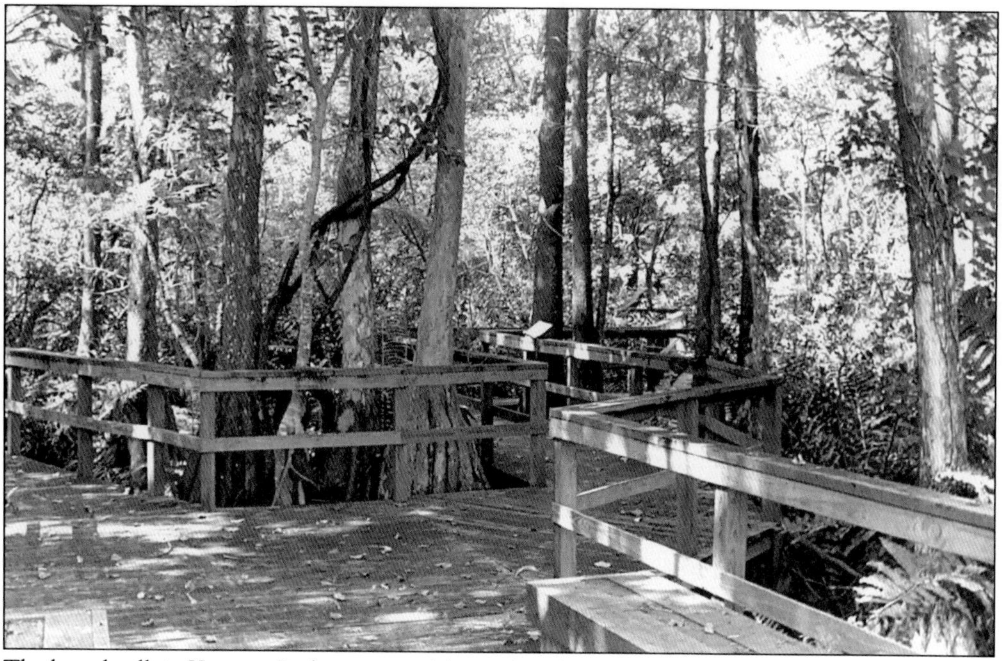

The boardwalk in Kiwanis Park was one of the earliest built in Coral Springs. Boardwalks provide places of quite retreat for contemplation, learning about nature, or just getting away from it all. (Courtesy of the City of Coral Springs.)

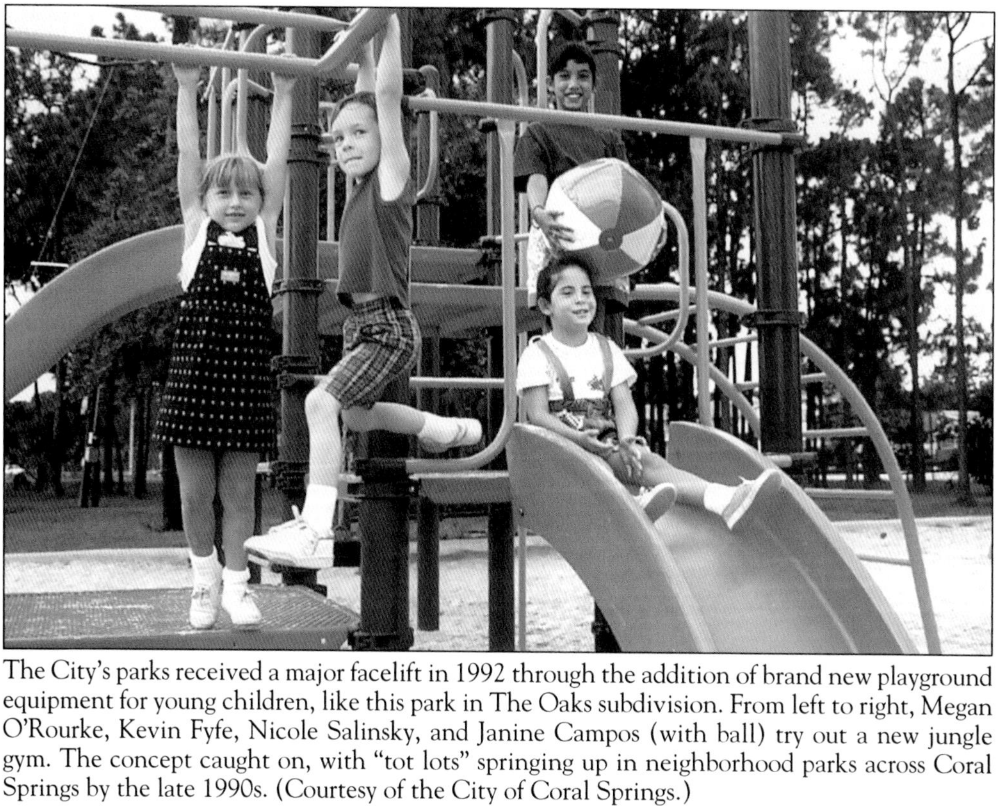

The City's parks received a major facelift in 1992 through the addition of brand new playground equipment for young children, like this park in The Oaks subdivision. From left to right, Megan O'Rourke, Kevin Fyfe, Nicole Salinsky, and Janine Campos (with ball) try out a new jungle gym. The concept caught on, with "tot lots" springing up in neighborhood parks across Coral Springs by the late 1990s. (Courtesy of the City of Coral Springs.)

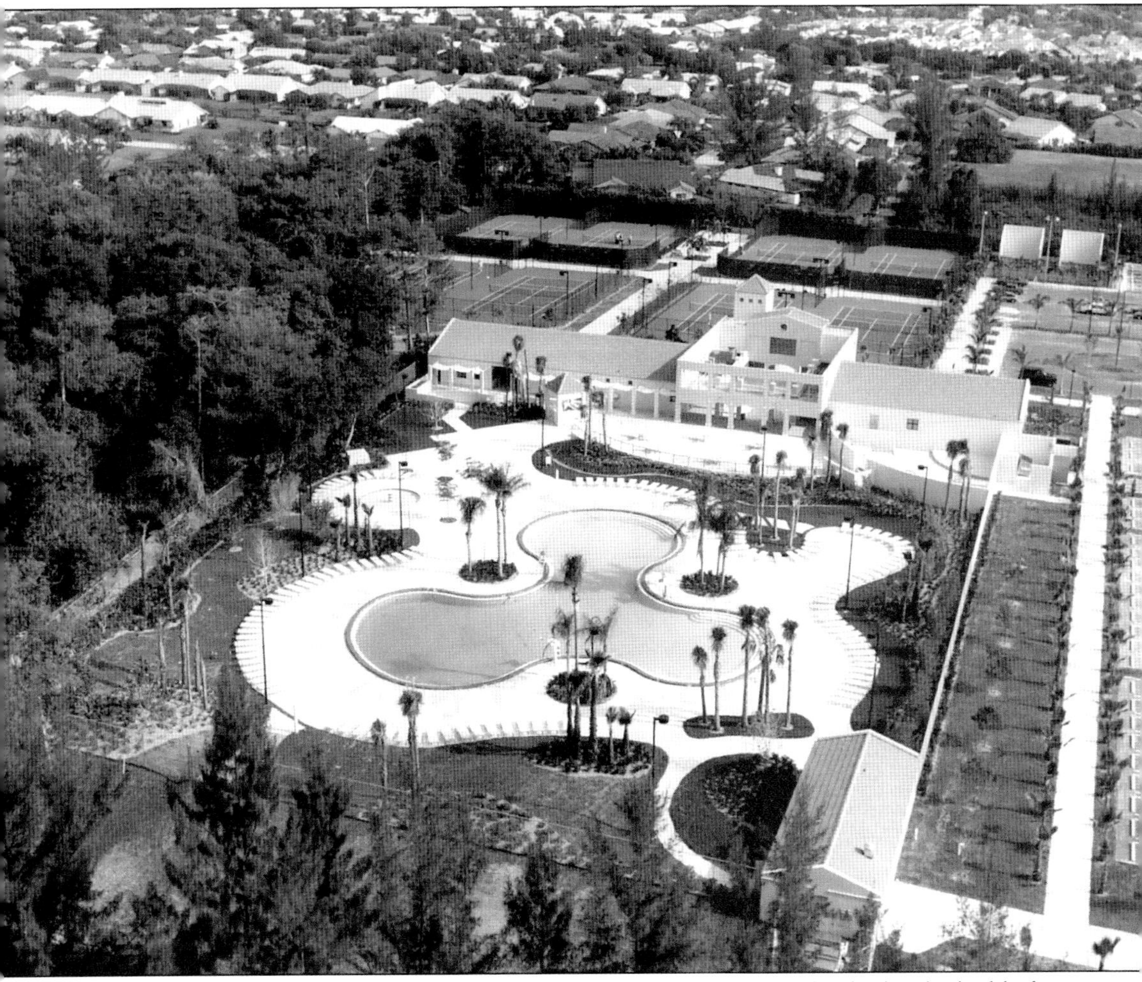

This 1989 picture of the cloverleaf pool at Cypress Park shows how the facility looked before the 2001 renovations made it into a water-themed park. The clubhouse is used by community groups for monthly meetings and special events. (Courtesy of the City of Coral Springs.)

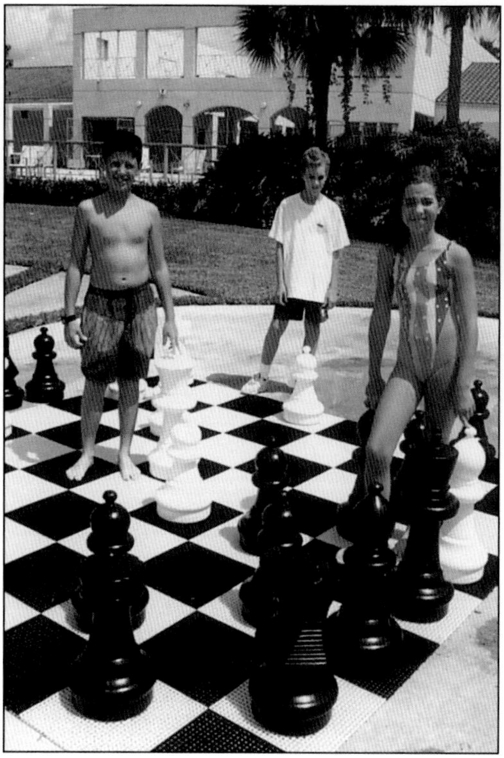

Kids play with the giant chess set added to Cypress Park in 1992. New equipment and activities are added to the city's parks every year to keep them fresh and interesting. (Courtesy of the City of Coral Springs.)

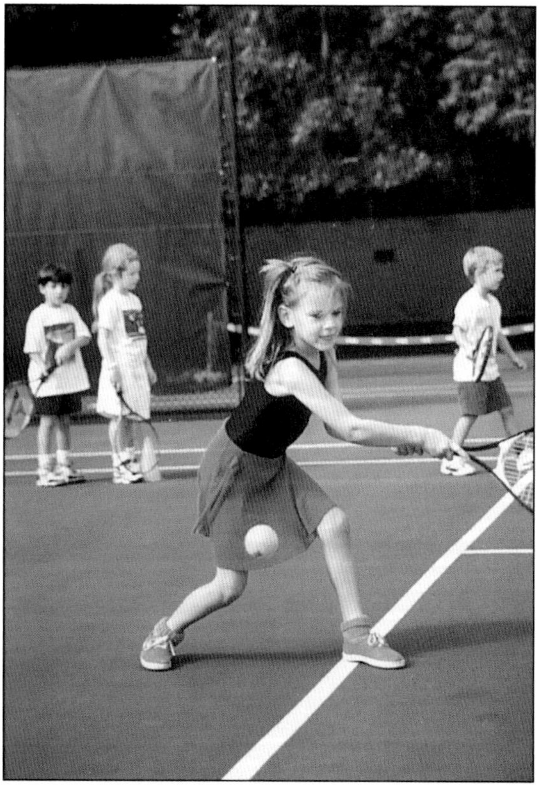

Cypress Park also provided the largest tennis facility available prior to the Tennis Center's opening in 1993. Here a young player practices her forehand. (Courtesy of the City of Coral Springs.)

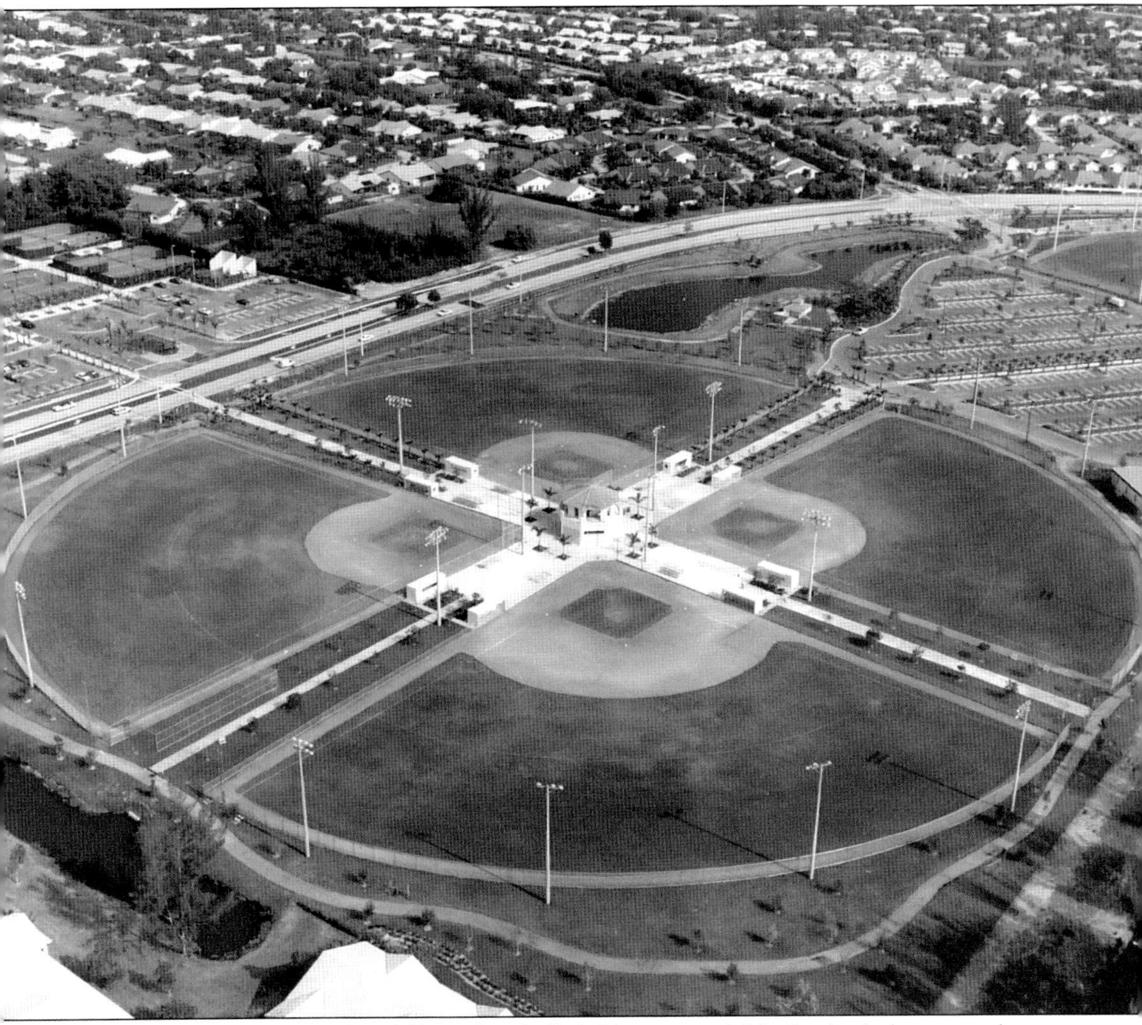

Typical of many city parks, full-size baseball fields are available for both league and open play, although constant use means there is a waiting list to get a field. (Courtesy of the City of Coral Springs.)

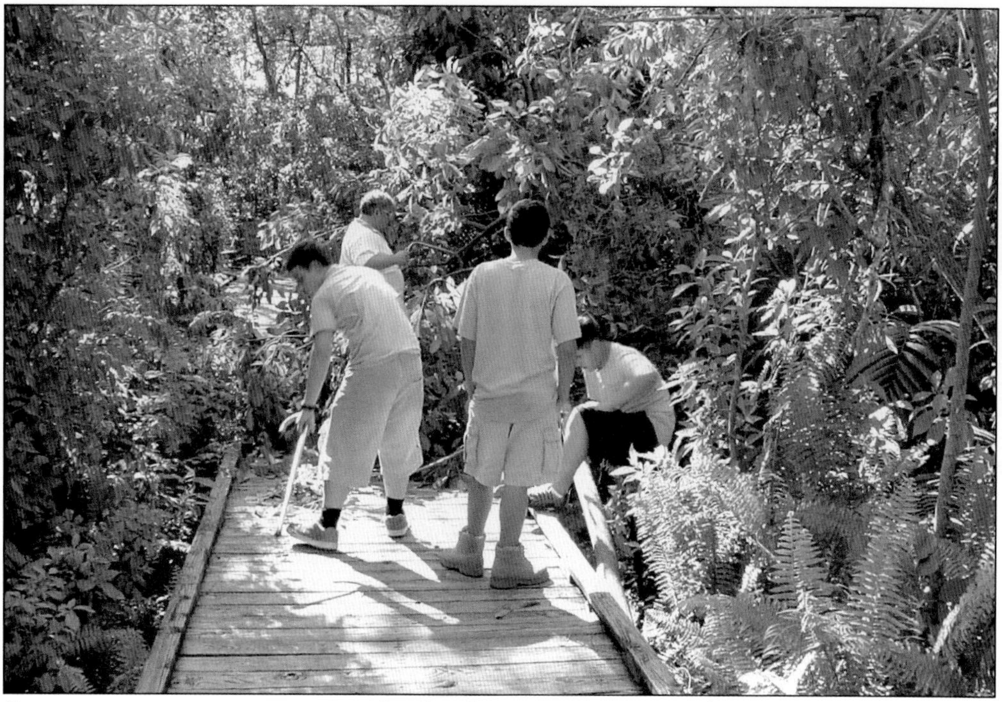

Scouts earn community service credits by clearing exotic tree saplings in Cypress Hammock Park, one of the many natural areas in the city. (Courtesy of the City of Coral Springs.)

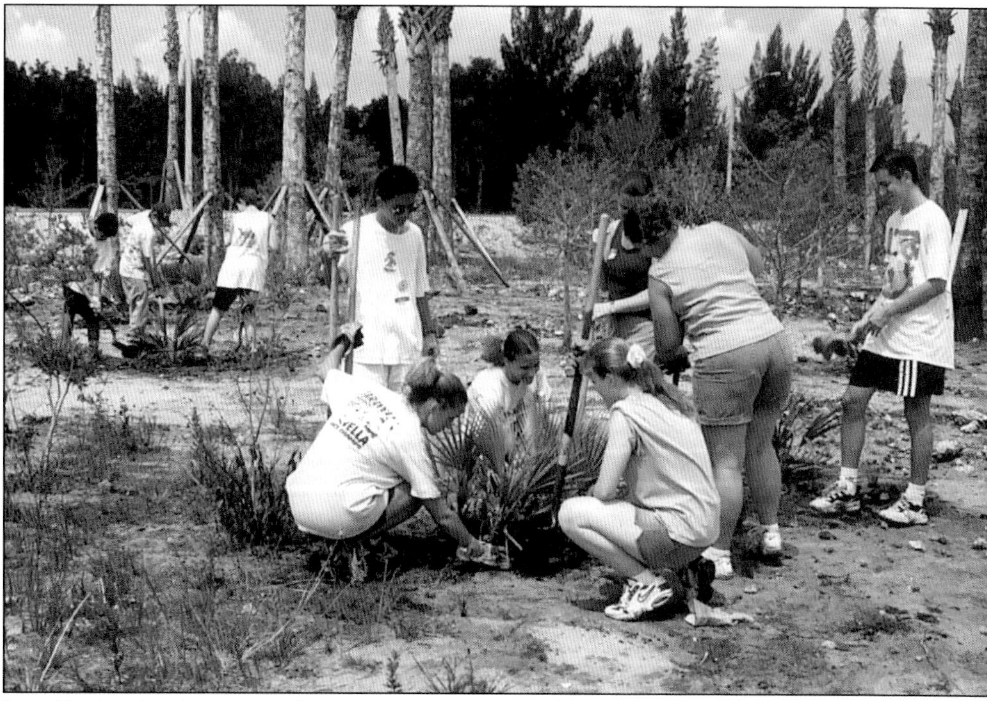

Local high school students plant trees in Sportsplex during the March 27, 1997 Youth Services Day, an annual event that allows young people to take part in keeping Coral Springs beautiful. (Courtesy of the City of Coral Springs.)

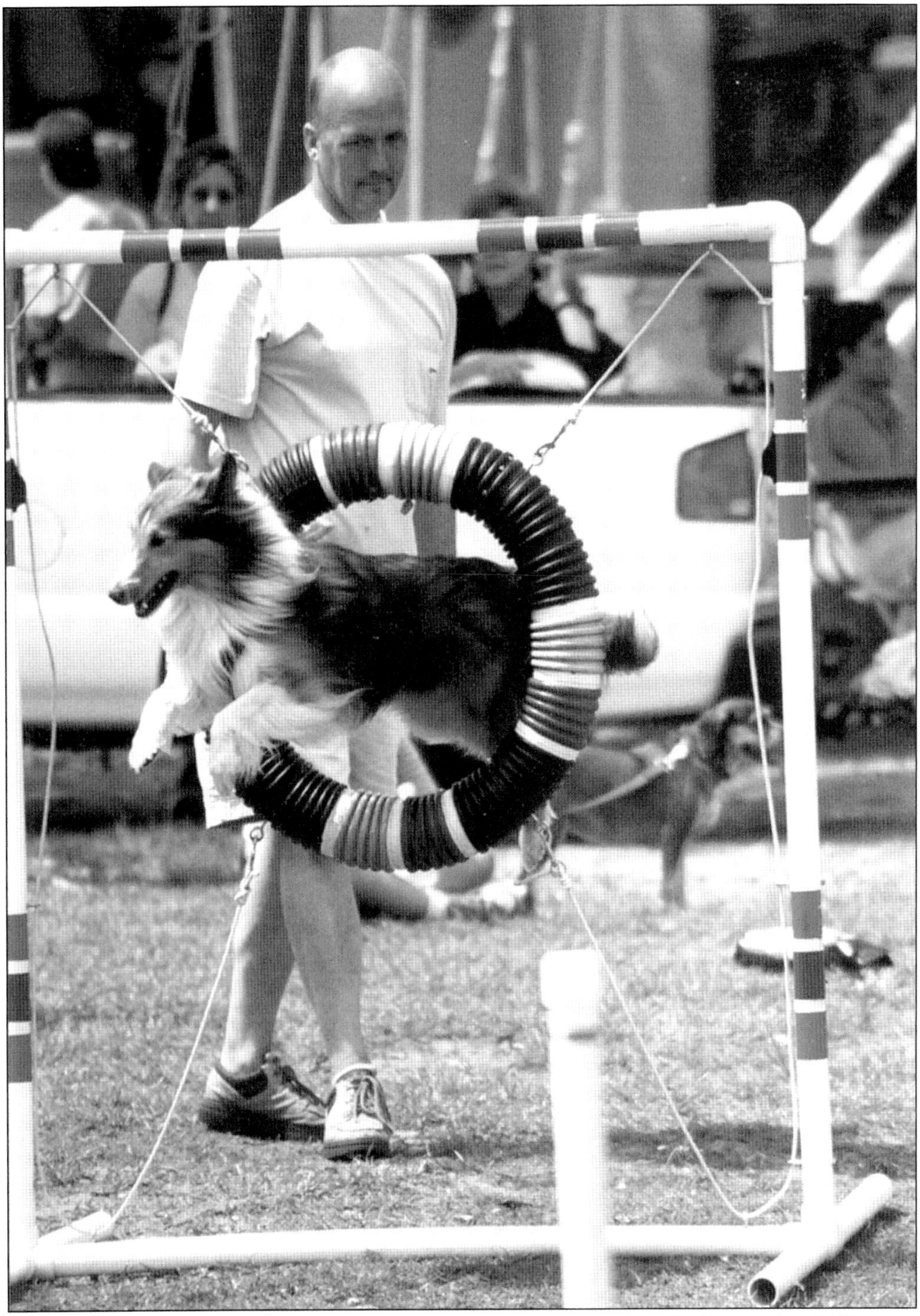

Located in Sportsplex regional park, Dr. Paul's Pet Care Center Dog Park provides challenging obstacles as well as open space for running and playing. It was one of the first pet-friendly parks in South Florida and draws hundreds of people and their pets every weekend. (Courtesy of the City of Coral Springs.)

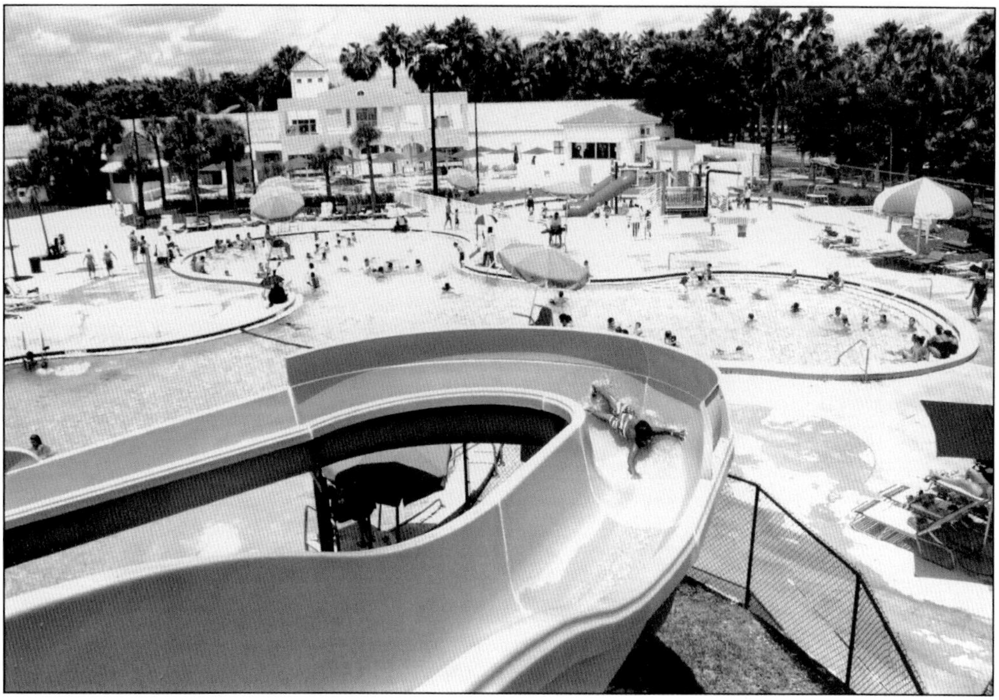

Water playground equipment was added to the Cypress Park pool in 2000, giving residents a fun way to cool off. This giant slide is one of the more popular attractions. (Courtesy of the City of Coral Springs.)

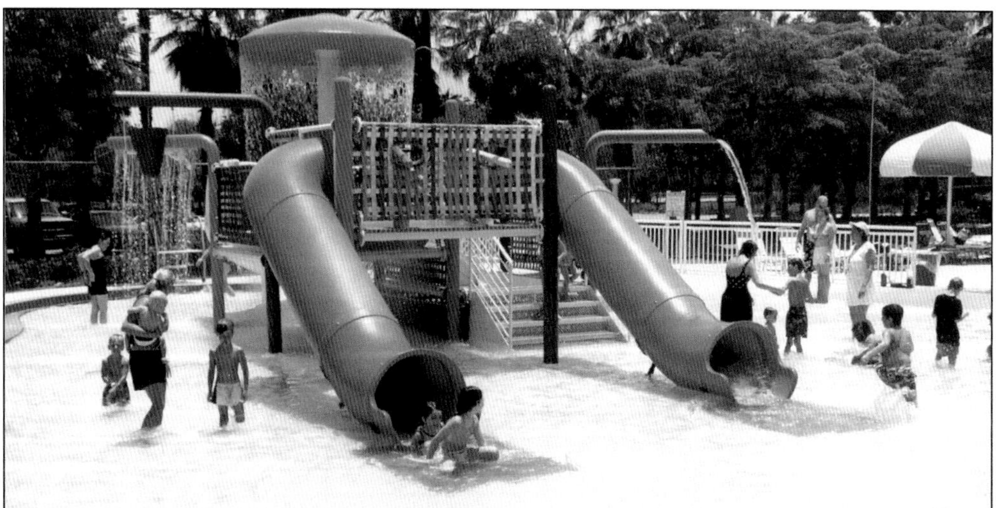

The new additions to Cypress Park pool included this wading pool with a water "umbrella," slides, waterfalls, and water cannons. Children of all ages come from all over to enjoy cooling off in this watery playground. (Courtesy of the City of Coral Springs.)

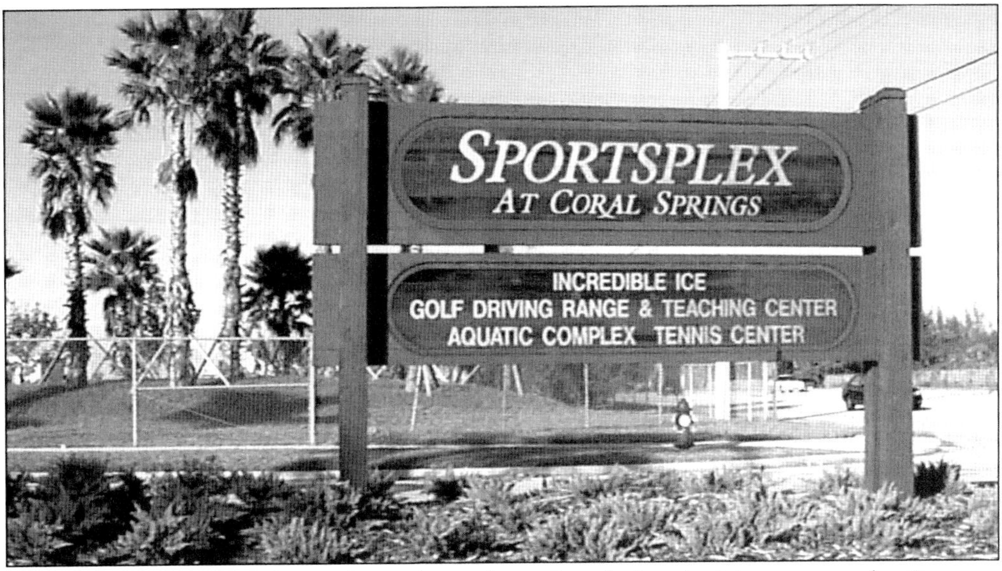

The north entrance to Sportsplex is located on Sample Road, right next to the Sawgrass Expressway and the Everglades. Sawgrass Springs Middle School is in the fenced area directly behind the sign. In 2004, a new high school will be added to the complex. Local resident Joan Kohl has been raising funds to develop a nature center and wildlife rescue hospital in Sportsplex also. (Courtesy of the City of Coral Springs.)

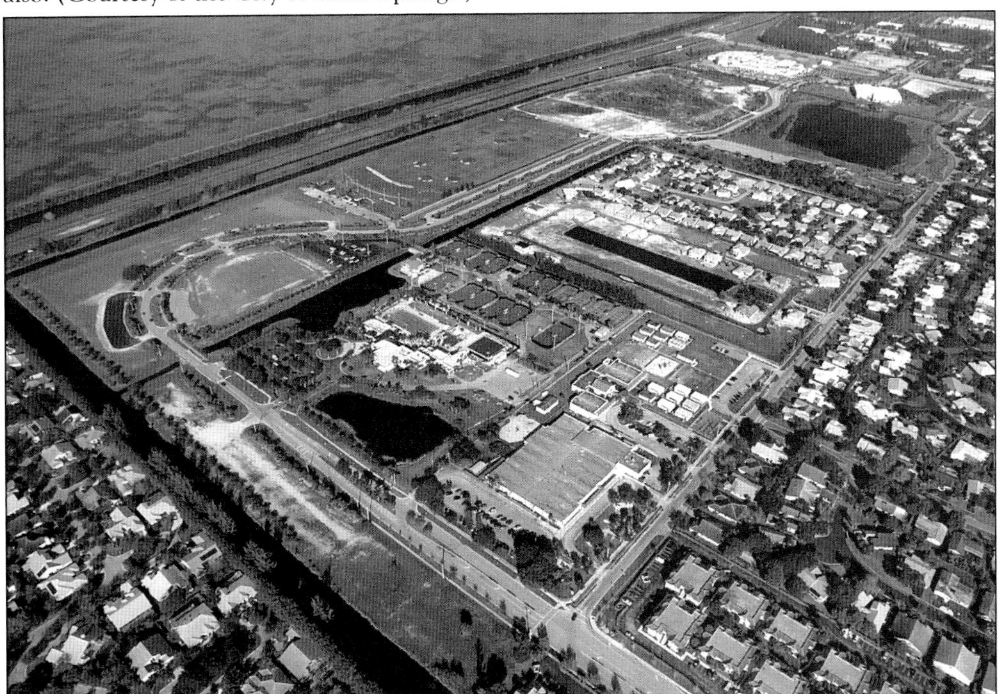

This aerial view of Sportsplex helps demonstrate the abundance of space set aside for parks in the city's master plan. Beyond the Sawgrass Expressway lies the Everglades. Just west (left) of the lake in the upper right hand corner is another of the city's environmentally-sensitive land sites. (Courtesy of the City of Coral Springs.)

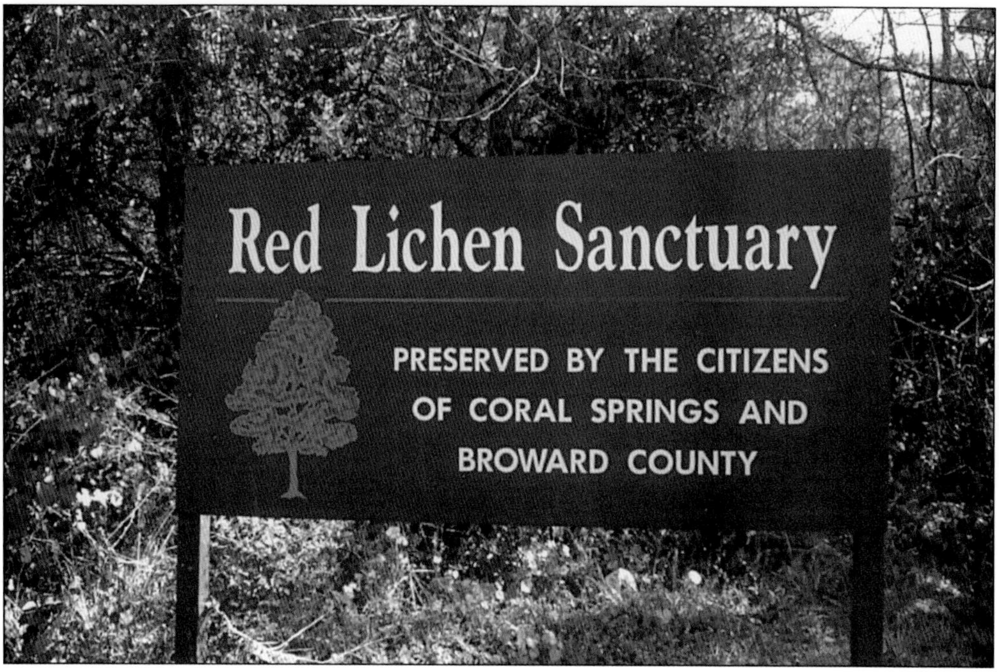

General Obligation Bonds totaling $7.5 million were approved by voters in 1995 to purchase environmentally-sensitive lands and keep them natural for the enjoyment and education of the community. Red Lichen Sanctuary was one of the first sites completed. (Courtesy of the City of Coral Springs.)

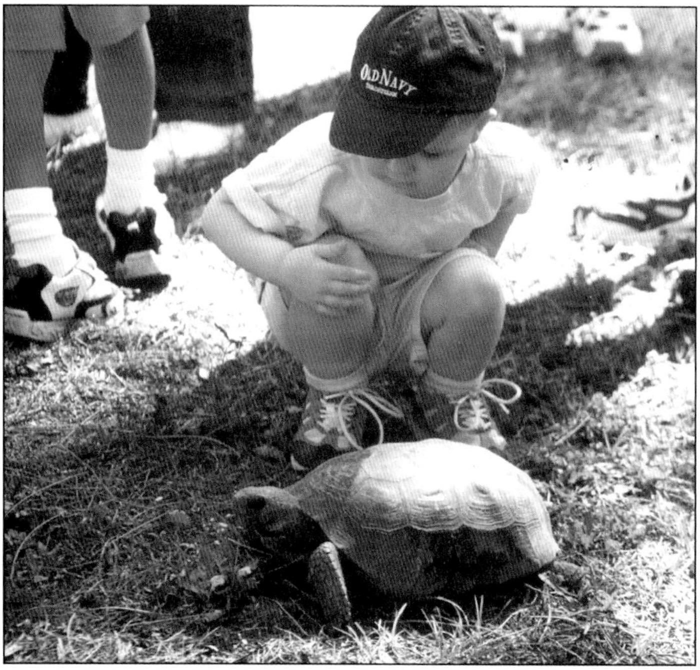

Here a protected gopher tortoise makes a home in Sandy Ridge Sanctuary as a young resident looks on during the annual Earth Day celebration. (Courtesy of the City of Coral Springs.)

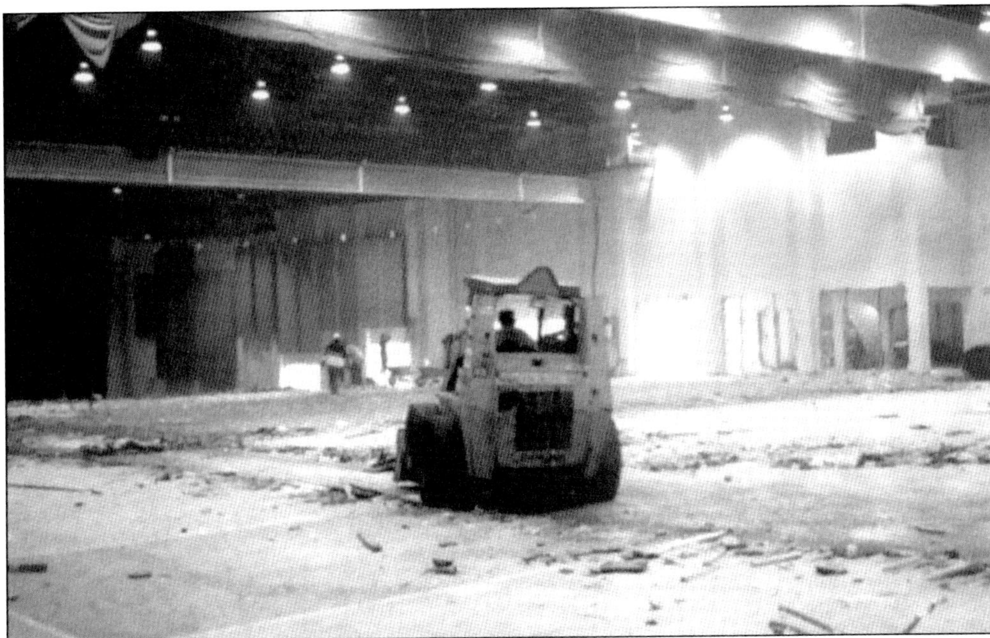

At the Coral Springs City Centre, a small bulldozer clears the maple gymnasium floor in preparation for the new balcony seating, lobby, and fine art museum. After the renovations, the city renamed the facility the Coral Springs Center for the Arts to emphasize the diverse activities held in the facility. (Courtesy of the City of Coral Springs.)

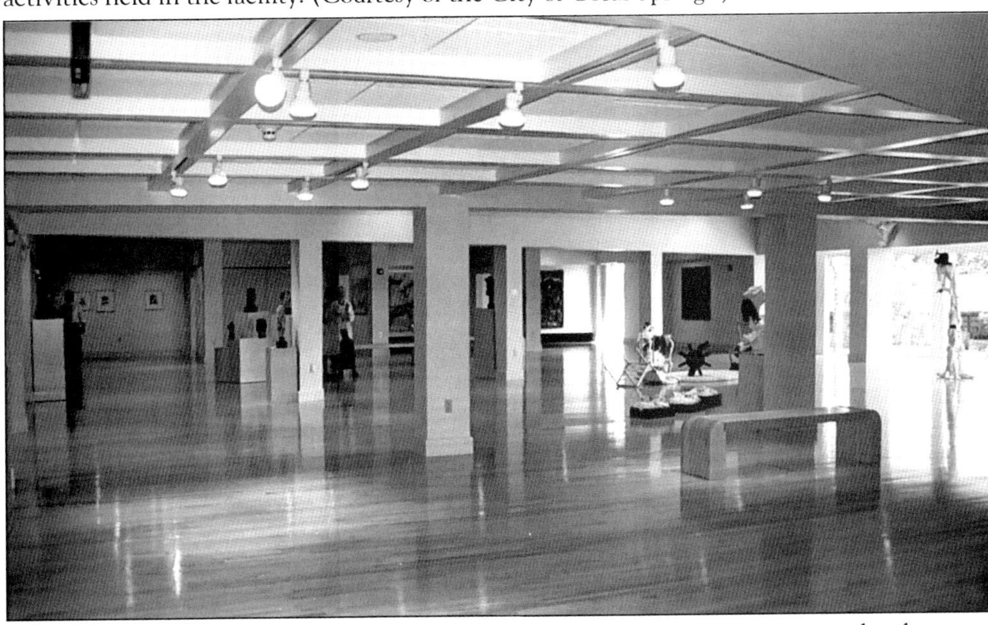

In 1994, the Coral Springs City Centre was renovated to improve acoustics in the theater as well as to add a 12,000-square-foot fine arts museum. This gallery space displays the work of the best artists who live and work in Florida, as well as many international artists. Originally named the Schacknow Museum of Fine Art in honor of a $1.4 million donation from Plantation resident and artist Max Schacknow, the city bought out the Schacknow Foundation in 1997 and renamed it the Coral Springs Museum of Art. (Courtesy of the City of Coral Springs.)

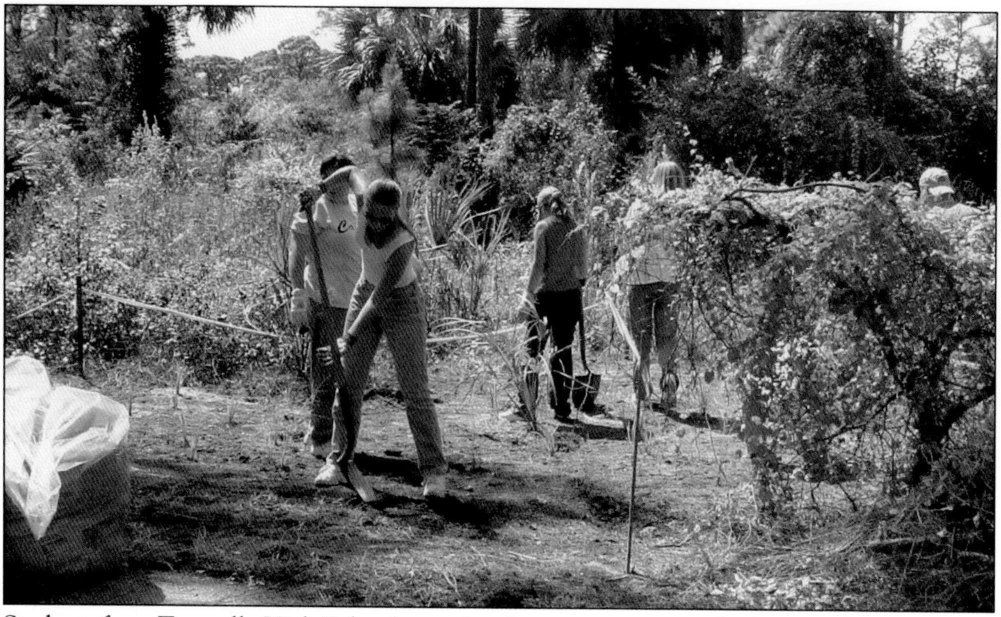

Students from Taravella High School get a hands-on environmental education by preparing a sample plot to study the principle of succession in Sandy Ridge Sanctuary. (Courtesy of the City of Coral Springs.)

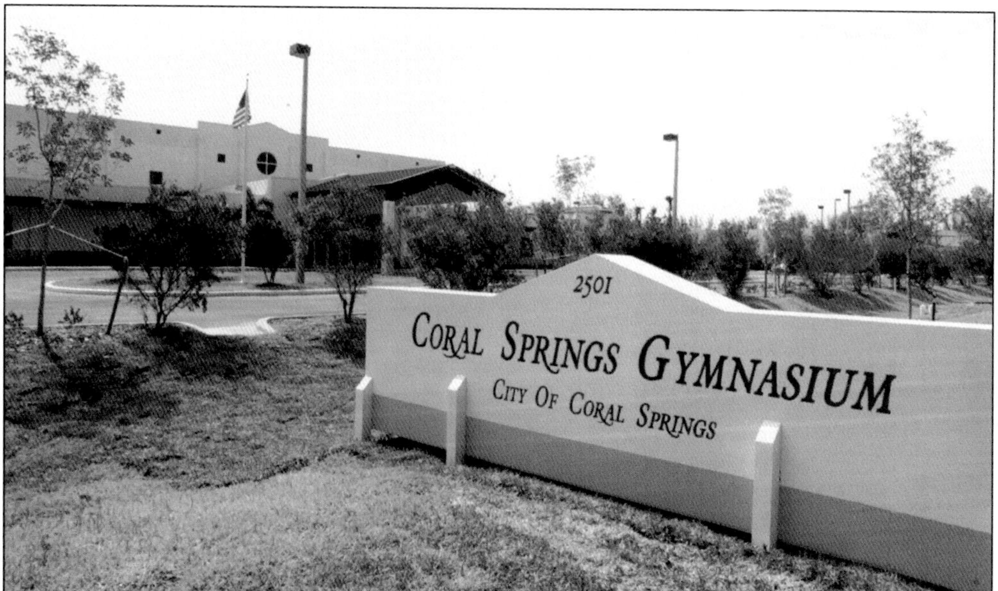

In 2000, the city opened an indoor gymnasium on the perimeter of Mullins Park, near the BMX Track and Public Safety Building along Coral Springs Drive. This facility was planned to replace the gymnasium that was removed in the Center for the Arts renovations. The facility features three full-size basketball courts, main court seating for 1,000 spectators, volleyball equipment, meeting rooms, a game room, and concession stand. (Courtesy of the City of Coral Springs.)

Nine

A Sterling Example

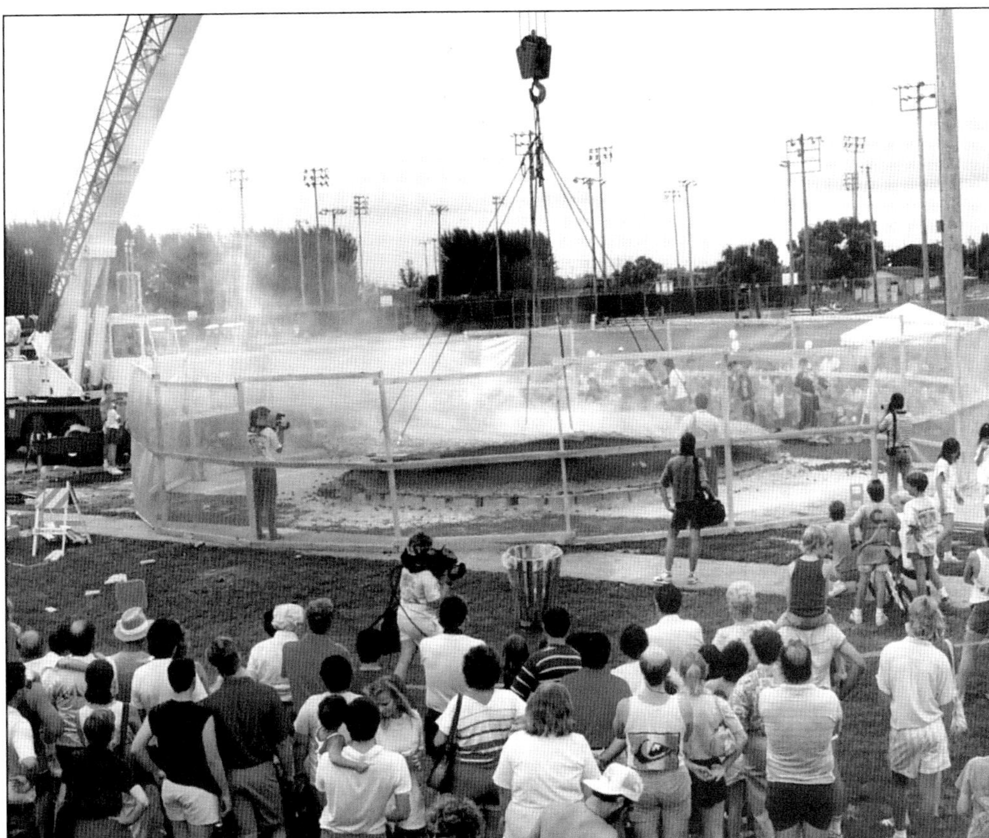

It's a bird—it's a plane—no, it's the world's largest burger! July 10, 1988 marked the 25th anniversary of the city. With a legacy of doing things in a big way, the following two *Guinness World Records* were broken that day: the world's biggest hamburger and the world's largest milk shake, prepared to order. (Courtesy of the City of Coral Springs.)

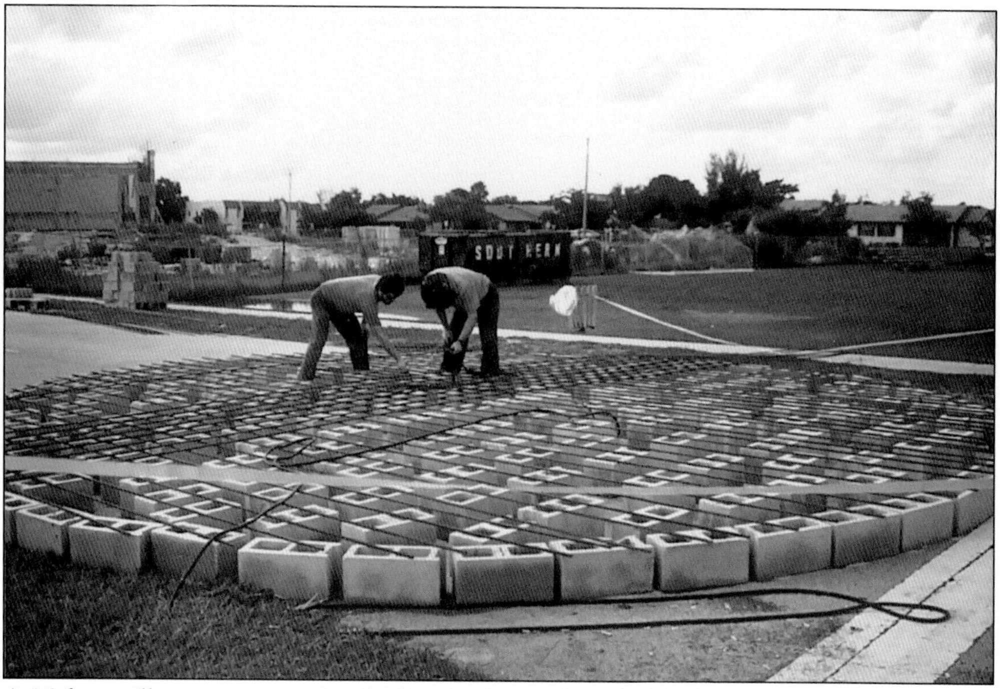

A 26-foot grill was constructed in Mullins Park out of cinder blocks, half-inch-thick steel bars that were cut and welded together at 8-inch intervals, and heavy mesh. Special flamethrowers lit 8,500 pounds of Royal Oak charcoal at 4 p.m. (Courtesy of the City of Coral Springs.)

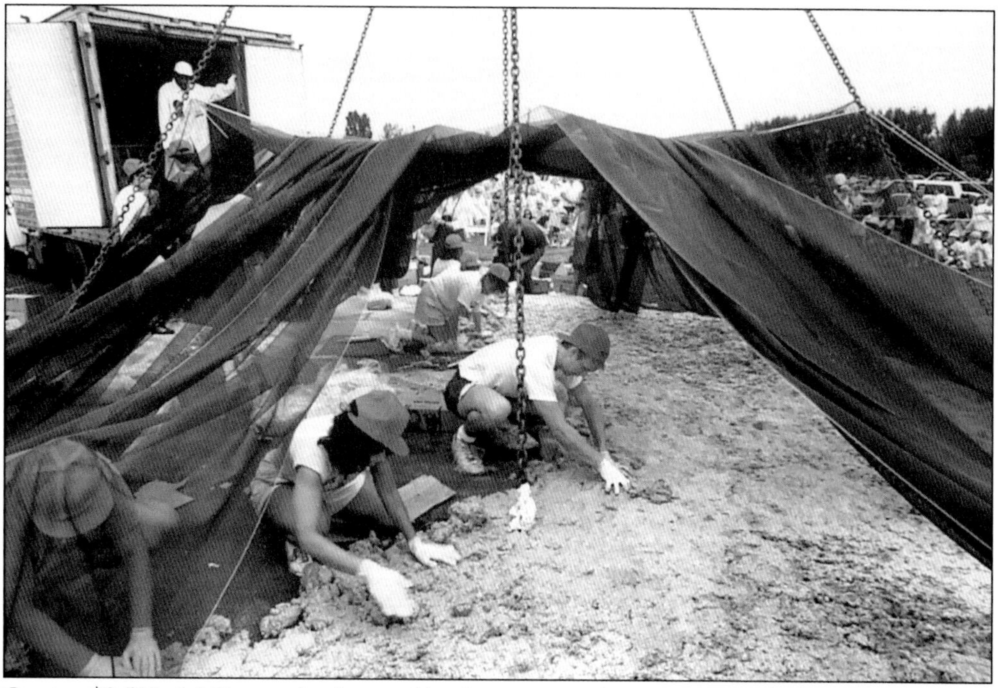

Costing $3,500, 5,063 pounds of ground beef were pressed onto a pan with gloved hands under a mesh teepee to keep away the flies. It was then swung over the fire by a crane to grill in the presence of a Broward County public health official. (Courtesy of the City of Coral Springs.)

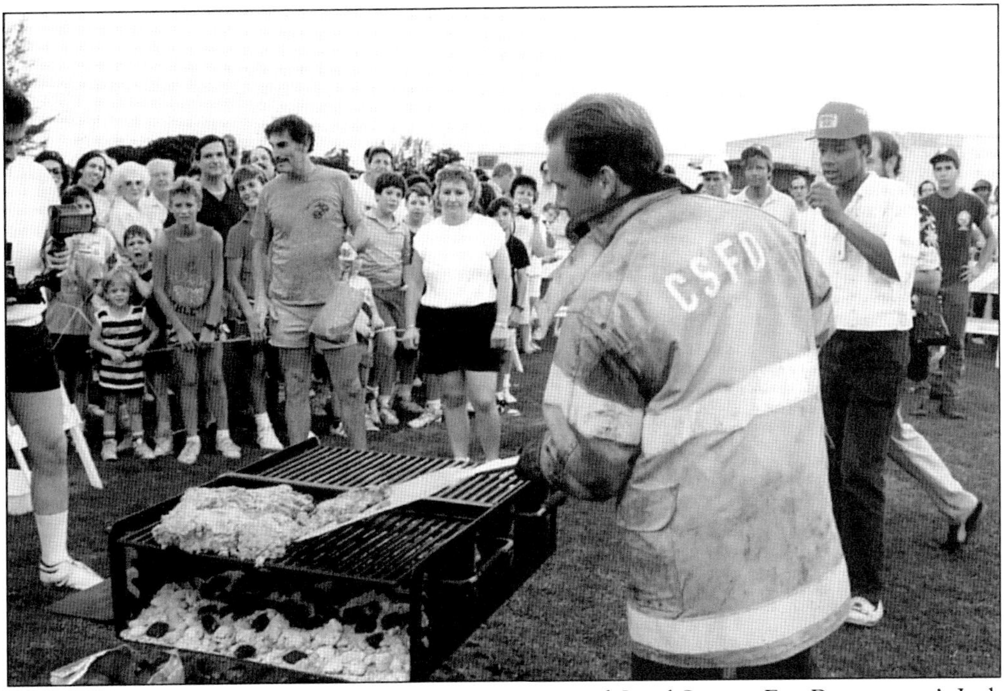

Flipping the burger at 5:27 p.m. required the assistance of Coral Springs Fire Department's Jack Reisenger and other firefighters, who turned it one piece at a time onto smaller grills. Twelve-thousand people stood in line for their serving. The event was B.Y.O.B. (bring your own buns). (Courtesy of the City of Coral Springs.)

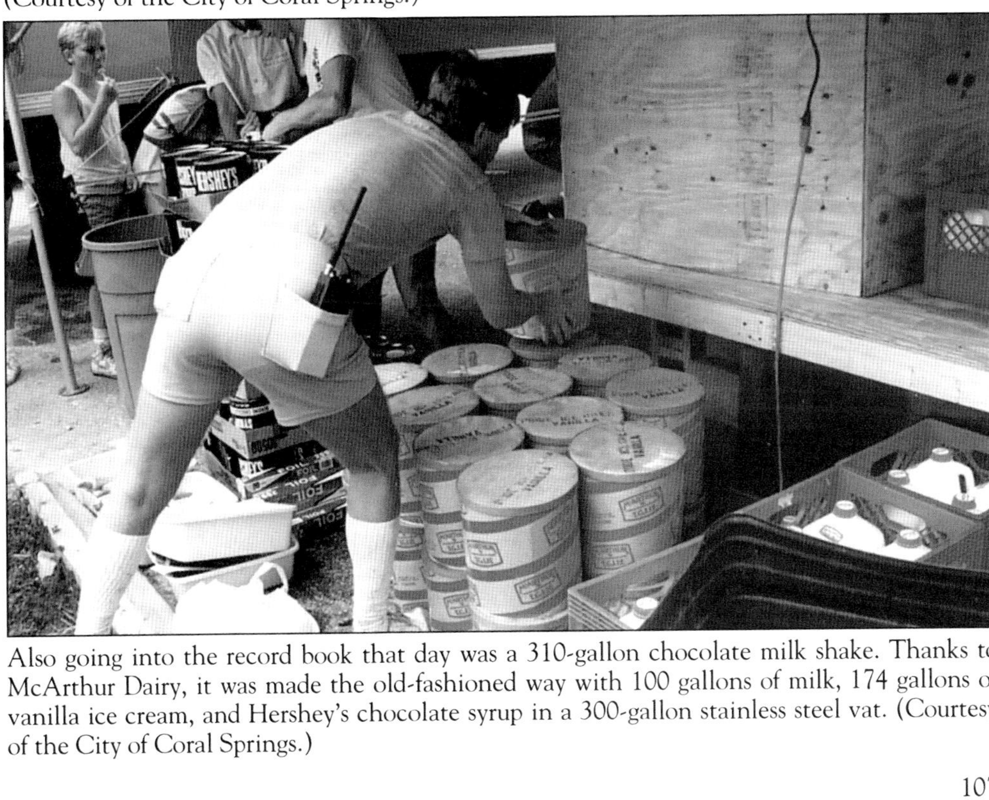

Also going into the record book that day was a 310-gallon chocolate milk shake. Thanks to McArthur Dairy, it was made the old-fashioned way with 100 gallons of milk, 174 gallons of vanilla ice cream, and Hershey's chocolate syrup in a 300-gallon stainless steel vat. (Courtesy of the City of Coral Springs.)

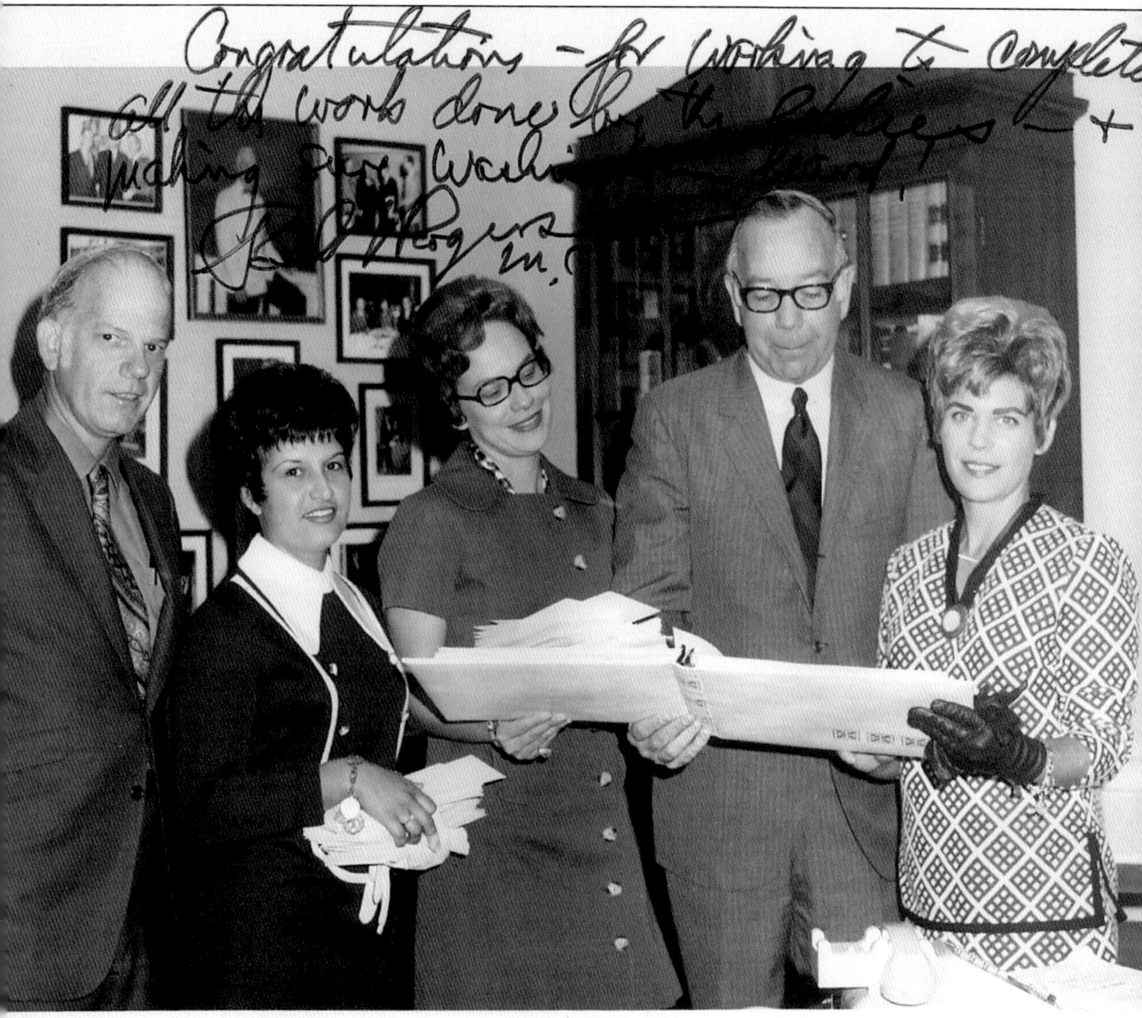

Before there were any schools in Coral Springs, the children were bused to Margate, Pompano Beach, and Coconut Creek. The ruling of the Fifth Circuit Court of Appeals would have required the children be cross-bused even farther away to achieve racial balance. The Coral Springs Chamber of Commerce Women's Division decided to take "positive and constructive action." They wrote to 50 state governors, 100 senators, and every representative, and personally delivered 50,000 letters of protest from Broward County and adjacent areas to the United States Supreme Court on October 9, 1970. As a result, the ruling was delayed a year—enough time to construct the first school and eliminate the need for busing children several hours a day. The ladies and gentleman who went to Washington were Edward Heafy, Alice Varvoutis, Sue Tisdale, and Marion Nolen, shown here meeting with Florida state representative Paul Rogers. (Courtesy of The Heafy Collection.)

In 1971, the only local news was written by Coral Ridge Properties management. Members of the Coral Springs Teen Center took issue with some of stories and decided to publish their own paper, *The Forum*. In the first issue on February 19, 1971, they wrote "This newspaper will tell you the good and the bad things that are happening in the city. This is not meant to be a propaganda sheet for you to send to your friends up north to lure them to our beautiful city. This is meant to be a newspaper." (Courtesy of The City of Coral Springs.)

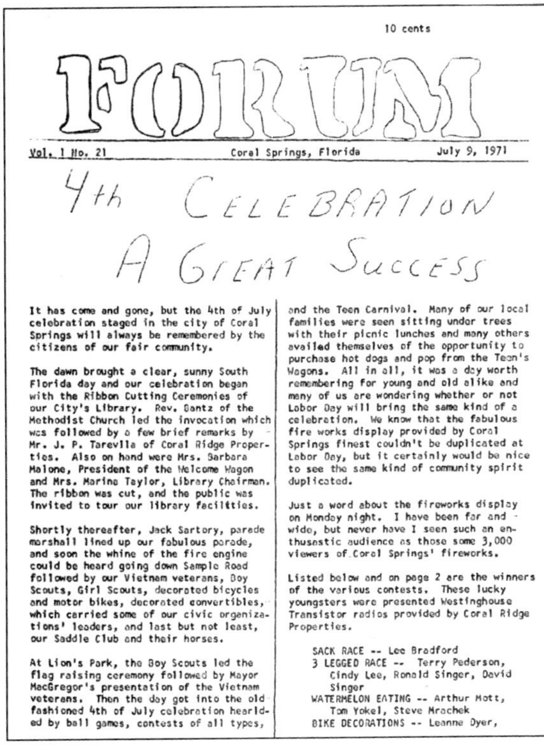

10 cents

FORUM

Vol. 1 No. 21 Coral Springs, Florida July 9, 1971

4th CELEBRATION A GREAT SUCCESS

It has come and gone, but the 4th of July celebration staged in the city of Coral Springs will always be remembered by the citizens of our fair community.

The dawn brought a clear, sunny South Florida day and our celebration began with the Ribbon Cutting Ceremonies of our City's Library. Rev. Bantz of the Methodist Church led the invocation which was followed by a few brief remarks by Mr. J. P. Tarevila of Coral Ridge Properties. Also on hand were Mrs. Barbara Malone, President of the Welcome Wagon and Mrs. Marine Taylor, Library Chairman. The ribbon was cut, and the public was invited to tour our library facilities.

Shortly thereafter, Jack Sartory, parade marshall lined up our fabulous parade, and soon the whine of the fire engine could be heard going down Sample Road followed by our Vietnam veterans, Boy Scouts, Girl Scouts, decorated bicycles and motor bikes, decorated convertibles, which carried some of our civic organizations' leaders, and last but not least, our Saddle Club and their horses.

At Lion's Park, the Boy Scouts led the flag raising ceremony followed by Mayor MacGregor's presentation of the Vietnam veterans. Then the day got into the old fashioned 4th of July celebration hearlded by ball games, contests of all types, and the Teen Carnival. Many of our local families were seen sitting under trees with their picnic lunches and many others availed themselves of the opportunity to purchase hot dogs and pop from the Teen's Wagons. All in all, it was a day worth remembering for young and old alike and many of us are wondering whether or not Labor Day will bring the same kind of a celebration. We know that the fabulous fire works display provided by Coral Springs finest couldn't be duplicated at Labor Day, but it certainly would be nice to see the same kind of community spirit duplicated.

Just a word about the fireworks display on Monday night. I have been far and wide, but never have I seen such an enthusastic audience as those some 3,000 viewers of Coral Springs' fireworks.

Listed below and on page 2 are the winners of the various contests. These lucky youngsters were presented Westinghouse Transistor radios provided by Coral Ridge Properties.

SACK RACE -- Lee Bradford
3 LEGGED RACE -- Terry Pederson, Cindy Lee, Ronald Singer, David Singer
WATERMELON EATING -- Arthur Mott, Tom Yokel, Steve Mrachek
BIKE DECORATIONS -- Leanne Dyer,

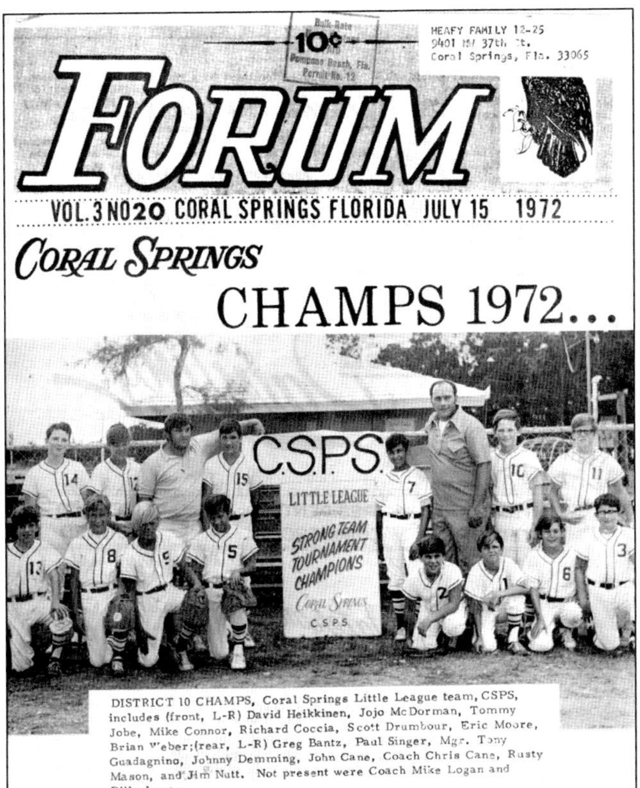

Bulk Rate 10¢ Pompano Beach, Fla. Permit No. 12

HEAFY FAMILY 12-25
9401 NW 37th St.
Coral Springs, Fla. 33065

FORUM

VOL. 3 NO 20 CORAL SPRINGS FLORIDA JULY 15 1972

CORAL SPRINGS CHAMPS 1972...

DISTRICT 10 CHAMPS, Coral Springs Little League team, CSPS, includes (front, L-R) David Heikkinen, Jojo McDorman, Tommy Jobe, Mike Connor, Richard Coccia, Scott Drumbour, Eric Moore, Brian Weber;(rear, L-R) Greg Bantz, Paul Singer, Mgr. Tony Guadagnino, Johnny Demming, John Cane, Coach Chris Cane, Rusty Mason, and Jim Nutt. Not present were Coach Mike Logan and Billy Logan.

The original newspaper was printed on 8 1/2-by-11-inch mimeographed paper and had hand-written headlines. By 1972 it sported printed headlines as well as a cover photograph, in this case the Little League Champions from District 10. The format changed to 8 1/2-by-14-inch paper on August 26, 1972. After many of the staff graduated from Coconut Creek High in 1972 (there was no local high school yet), Larry Mailloux became the publisher of *The Forum* and a paid staff was hired. Editions after October 26, 1972 used newsprint. (Courtesy of the City of Coral Springs.)

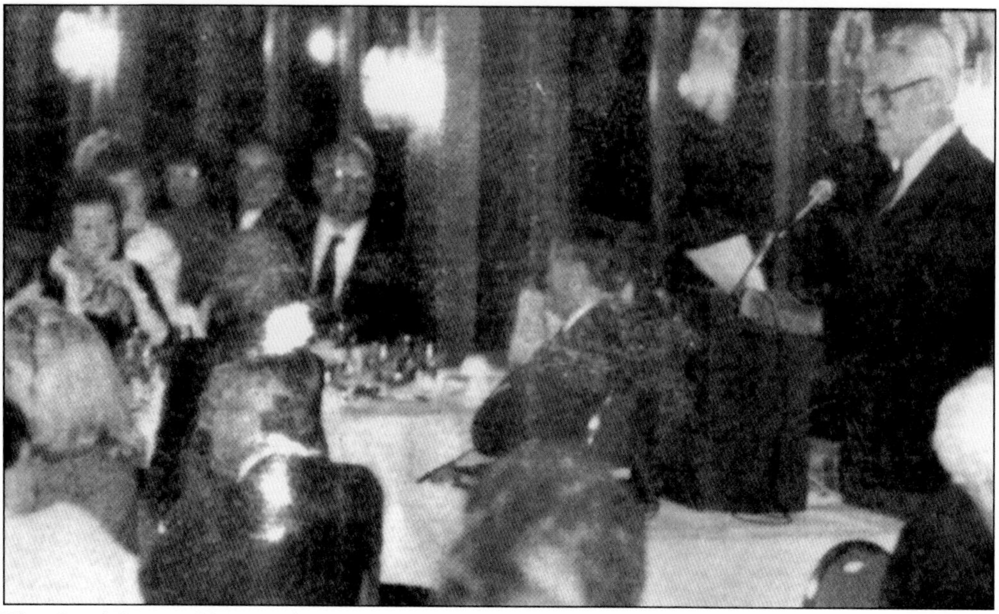

The Coral Springs Historical Society was organized on May 19, 1976 through the efforts of Emily Heafy and Gordon Ickes. As a Coral Ridge Properties spokesman, Ickes secured a complete pictorial history of the city. One of the society's first acts was the bury the Bicentennial Time Capsule. Their mission was to collect, archive, and display the city's history. That goal has since been passed on to the Coral Springs Historical Advisory Committee. Gordon Ickes addresses the Coral Springs Historical Society in December 1989 at their first-ever dinner meeting.

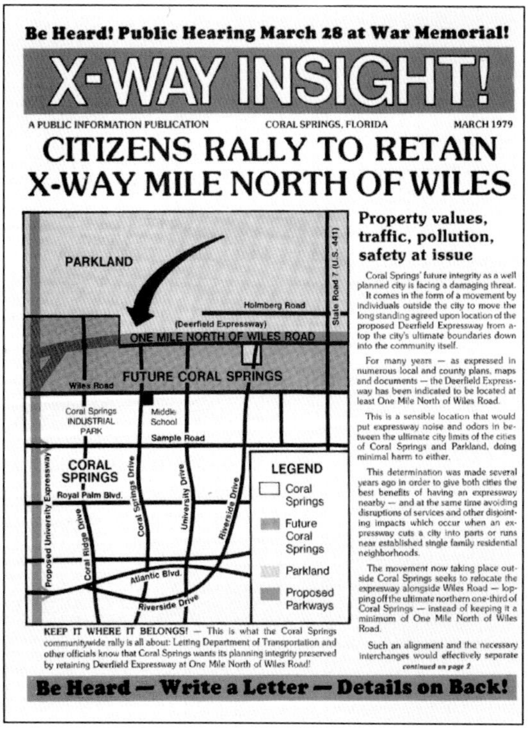

Be Heard! Public Hearing March 28 at War Memorial!

X-WAY INSIGHT!

A PUBLIC INFORMATION PUBLICATION CORAL SPRINGS, FLORIDA MARCH 1979

CITIZENS RALLY TO RETAIN X-WAY MILE NORTH OF WILES

KEEP IT WHERE IT BELONGS! — This is what the Coral Springs communitywide rally is all about: Letting Department of Transportation and other officials know that Coral Springs wants its planning integrity preserved by retaining Deerfield Expressway at One Mile North of Wiles Road!

Property values, traffic, pollution, safety at issue

Coral Springs' future integrity as a well planned city is facing a damaging threat.

It comes in the form of a movement by individuals outside the city to move the long standing agreed upon location of the proposed Deerfield Expressway from atop the city's ultimate boundaries down into the community itself.

For many years — as expressed in numerous local and county plans, maps and documents — the Deerfield Expressway has been indicated to be located at least One Mile North of Wiles Road.

This is a sensible location that would put expressway noise and odors in between the ultimate city limits of the cities of Coral Springs and Parkland, doing minimal harm to either.

This determination was made several years ago in order to give both cities the best benefits of having an expressway nearby — and at the same time avoiding disruptions of services and other disjointing impacts which occur when an expressway cuts a city into parts or runs near established single family residential neighborhoods.

The movement now taking place outside Coral Springs seeks to relocate the expresway alongside Wiles Road — lopping off the ultimate northern one-third of Coral Springs — instead of keeping it a minimum of One Mile North of Wiles Road.

Such an alignment and the necessary interchanges would effectively separate

continued on page 2

Be Heard — Write a Letter — Details on Back!

This brochure, distributed by Coral Ridge Properties, warns residents, "Coral Springs' future integrity as a well planned city is facing a damaging threat. It comes in the form of a movement by individuals outside the city to move the longstanding agreed upon location of the proposed Deerfield Beach Expressway . . . along side Wiles Road . . . instead of keeping it a minimum of One Mile North of Wiles Road." (Courtesy of the City of Coral Springs.)

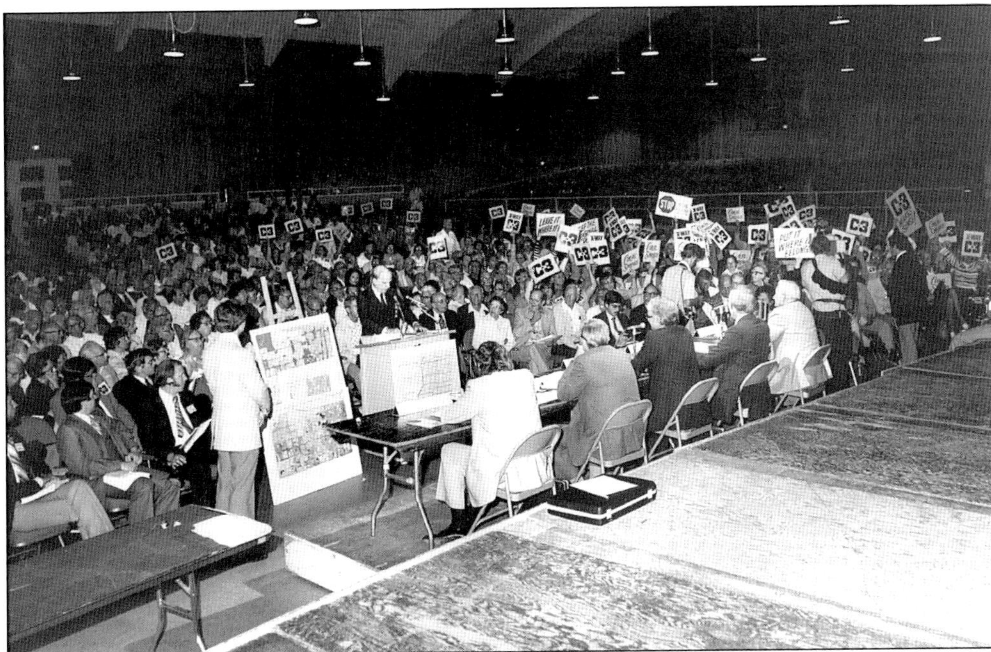

On March 28, 1979, the Florida Department of Transportation held a public hearing at the War Memorial Auditorium in Ft. Lauderdale to discuss the location of the expressway. The "C-3" on the placards refers to the C-3 Canal running one mile north of Wiles Road, which was the preferred site for the expressway by hundreds of Coral Springs residents, who came to the hearing by car and four chartered buses. Vice Mayor Edward Heafy is seen at the podium. (Courtesy of Coral Ridge Properties.)

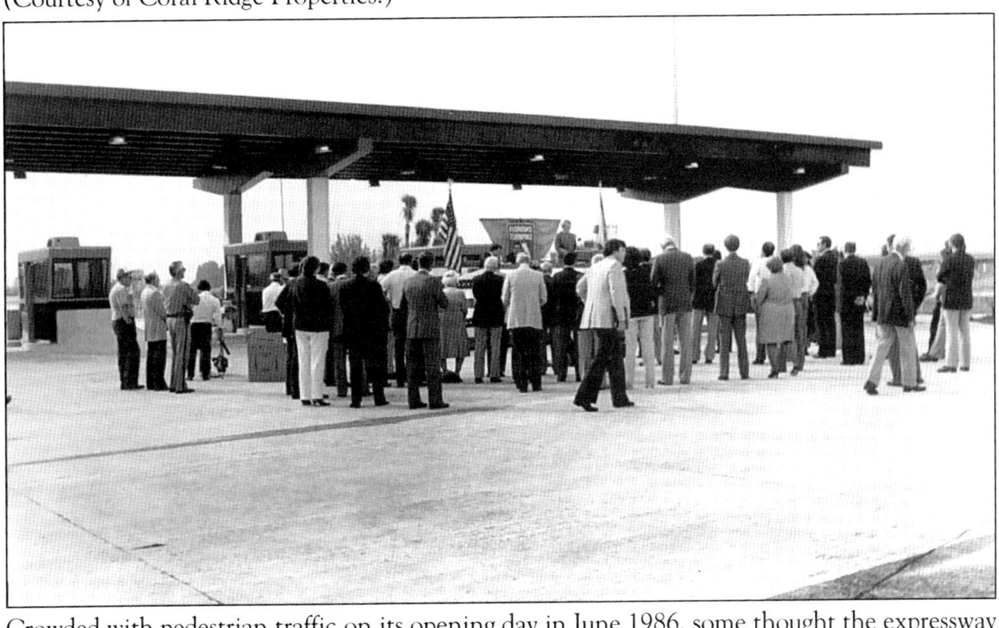

Crowded with pedestrian traffic on its opening day in June 1986, some thought the expressway was a waste of taxpayers' money, considering how few drivers would use it. Originally intended to continue to I-95, the expressway stopped at Florida's Turnpike, so it was then given the more suitable name of Sawgrass Expressway. (Courtesy of Coral Ridge Properties.)

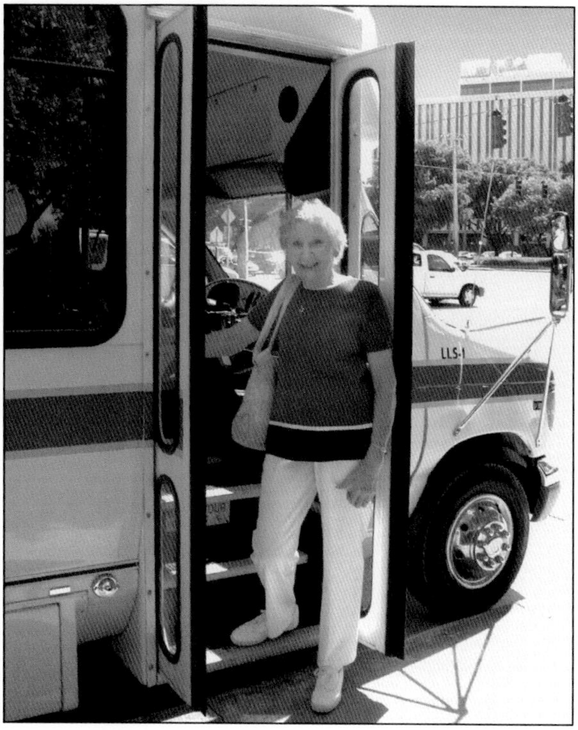

A free city bus service operates weekdays along two routes—the green route runs through the north side of the city and the blue route runs through the south side. Anna Lee Cannon takes advantage of the convenience of traveling around town without driving. (Courtesy of the City of Coral Springs.)

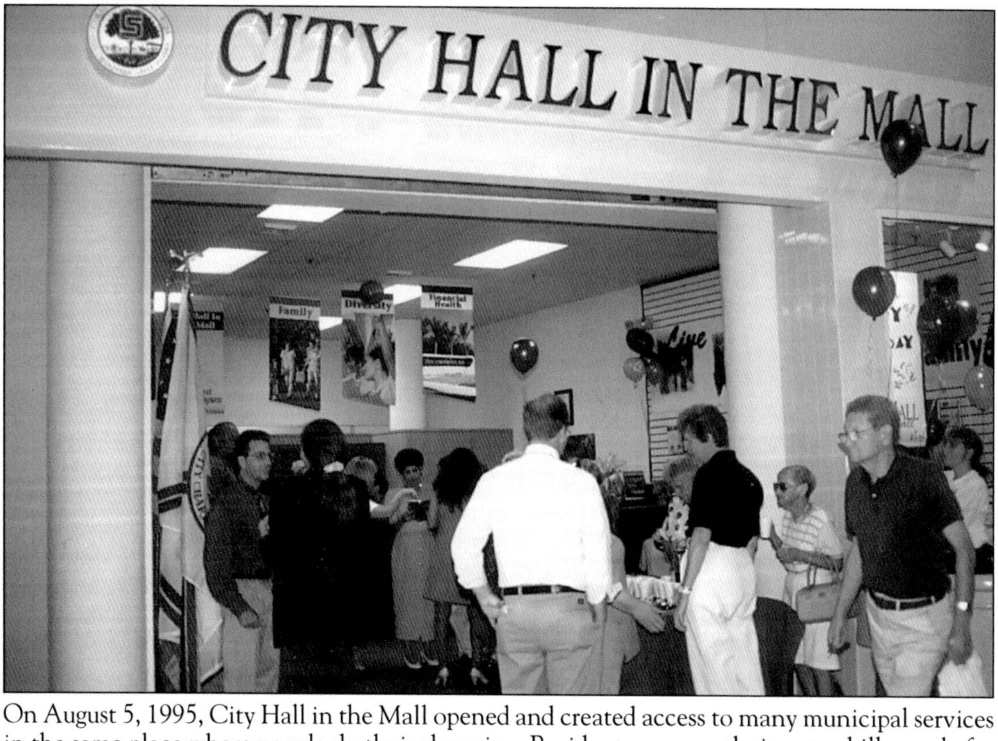

On August 5, 1995, City Hall in the Mall opened and created access to many municipal services in the same place where people do their shopping. Residents can pay their water bills, apply for a homestead exemption, register to vote, apply for a passport, or renew an old one, as well as check out city recreational programs. (Courtesy of the City of Coral Springs.)

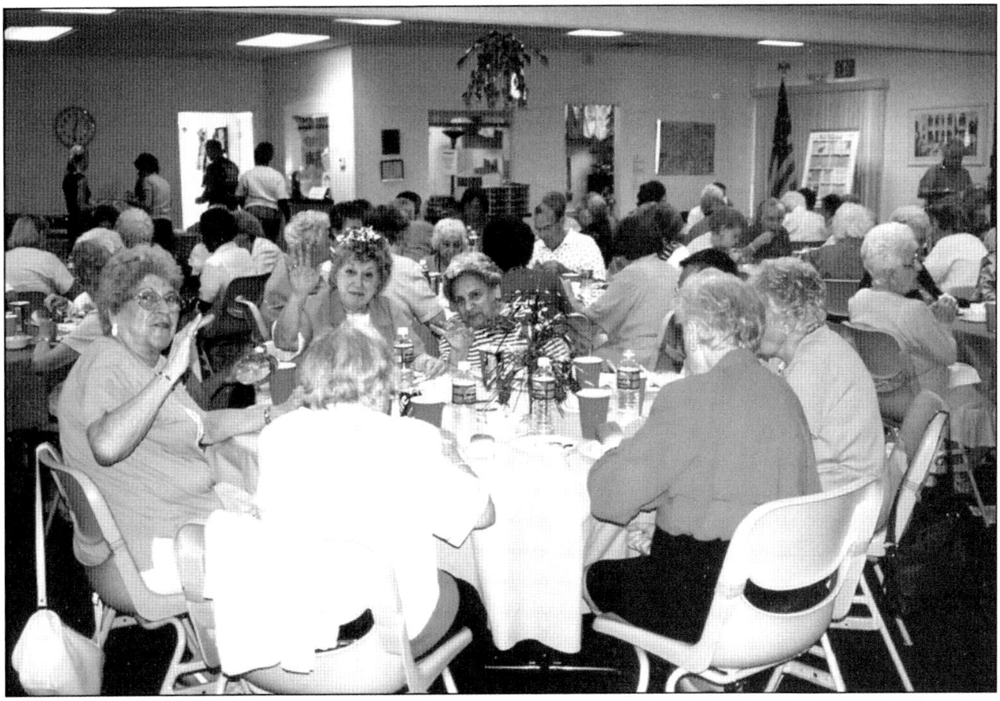

Sartory Senior Center is a recreational facility located in Mullins Park. Sponsored by the City of Coral Springs, the center offers monthly excursions, free classes, and entertainment. It also serves as a place to play cards, watch a movie, get in shape, or just visit, as at this St. Patrick's Day party. (Courtesy of the City of Coral Springs.)

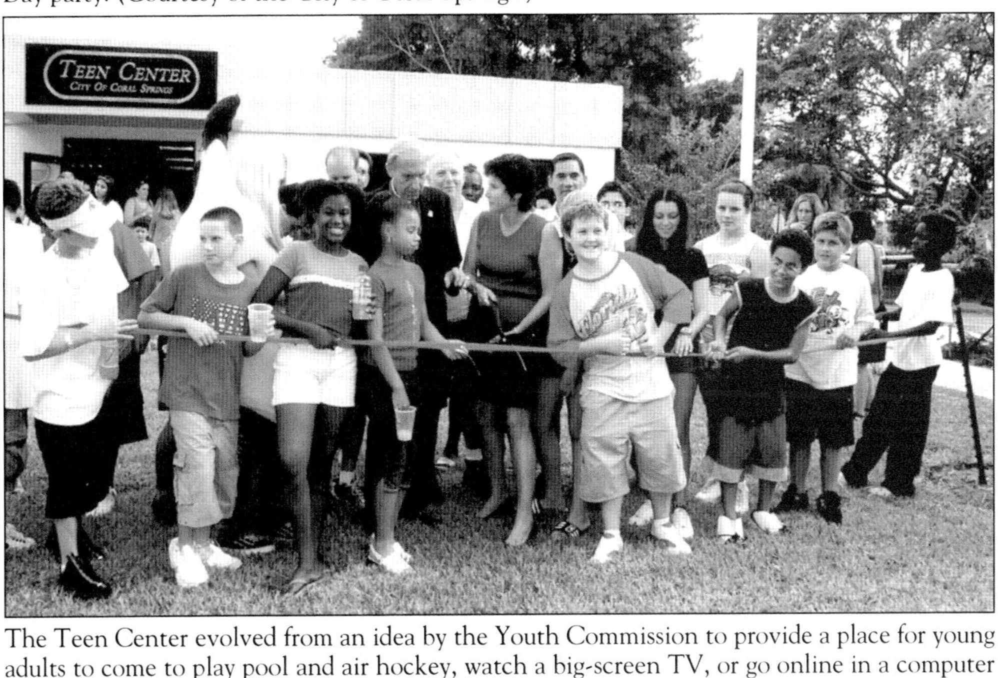

The Teen Center evolved from an idea by the Youth Commission to provide a place for young adults to come to play pool and air hockey, watch a big-screen TV, or go online in a computer center. Here Bishop John Erbelding and commissioner Rhonda Calhoun prepare to cut the ribbon at the grand opening. (Courtesy of the City of Coral Springs.)

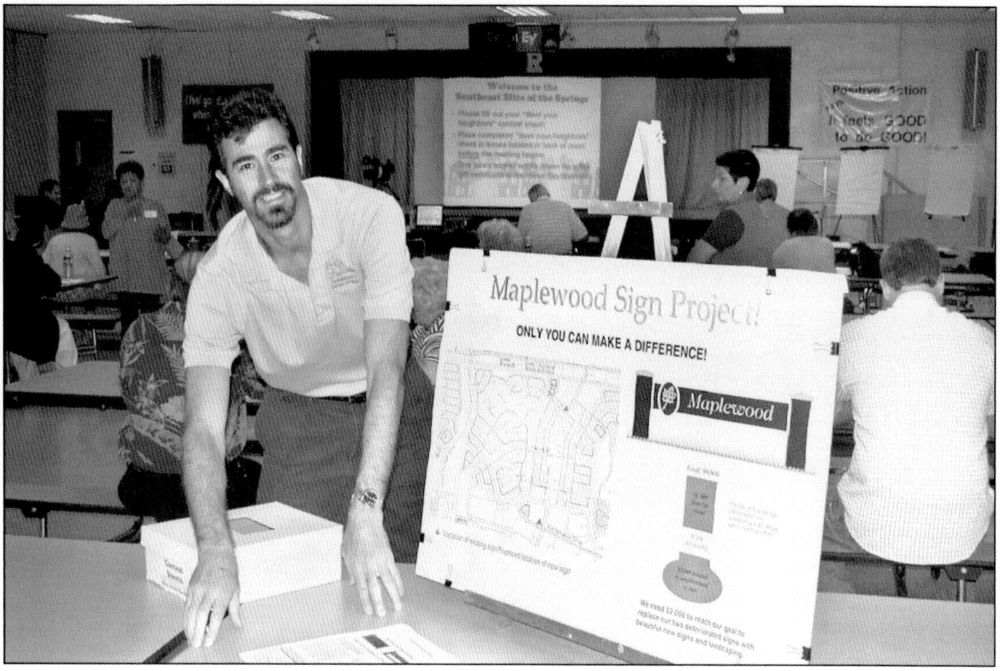

Slice of the Springs town meetings began in 1996 to keep residents informed and involved with their community. City-sponsored programs are discussed and local code-enforcement officers and police are present to answer questions. They rotate among six different parts of town in order to address local issues. Neighborhood planning analyst Marty Schneider is seen here setting up a display. (Courtesy of the City of Coral Springs.)

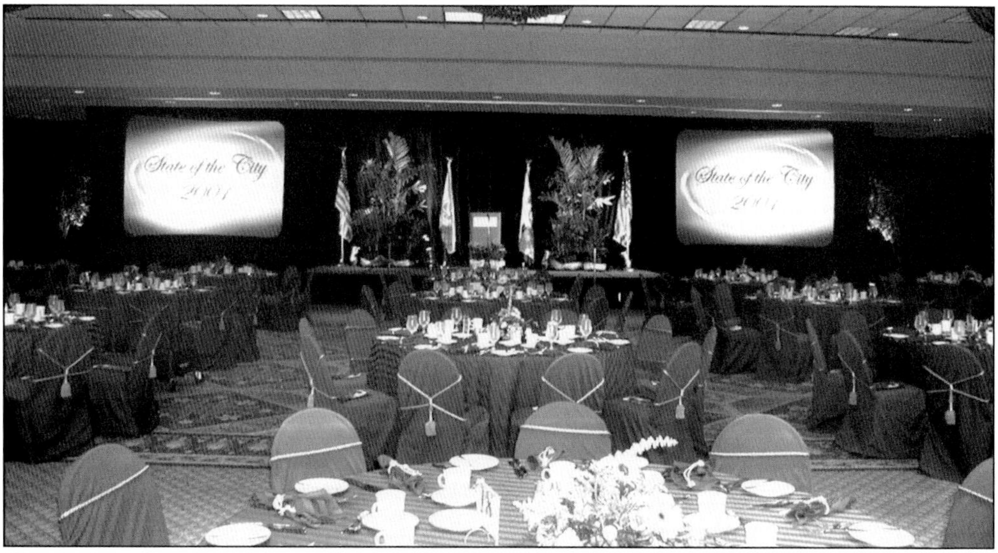

"State of the City" is an annual event that recognizes the approximately 350 volunteers who work on the many boards and advisory committees. Some of these include the Historical Advisory Committee, the Multi-Cultural Advisory Committee, the International Partnership Committee, the Martin Luther King Jr. Advisory Committee, the Youth and Family Advisory Committee, the Neighborhood and Environment Advisory Committee, and the Financial Advisory Committee. (Courtesy of The City of Coral Springs.)

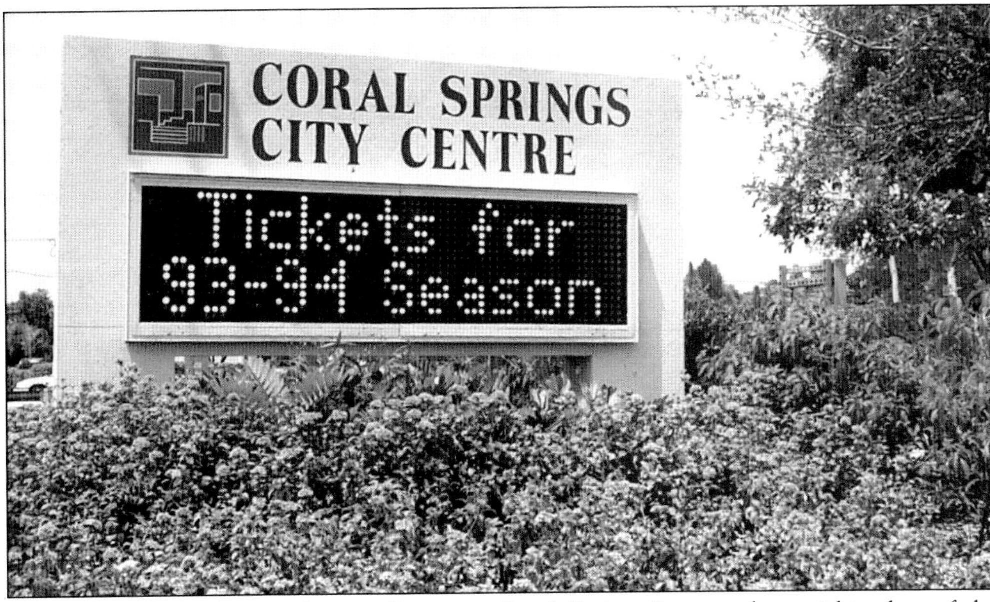

Headlines, such as "Times Square Comes to Coral Springs," cropped up within days of the installation of the City Centre's new marquee in 1993. Due to the city code that allows only modest monument signs for public facilities (such as parks and churches), the lighted message board required a special variance by the city commission. It was the only sign of its kind in Coral Springs. It is now history, however, as it was replaced in 2002 with a monument sign that conforms to code. (Courtesy of the City of Coral Springs.)

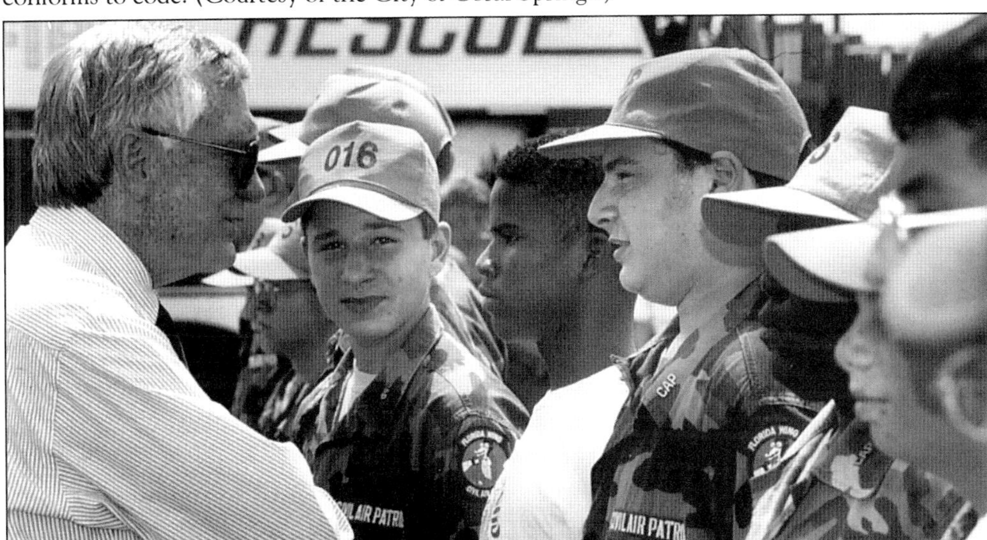

Gov. Lawton Chiles inspects cadets of the Coral Springs Cadet Squadron of the Civil Air Patrol during a visit on July 25, 1996. In the background is the side of the Broward County Sheriff's Office search-and-rescue helicopter, which was demonstrated on that day as well. The Civil Air Patrol is just one of many volunteer opportunities for area youth. (Courtesy of the City of Coral Springs.)

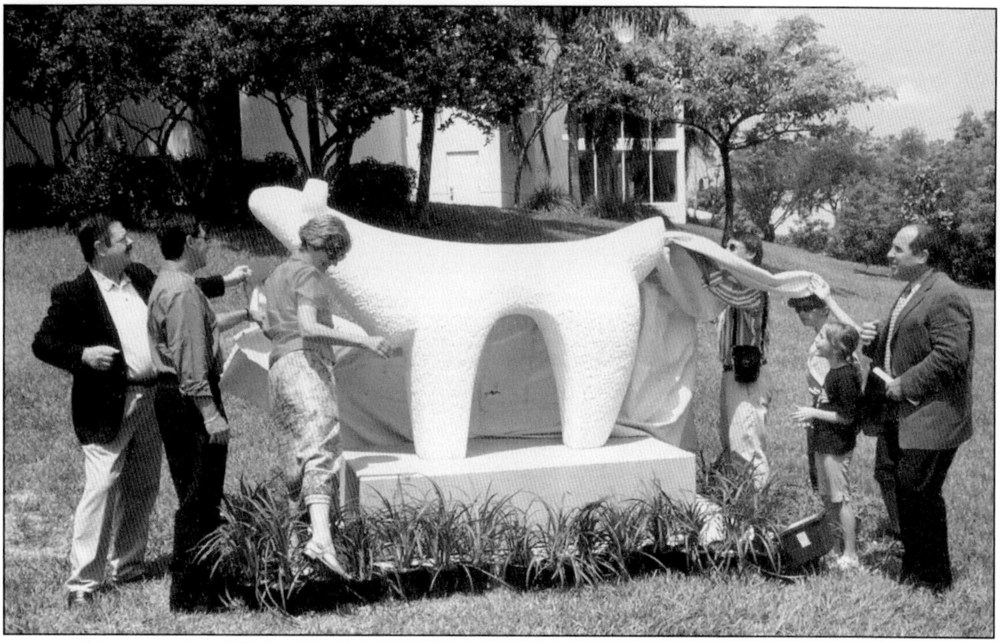

Pictured here is the 2002 unveiling of the city's first "Art in Public Places" project, on the grounds of the Coral Springs Center for the Arts. From left to right, Mayor John Sommerer, Commissioner Scott Brook, museum director Barbara O'Keefe, artist Lothar Nickel, two young participants in the Master Class, and City Manager Mike Levinson unveil the marble sculpture "Himalama." Carved on the museum grounds from a 8,500-pound block of Italian Carrera marble, the sculpture took three months to complete. (Courtesy of the City of Coral Springs.)

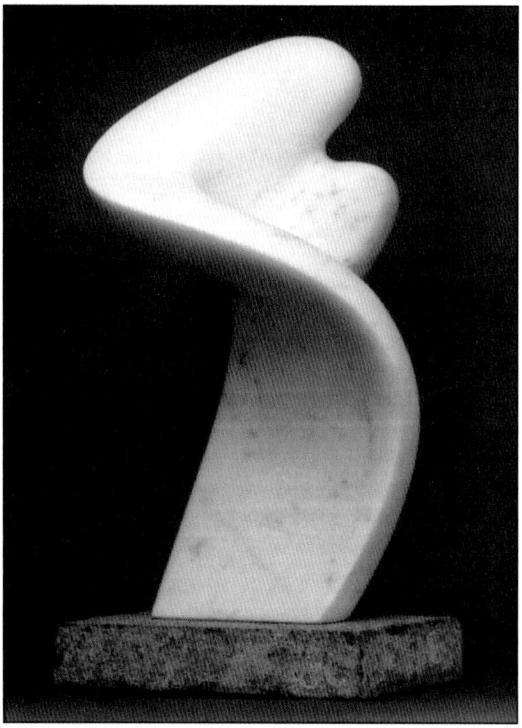

Also carved by artist Lothar Nickel from imported Carrara *statuario* marble, the sculpture "Striding" was the museum's first commission, created as part of the 2001 Artist-in-Residence program. The program gave city residents the opportunity to work shoulder-to-shoulder with a professional artist whose work appears in collections and museums in Europe and the United States. (Courtesy of the City of Coral Springs.)

The "Everglades Room" at Eagle Ridge Elementary School was part of a series of student projects centered around learning more about the ecosystem of the "River of Grass," Florida's Everglades. The mural was painted by art teacher Jan Avis and depicts a wetlands environment. (Courtesy of the City of Coral Springs.)

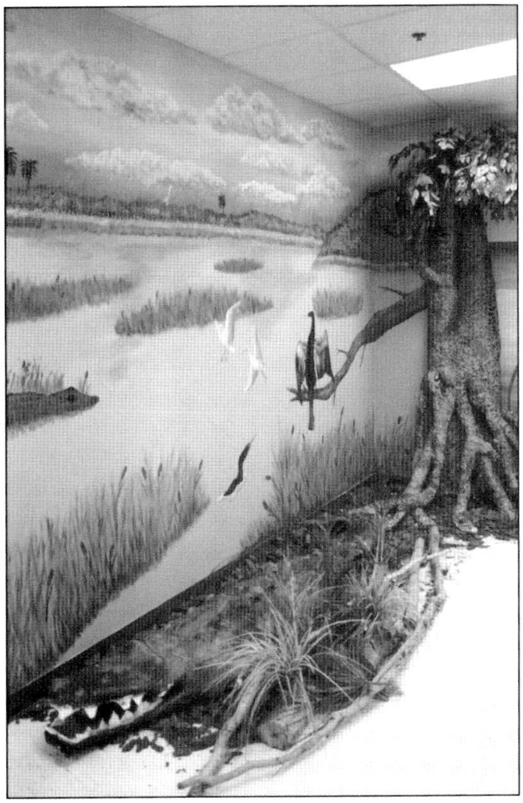

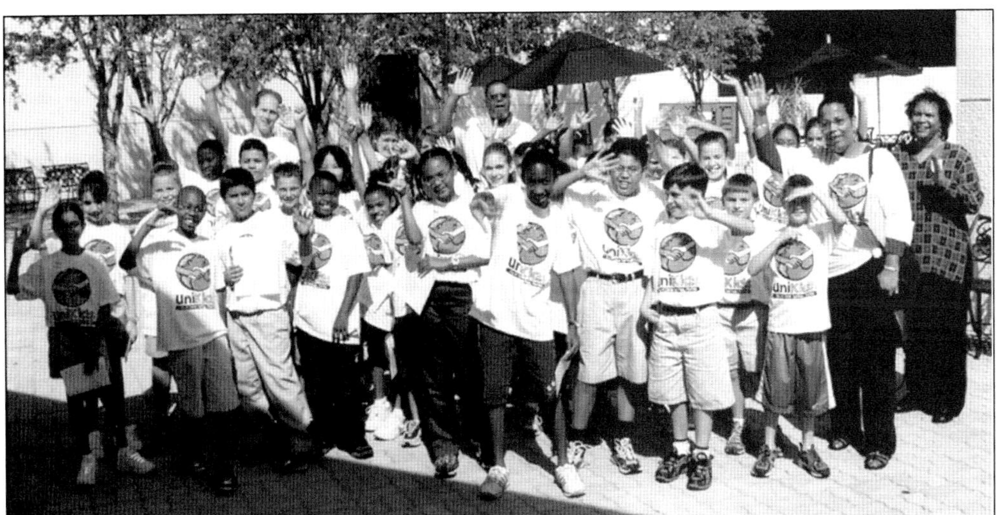

Some of the 150 participants in the first-annual UniKids youth leadership training program gather in the Center for the Arts courtyard. The program is geared to elementary school students where values of citizenship, friendship, and racial harmony are emphasized. (Courtesy of the City of Coral Springs.)

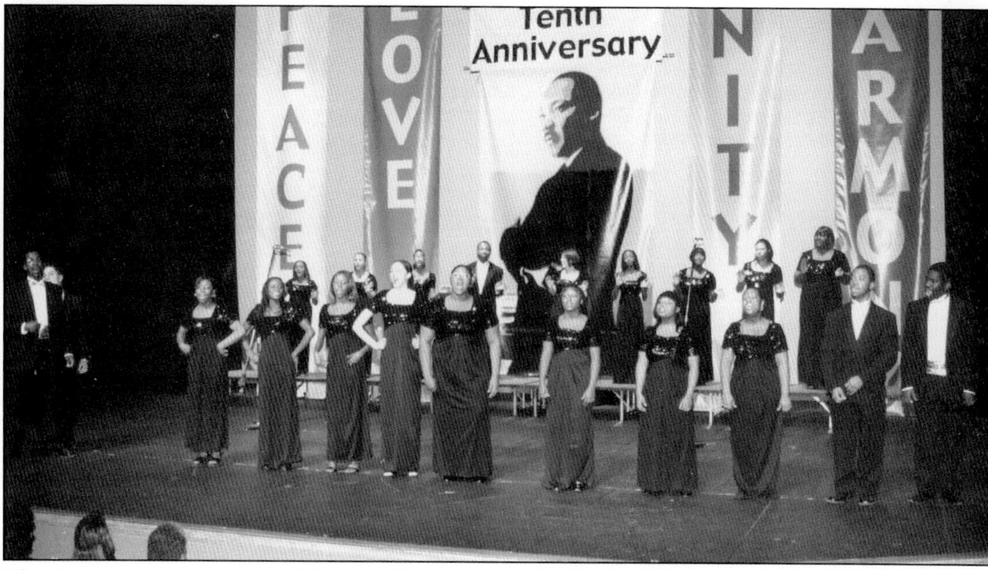

The City sponsors an annual Martin Luther King Jr. Day celebration in January that features guest speakers such as Yolanda King, Martin Luther King III, Ruby Dee, Andrew Young, Harry Belafonte, Kweisi Mfume, and Ernest Green. An art contest, luncheons, concerts, speeches, and presentation of scholarships are part of the three-day celebration. In this photograph, a choir takes the stage at the Center for the Arts in 2001, the celebration's tenth anniversary. (Courtesy of the City of Coral Springs.)

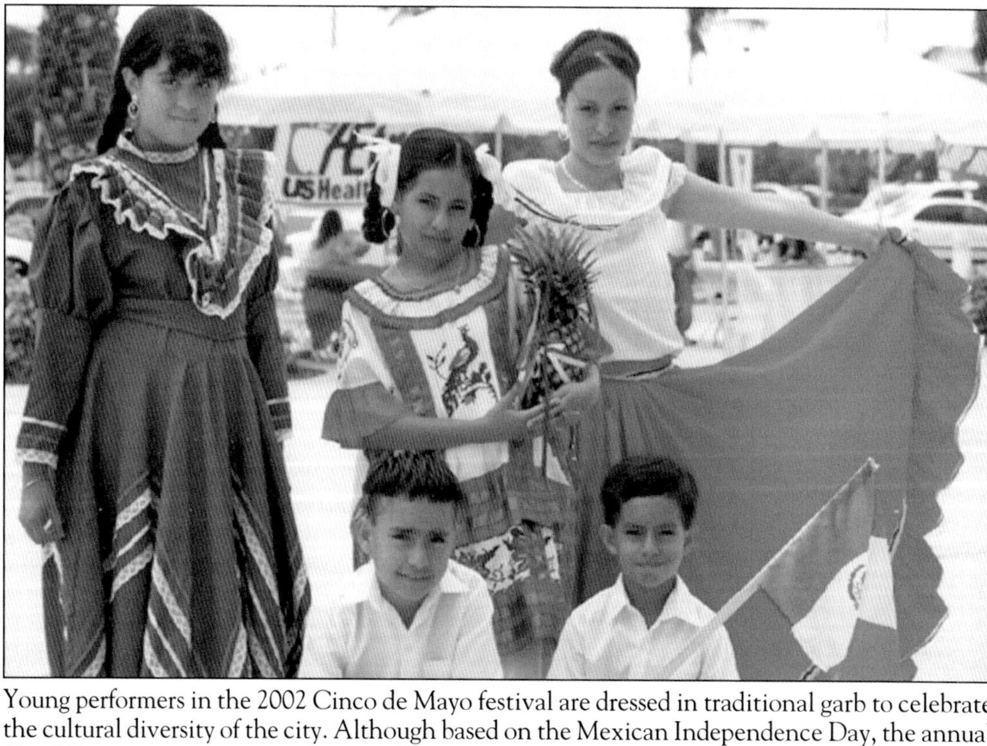

Young performers in the 2002 Cinco de Mayo festival are dressed in traditional garb to celebrate the cultural diversity of the city. Although based on the Mexican Independence Day, the annual Coral Springs event commemorates all Latin cultures represented in the city. (Courtesy of the City of Coral Springs.)

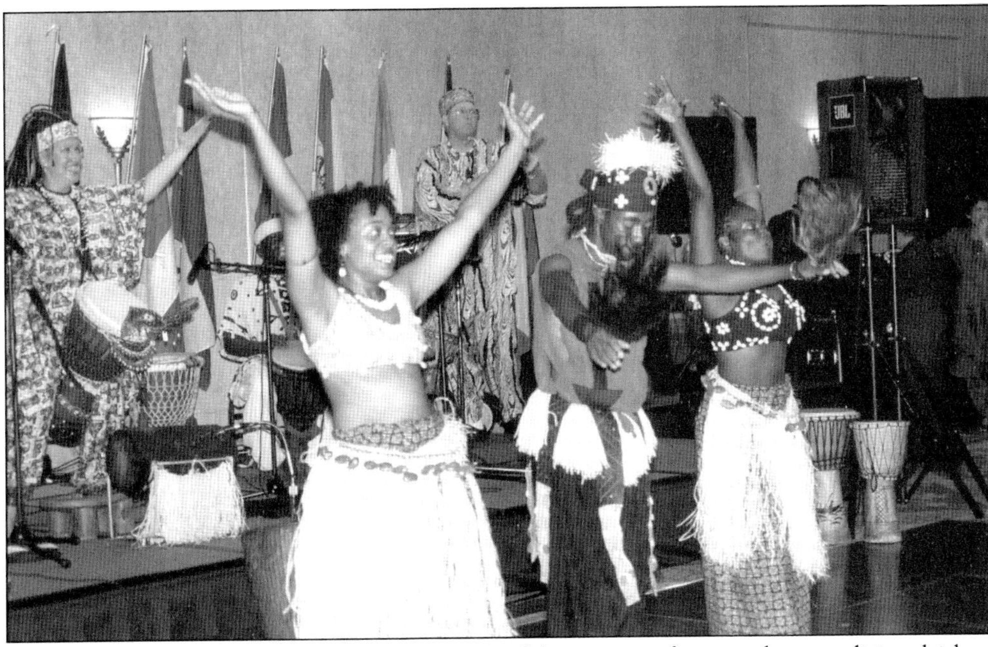

At the annual "International Dinner Dance" celebration, performers share traditional island dances with hundreds of attendees. Each year, a different culture is celebrated. Coral Springs sees itself as part of a global community and has an international partnership with the city of Paraiso, Costa Rica. (Courtesy of the City of Coral Springs.)

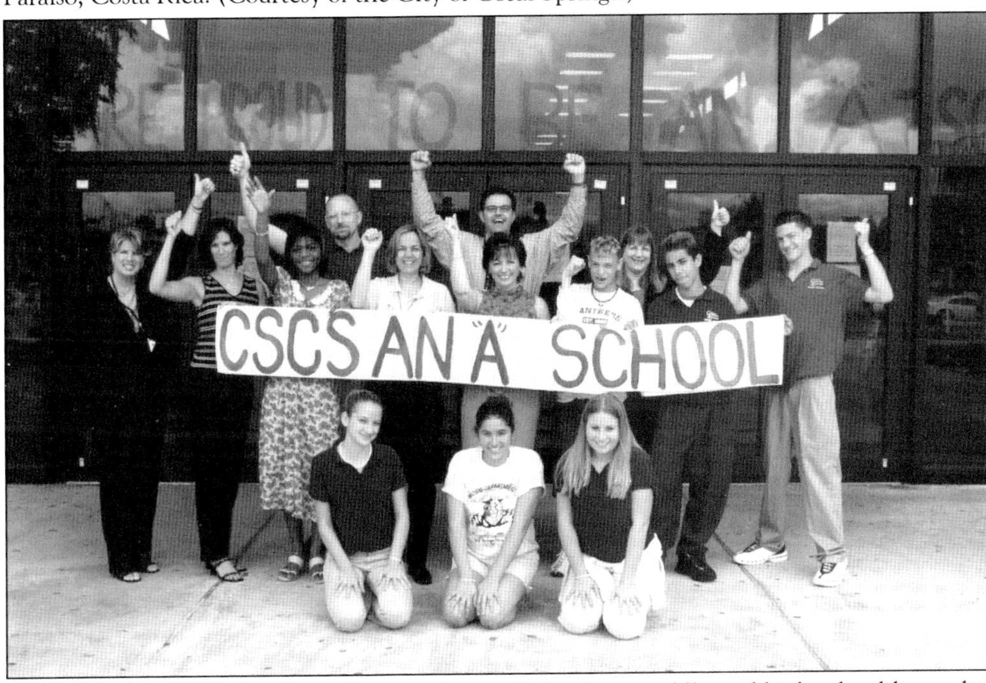

After only two years, the Coral Springs Charter School—a middle and high school located in the renovated Coral Springs Mall and managed by the City of Coral Springs—was awarded an "A" rating by the State Department of Education. Principal Estelle Strader, center, middle row, attributes the school's success to good planning. (Courtesy of the City of Coral Springs.)

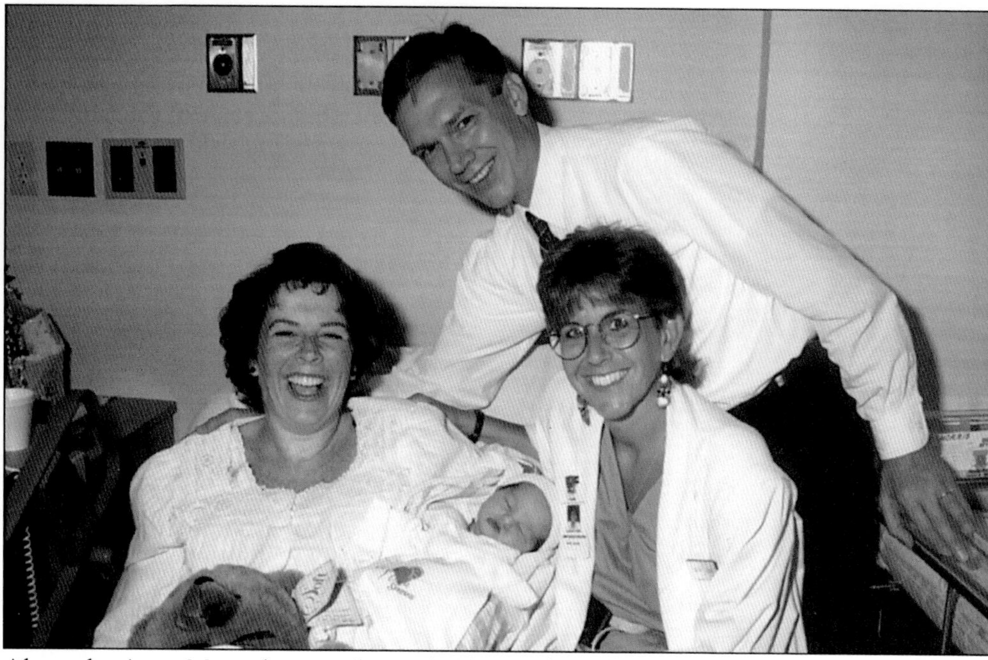

Alexandra Anne Morris became the city's 100,000th resident when she was born at 6:54 p.m. on June 6, 1996 at the Coral Springs Medical Center. Here she celebrates with her parents, Marybeth and Joseph Morris, and midwife Kathy Fair. (Courtesy of the City of Coral Springs.)

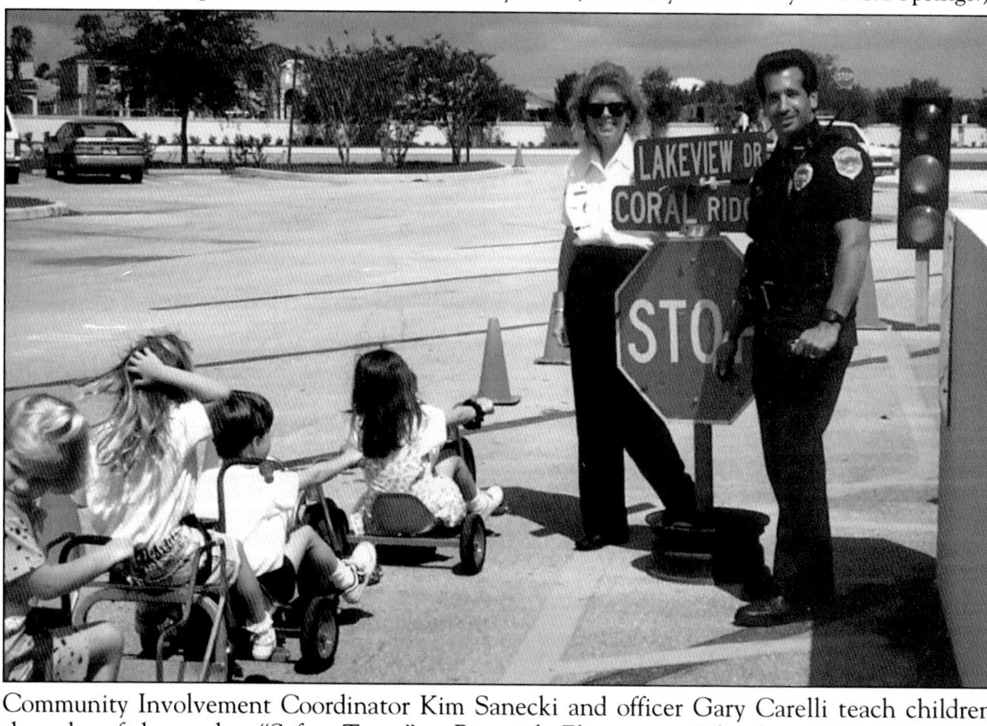

Community Involvement Coordinator Kim Sanecki and officer Gary Carelli teach children the rules of the road at "Safety Town" at Riverside Elementary School in 1992. Small-scale intersections with working lights have been recreated to help children learn how to be safe. (Courtesy of the City of Coral Springs.)

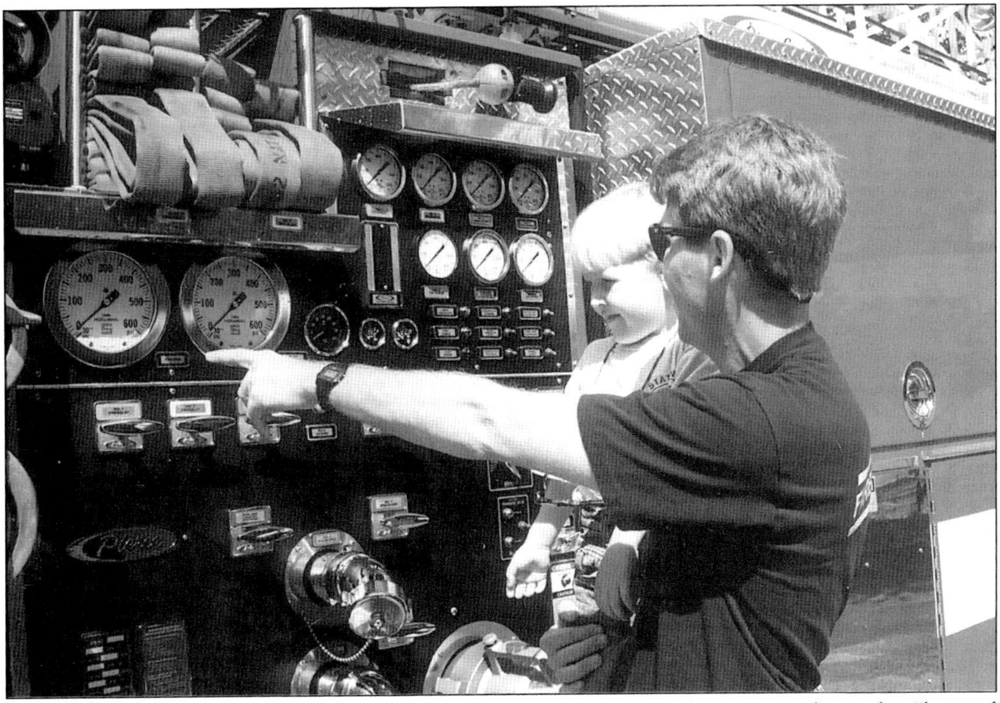

Youngsters always enjoy visiting the city's five fire stations and learning about the "big red trucks," such as this ladder truck. Not only does the city welcome visitors to public facilities like the fire stations, but a number of educational programs are also brought into the city's 23 public schools throughout the year. (Courtesy of the City of Coral Springs.)

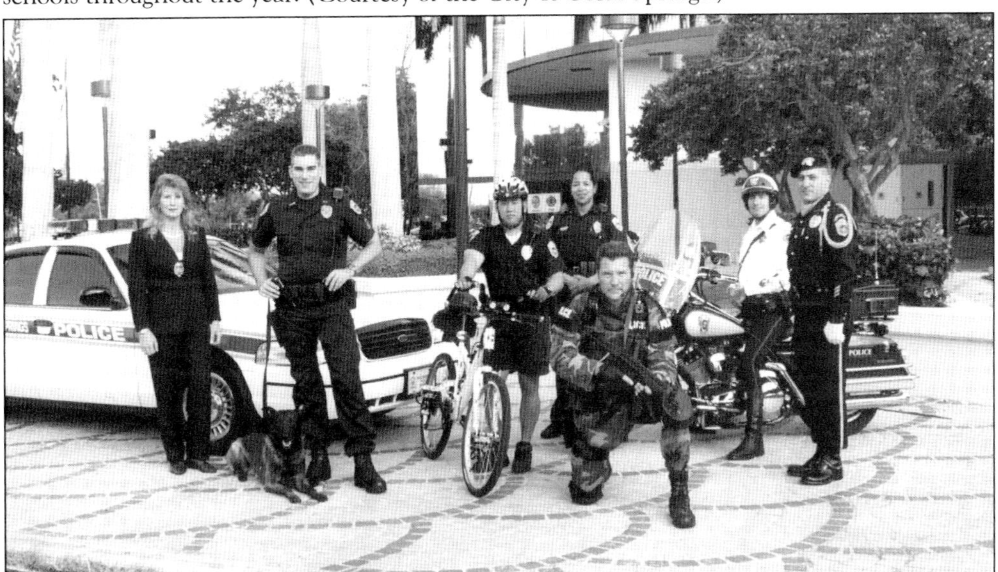

With almost 200 uniformed officers, the Coral Springs police department has come a long way in a short time. From the left, officer Sherry Raczka, officer William Floyd and his K-9 partner "Boris," bicycle officer Peter Kim, youth liaison officer Lisa Jo Faircloth, special response team officer Stephen Bilous, motorman officer John Harrison, and officer David Agata are seen in dress uniform. (Courtesy of the City of Coral Springs.)

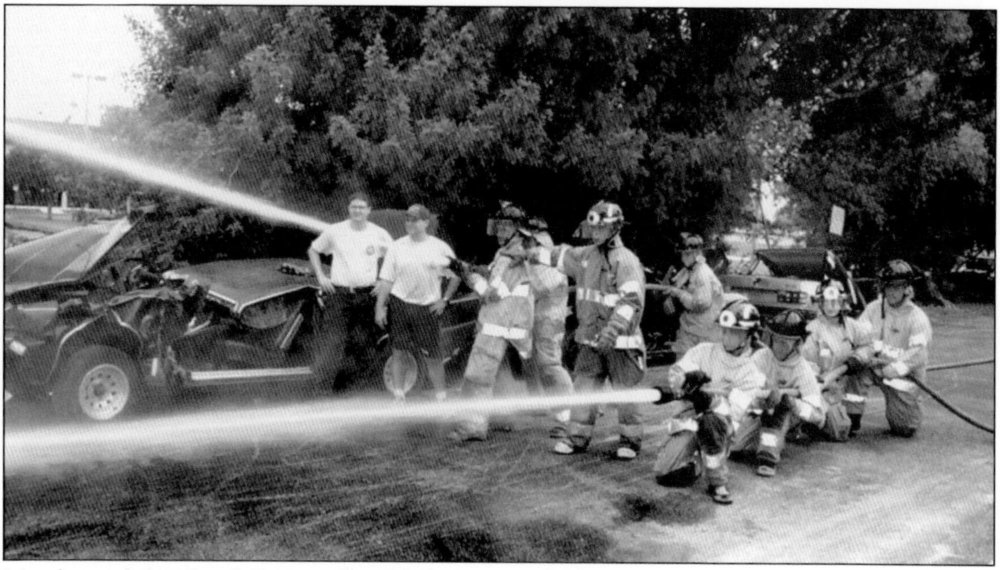

Members of the Coral Springs Fire Explorers, a teen program, learn how to operate various suppression devices, such as these fire hoses. Programs like this and the Police Explorers give area youth the opportunity to serve the community while receiving valuable training for possible future careers in public safety. (Courtesy of the City of Coral Springs.)

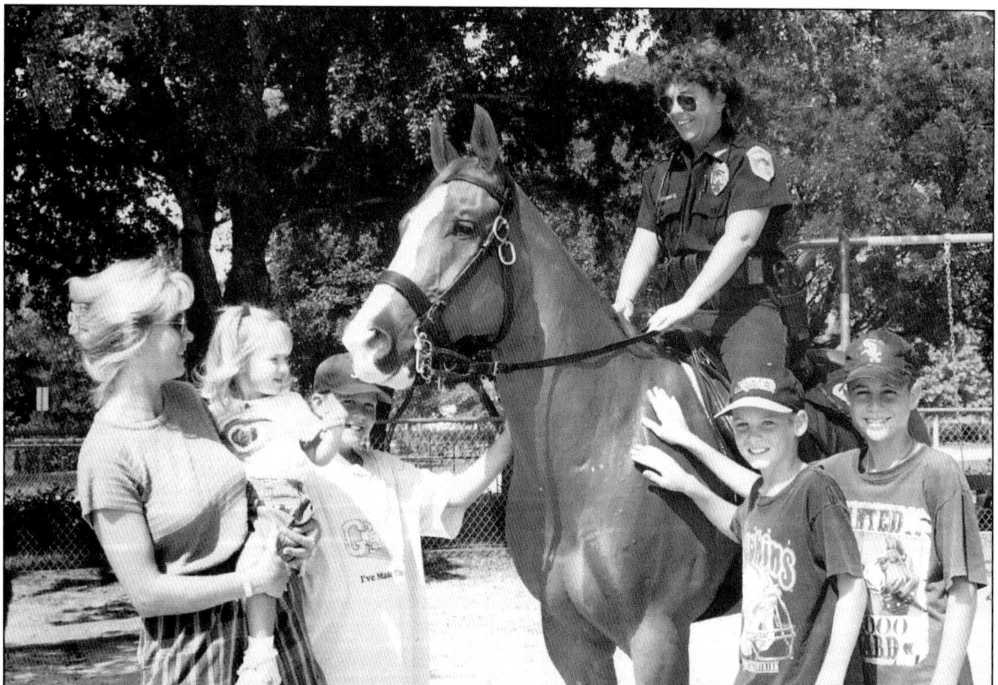

During the mid-1990s, officer Cheryl Lumm would ride "Stormy" on park patrol, one of four horses used at various times for mounted patrol. The equestrian officers were a favorite with park visitors. Today, officers patrol the parks on bicycles. From left to right are Julie Ritthaler, Mallory Ritthaler, Greg Moyer, officer Cheryl Lumm, Ryan Moyer, and Nick Dalu. (Courtesy of the City of Coral Springs.)

Fifteen years after the Landmark Restoration Committee rescued the original sales building from the fire department's training activities, this burn tower was built in 1992 to provide hands-on training to volunteers and career firefighters. Here, a firefighter practices his rappelling skills down the side of the tower. (Courtesy of the City of Coral Springs.)

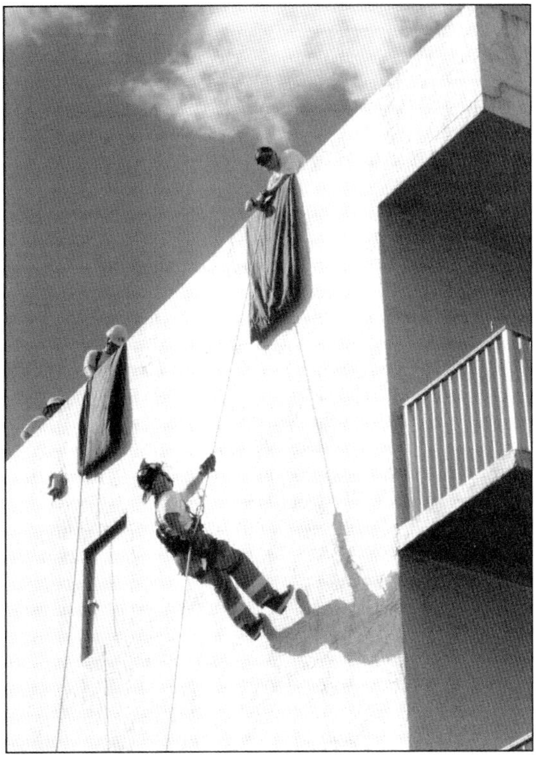

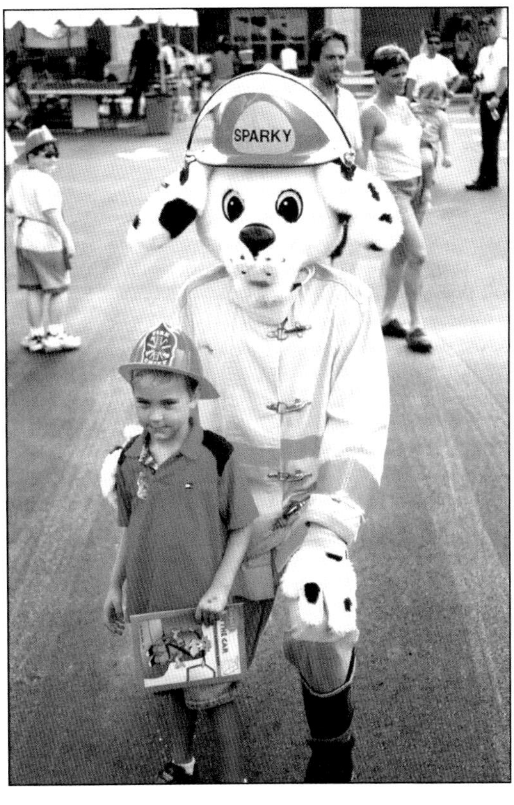

"Sparky" is one of the many community outreach programs of the Coral Springs Fire Department. The department is a unique combination of volunteer and professional firefighters and paramedics. The department provides such high-quality services that a neighboring city contracts with Coral Springs for EMS services. (Courtesy of the City of Coral Springs.)

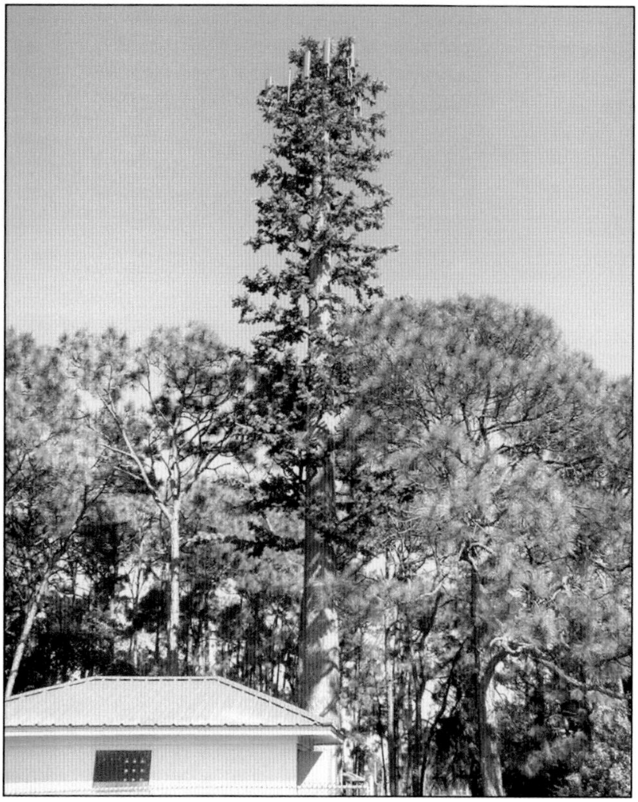

In an effort to keep the natural feel of the city while delivering the latest technology, Coral Springs uses "stealth" cell towers like this one in Lion's Park. While taller than the trees surrounding it, towers like this resemble the real thing enough to blend in with its surroundings. (Courtesy of the City of Coral Springs.)

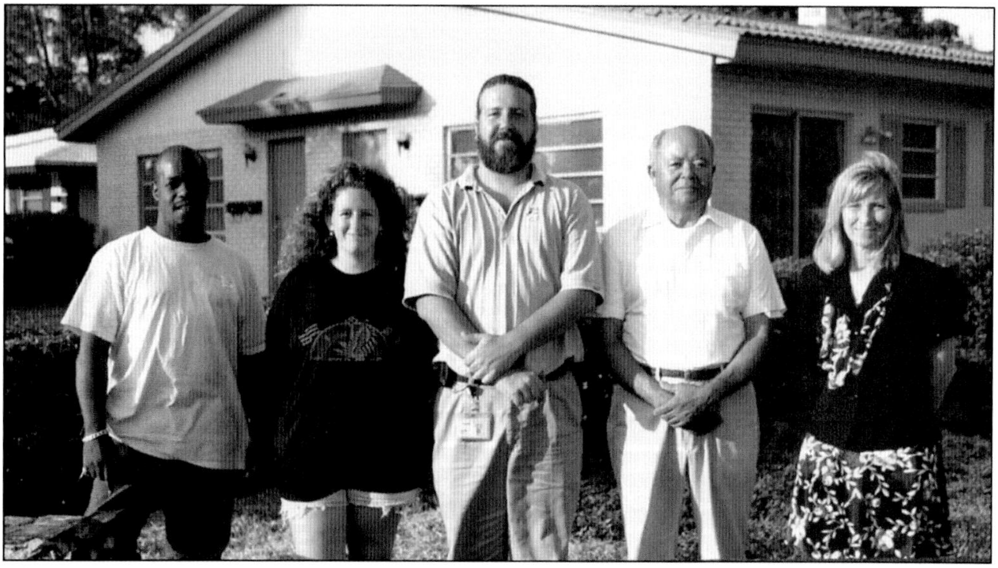

The city partners with neighborhoods through grant and consulting programs for revitalization efforts that help protect property values and improve the aesthetics of the community. In 1999, Forest Hills won the Neighborhoods USA assocation's "Neighborhood of the Year" award. This committee, representing the Meadows and Dells subdivisions, took home the Neighborhoods USA 2002 "Neighborhood of the Year" award. From left to right are two unidentified people, David Jukes, Joseph McKenzie, and Samantha Fagnoni. (Courtesy of the City of Coral Springs.)

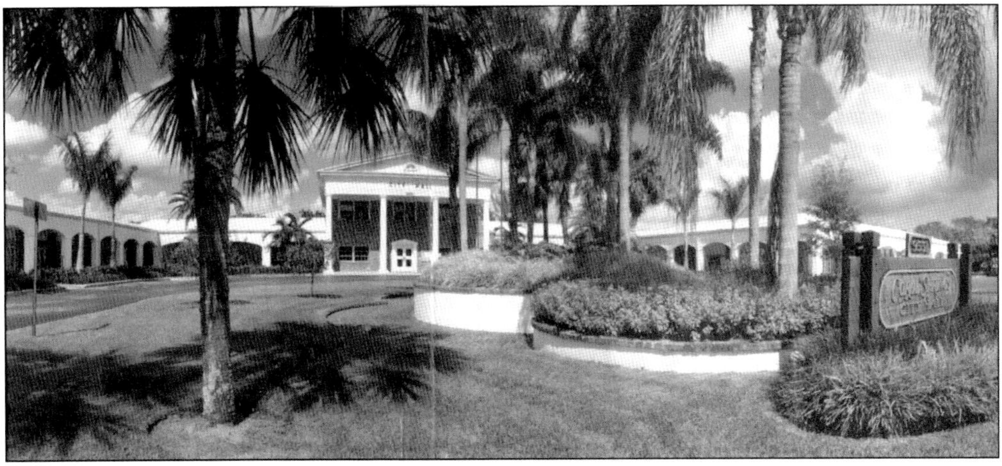

City Hall is seen here as it appeared at the dawn of the 21st century, almost forty years after serving as the Coral Ridge Properties administration building. Little has changed on the facade. (Courtesy of the City of Coral Springs.)

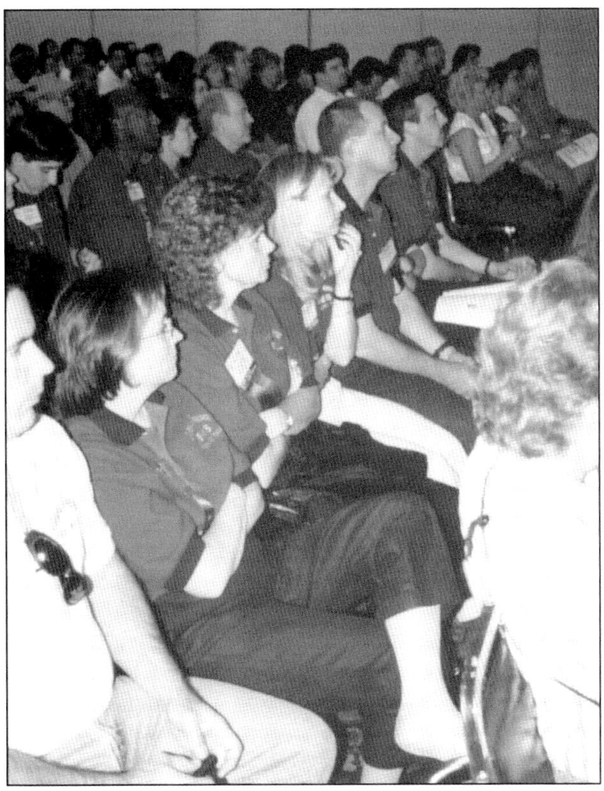

City staff attend numerous quality training events throughout the year to keep their customer service skills at their peak. Shown here, in the center row from left to right, are Donald Petito, Laura Norwalk, Chris Heflin, Nancy Morando, Scott Mathis, and former fire chief William Fyfe. These employees were members of the "Time=Life Team" that won the state's quality showcase, where quality improvement teams from top companies compete against each other. The team also placed fourth in the national competition in Las Vegas. (Courtesy of the City of Coral Springs.)

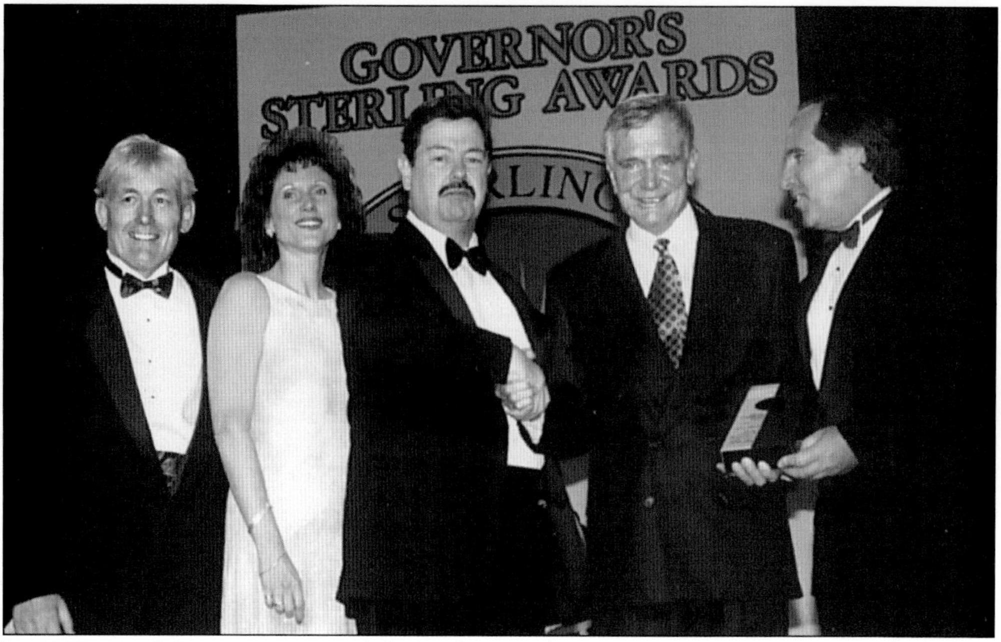

In 1997, Coral Springs was awarded Florida Governor's Sterling Award, making it the first municipality in the nation to be awarded a state-sanctioned Baldrige-based quality award. From left to right are Commissioner Bill Stradling, Commissioner Rhonda Calhoun, Mayor John Sommerer, Gov. Lawton Chiles, and City Manager Mike Levinson. (Courtesy of the City of Coral Springs.)

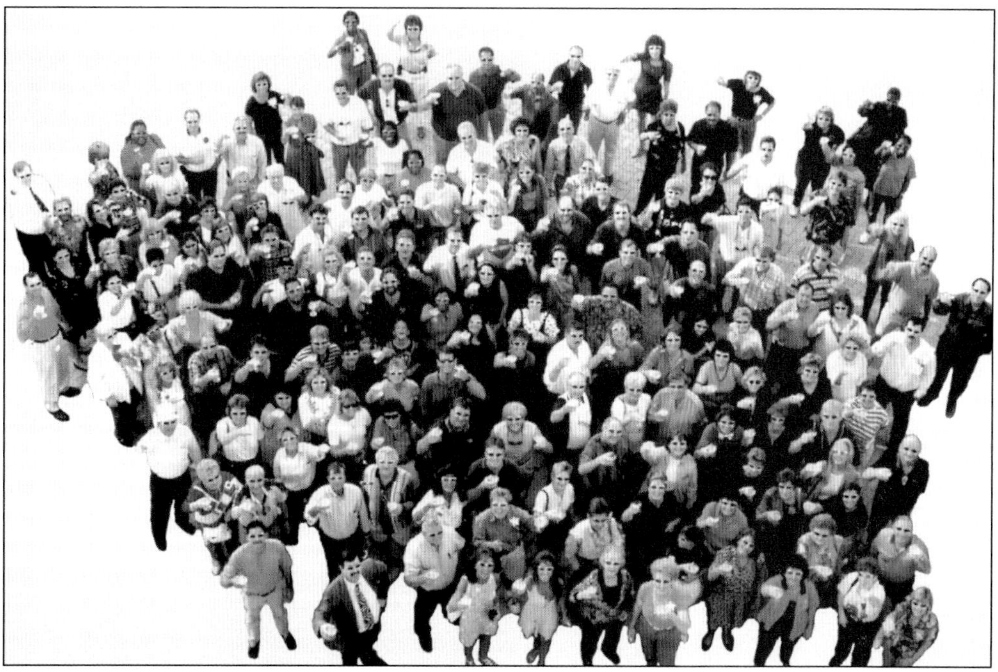

Assembled in the courtyard at the Center for the Arts in 1997, city employees donned silver-rimmed glasses and raised a toast in honor of the unique recognition of their city by the state. (Courtesy of the City of Coral Springs.)

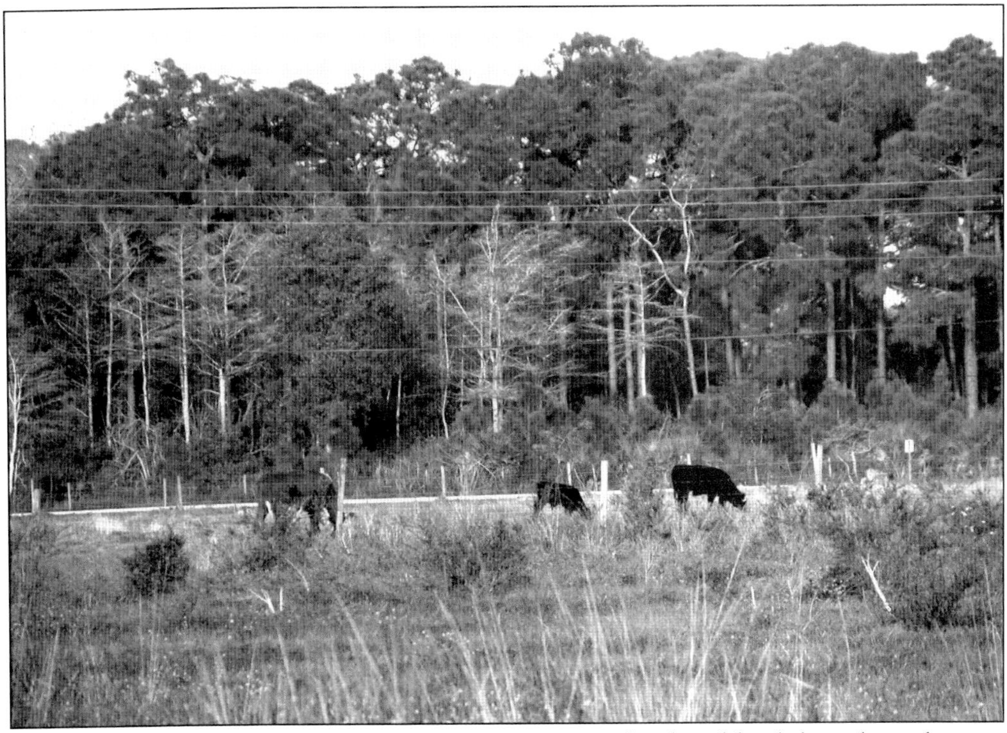

Until recently, it was common to see cows grazing in undeveloped land throughout the city, providing a glimpse of Coral Springs as it was at its founding. Today, only two small parcels have grazing animals and both are slated for development in the near future. (Courtesy of the City of Coral Springs.)

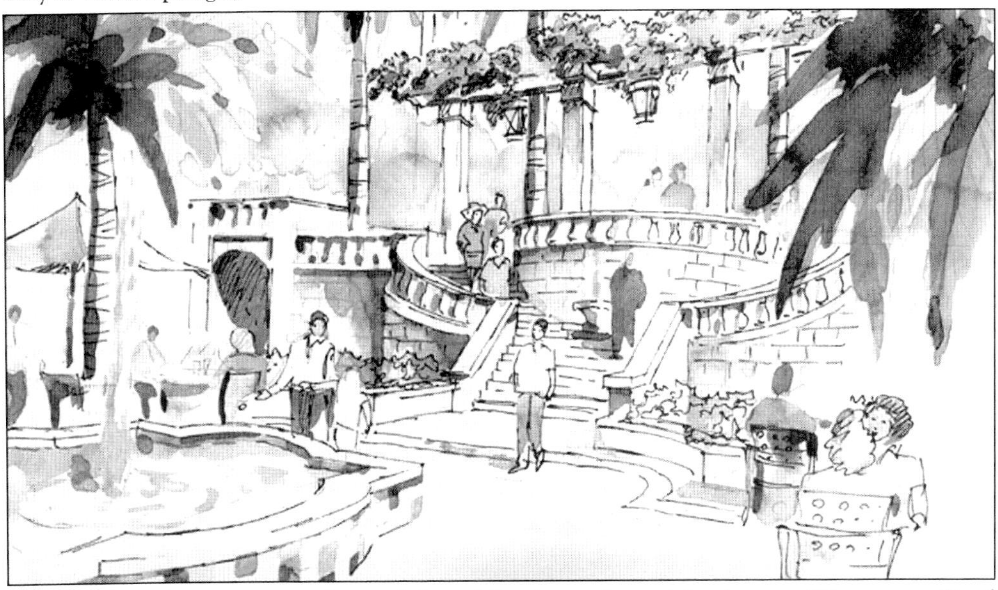

This is an artist's conception of one of the public plazas planned for the new "Downtown Coral Springs" project, a redevelopment of the original intersection at Sample Road and University Drive. As the master plan continues to evolve, the city redesigns itself, continuously improving the community aesthetics. (Courtesy of the City of Coral Springs.)

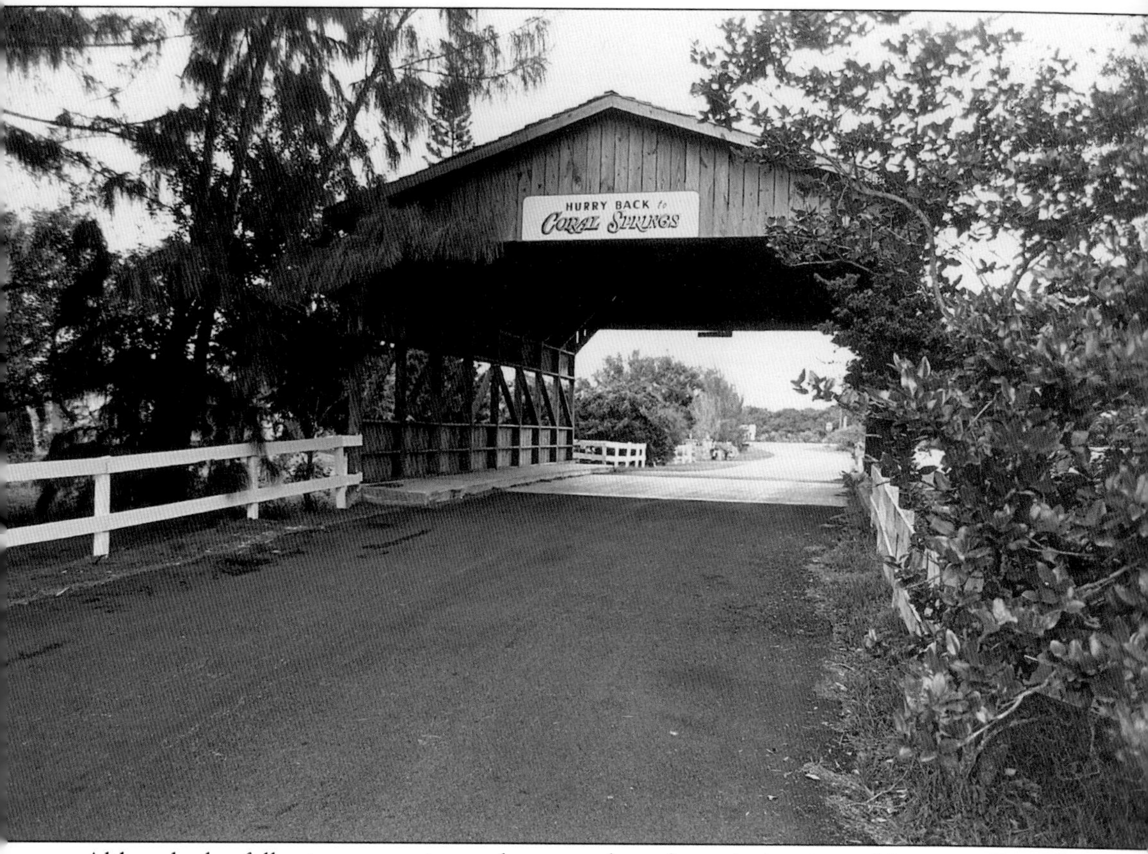

Although the following was written about another planned city, it could very well apply to the city of Coral Springs: [The city] "was created for a definite purpose and has been developed, with many modifications, according to a definite plan. Therein lives its unique distinction among American cities." (From *WPA Guide to Washington*, 1942.) (Courtesy of Coral Ridge Properties.)